Moscow and Greek Communism, 1944–1949

Moscow and Greek Communism, 1944–1949

by PETER J. STAVRAKIS

Cornell University Press, *Ithaca and London*

First published 1989 by Cornell University Press.

International Standard Book Number 0-8014-2125-x
Library of Congress Catalog Card Number 88-47767

Printed in the United States of America

Librarians: Library of Congress cataloging information appears on the last page of the book.

The paper in this book is acid-free and meets the guidelines for permanence and durability of the Committee on Production Guidelines for Book Longevity of the Council on Library Resources.

To Regina Vassiliki Stavrakis

CONTENTS

Preface   ix

Abbreviations   xiii

Transliteration and Documentation   xv

Map   xviii

1 INTRODUCTION: THE GREEK CIVIL WAR AND
   SOVIET FOREIGN POLICY   1

2 CONSOLIDATING WARTIME GAINS, 1944–1945   7

3 POSTWAR SOVIET OBJECTIVES AND GREEK
   COMMUNIST GRADUALISM, 1945–1946   48

4 FROM DUALISM TO DEFEAT, 1946–1949: THE
   SOVIET IMPACT ON THE THIRD ROUND OF THE
   CIVIL WAR   127

5 ELITE CONFLICT AND SOVIET POLICY IN GREECE   186

6 THE IMPACT OF SOVIET POLICY ON POSTWAR
   BALKAN POLITICS   203

Appendix: Historical Narrative and Path Analysis   217

Bibliography   221

Index   233

PREFACE

Few postwar events have had as profound an effect on Western perceptions of Soviet international behavior as the Greek Civil War. The political instability and Communist insurgency in Greece, coinciding with Soviet pressure on the fragile Turkish and Iranian governments, convinced the West it was confronted by an ideologically militant Soviet Union pursuing a policy of global revolutionary expansionism. With the Truman Doctrine, the United States served notice that Greece was to be America's first test of a policy of containment of Soviet expansionism. Although victory in the Greek Civil War was important to the United States at the time, the conflict's long-term importance lies in the American perceptions it created about the means and motives of Soviet foreign policy. More than four decades later, that legacy of the Greek Civil War continues to affect U.S. calculations of Soviet behavior.

Greece's strategic location and the occurrence of civil war there during a historic transformation of the international system naturally assured the examination of the Communist insurgency. What is surprising is the extent to which assumptions about Soviet conduct in the Balkans have remained unexamined. No investigation has ever determined *actual* Soviet involvement in Greece; no persuasive explanation of Soviet policy during the years 1944–49 has ever emerged. In this book, using a variety of sources (Greek Communist, in particular), I have tried to determine as precisely as possible the extent and impact of Soviet activity in Greece. Beyond this, I have integrated the historical evidence into an interpretation that, without sacrifice of complexity, adequately explains Soviet policy. The result, I hope, provides the basis for a more careful evaluation of Soviet conduct in the first years of the Cold War.

The study of the Greek Civil War, because it draws in virtually every factor important in the explanation of Soviet foreign policy generally, can illuminate the extent to which the Soviet Union was driven by ideological rather than pragmatic considerations; Soviet willingness to pursue objectives within the existing state system; the relative importance to the Soviets of subordinating all Communist parties to the Soviet state; and the extent to which Stalin would risk Soviet gains to take advantage of an adversary's weakness. Case-study limitations aside, studying the Greek Civil War also makes it possible to test assumptions about Soviet conduct because the war coincided with the evolution of a new strategic relationship among the major powers in the international system. Postwar Stalinist foreign policy derived part of its character and style from this crucial episode; for those early postwar events established the limits and patterns of foreign policy that have affected succeeding generations of Soviet leaders down to the present.

The scarcity of information on Soviet behavior always tests the creativity of scholars. My extensive use of Greek Communist, British, and American sources means my analysis is based largely on *perceptions* of Soviet conduct rather than on the conduct itself. No analysis of foreign policy is ever, of course, free of perceptual problems. Perhaps mine is not the sole defensible interpretation of events in postwar Greece; the information I have used may yield alternative ones. Mine is shaped by my focus on the Soviet contribution to developments in postwar Greece; I hope its coherence and scope enables it to stand up to comparison with the alternatives.

As in all historical research, the validity of some information, as well as the meaning of certain documents, is open to question; some documents reflect opinions, rather than the facts; and there is the possibility of deliberate falsehoods. Yet, converging lines of evidence from a variety of sources do allow for an intersubjective evaluation of the data. Where possible, I have treated information that appears in both Western and Greek Communist archives as possessing higher-order validity than data found in only one of these sources. Furthermore, whatever doubts there may be about the validity of Communist sources, the Greek Communists were in much closer contact with the Soviets than Western officials were. And there is simply no other currently available source of information on the Soviet role in the Greek Civil War.

I cannot begin here to acknowledge all those who have contributed to this book or describe the ways my life has been enriched in the process. I trust that all will understand that it is not from ingratitude that I restrict myself to the major contributors. I owe a special debt to John Armstrong for the time he has taken to comment upon early drafts. Because he was my major adviser, his understanding and encouragement were important to me; his straightforward manner, honesty, and devotion to serious scholarship have been my model. I am grateful to my undergraduate adviser, Yaroslav Bilinsky, because his courses sparked my interest in Soviet politics. Patrick Riley has always inspired my intellectual endeavors; through his example, I have come to appreciate the pursuit of knowledge for its intrinsic rewards. I also thank Michael Petrovich and Melvin Croan for providing useful comments and criticisms early in my project.

John Iatrides and Ole Smith encouraged and supported my work in its initial phases and then took the time to read a draft of the completed manuscript. Ivo Banac reviewed a later version. Their comments were especially valuable in the long task of revision; I hope that I have done justice to their criticisms and observations. Prokopis Papastratis generously assisted me while I was doing my research in Greece. The kindness and patience of those who helped me remain a source of great satisfaction.

Of course no project of this kind is possible without financial assistance. The Russian Area Studies Program at the University of Wisconsin-Madison generously awarded me three Title VI Foreign Language and Area Studies Fellowships, which permitted me to carry out research in Greece and to write up the findings on my return. In addition, the University of Wisconsin Graduate School provided me with foreign and domestic travel grants to complete basic research at the Public Records Office in London and at the National Archives in Washington, D.C. I was also fortunate to receive assistance in order to carry out the supplementary research essential for revision. A research grant provided by the American Philosophical Society and the University of Vermont's Summer Research Fellowship made possible my return to Greece and Britain to acquire further materials. Terry Walsh of the University of London kindly provided housing for me and my wife, making our stay in Britain as pleasant as it was productive. Finally, John Iatrides, Nikiforos Diamandouros, Nicholas Rizopoulos, and Lars Baerentzen were kind enough to invite me to a conference on the Greek Civil War, sponsored by the Lehrman Institute, where I received valuable comments on my work, along with intellectual stimulation.

Perhaps the greatest benefit, however, has been the personal support of those close to me and the new friendships I formed in my travels. These alone were worth the effort. My "family in Greece" was a source of great support to me. Dimitris and Aliki Georgalas, Elly Triandafillidou, and Olga Miltiadovna went out of their way to make my stay in Greece as pleasant as possible. I was also fortunate to have the generous hospitality of Julie Mylona, Christina Antzoulatou, and Dionysios and Paraskevoula Antzoulatou. Finally, my travels while researching this book provided my happiest experience, meeting Regina Romanos, who later became my wife. Regina's subsequent patience and endurance were vital to my own success, since intellectual investigation takes its toll on more than just one person. I am grateful that she put up with me through such trying times.

Of course, not even the first few steps would have been possible without the moral and financial support of my parents, Peter and Helen Stavrakis. Because they value a good education, I have been able to receive one. In a sense, my work is an extension of their lives; for having survived the excesses of Stalinism, as displaced persons in Greece after the war they were plunged into four more years of chaos and bloodshed. They never had the chance (or the desire) to go back over that painful terrain in order to examine the larger forces that dominated their lives during those years; that is something I hope my study achieves to some small degree.

PETER J. STAVRAKIS

Burlington, Vermont

ABBREVIATIONS

AMFOGE	Allied Mission for Observing the Greek Elections
ASNOM	Antifašističkoto sobranije na narodnoto osloboduvanije na Makedonija (Antifascist Assembly of the National Liberation of Macedonia)
ASO	Antifasistikis Stratiotikis Organosis (Antifascist Army Organization)
AVNOJ	Antifašističko veće narodnog oslobodenija Jugoslavije (Antifascist Council for the National Liberation of Yugoslavia)
CPSU	Communist Party of the Soviet Union
DSE	Dimokratikos Stratos tis Elladas (Democratic Army of Greece)
DSR	Department of State Records, United States National Archives
EAM	Ethniko Apeleftherotiko Metopo (National Liberation Front)
EDES	Ethnikos Dimokratikos Ellinikos Syndesmos (National Republican Greek League)
EEAM	Ergatiko Ethniko Apeleftherotiko Metopo (Workers' National Liberation Front)
EKKA	Ethnikis kai Koinonikis Apeleftherosis (National and Social Liberation
ELAS	Ellinikos Laïkos Apeleftherotikos Stratos (Greek Popular Liberation Army)
ERGAS	Ergatikos Antifasistikos Syndesmos (Workers' Antifascist League)
FO	Foreign Office Files, Public Records Office, London

GSEE	Geniki Synomospondia Ellinikon Ergazomenon (General Confederation of Greek Workers)
KKE	Kommounistiko Komma tis Elladas (Communist Party of Greece)
KOA	Kommounistikis Organosis tis Athinas (Communist Organization of Athens)
KOSSA	Kommounistikis Organosis Stratou kai Somaton Asfaleias (Communist Organization of the Army and Security Forces)
NOF	(See SNOF)
OSS	Office of Strategic Services Reports, United States National Archives
PCB	Parti Communiste de Belgique (Communist Party of Belgium)
PCF	Parti Communiste Français (Communist Party of France)
PCI	Partito Comunista Italiano (Communist Party of Italy)
PEEA	Politiki Epitropi Ethnikis Apeleftherosis (Political Committee of National Liberation
SNOF	Slovenomakedonski narodnoosloboditelen front (Slavo-Macedonian National Liberation Front)
UNA	United Nations Archives
UNRRA	United Nations Relief and Rehabilitation Administration

TRANSLITERATION
AND DOCUMENTATION

There are always problems to be confronted in using another language in research. I have tried to minimize the difficulties by translating as much as possible from original Greek and Russian sources, but this still leaves the necessity of transliterating proper names and the titles of articles, books, and monographs. For the Russian, I have used the Library of Congress System throughout the text. Modern Greek is more of a problem; for there appears to be no commonly accepted system of transliteration that seeks to minimize the burden on the non-Greek-speaking reader. Indeed, the *Chicago Manual of Style* deals only with classical Greek; the United States Government Printing Office's *Style Manual* suggests using a standard transliteration, regardless of pronunciation, but the inclusion of various diacritical marks makes the text tedious and difficult to absorb. Since my primary objective is to have the various Greek citations blend as smoothly into the text as other passages without producing confusion, I have adopted the *Style Manual*'s suggestion but with several important changes. Greek letters are transliterated as follows: a, v, g, d, e, z, i, th, i, k, l, m, n, x, o, p, r, s, t, y, f, ch, ps, o. The only exceptions are several vowel-and-consonant combinations in which the sound changes significantly. Hence, "ευ" and "αυ" become "ev/ef" and "av/af," respectively; "ντ" becomes "d" at the beginning of words; "μπ" is given as "mb/mp/b"; and "γγ/γκ" appears as "g/ng."

Even so, transliteration in the text will differ from English-language documents that contain various translations of original Greek sources within them. I have left the documents unchanged, but introduced minor changes in brackets where grammatical errors or stylistic differences in the original documents require clarification. This is especially necessary in the excerpts from the Greek Communist archives, because they are replete with aliases, omissions, contractions, and occasional grammatical errors. In all cases, the changes I introduce appear in brackets; parentheses in a citation indicate that the material was in the original source. Preserving the form of the original documents inevitably produces differences in names between the text and quotations. In most instances these are understandable without insertions or corrections, since the variations involve little more than one or two letters. I am confident the reader will be able to recognize that "Zachariades" refers to Nikos Zachariadis, "Themistocles Sophoulis" to Themistoklis Sofoulis, "Ioannides" to Iannis Ioannidis, and so on. Only in cases where it is likely that the original transliteration will be misleading have I inserted appropriate corrections. Prominent place names have been retained in their commonly accepted English transliteration for the reader's convenience.

In many instances, pseudonyms and aliases have been used, and I have provided real names when they are known. The Greek Communists' contacts in the Balkan countries pose a special problem, because in some instances one can ascertain neither nationality nor individual identity. "Zhivkov," for example, is mentioned several times by Zachariadis while he was in Belgrade, but it is as yet impossible to determine conclusively whether Zhivkov is a pseudonym, or even whether he is Soviet or Bulgarian. As a general rule, I have used the names provided in the documents available to me and have indicated the identity of individuals only when I am certain. Where two different spellings appear for what is clearly one person, I have used one in the text and placed the alternative form in an accompanying note.

Another problem arises in citing authors of Greek origin who have published works in languages other than Greek. When those works are in English, I have kept the name as it appears in the published work. Greek-name authors in other languages have been transliterated from the language in which the work was published. For example, the author of *Grazhdanskaia voina v Gretsii, 1946–1949* is given as G. D. Kir'iakidis, despite the fact that having his name transliterated from Greek would yield "Kyriakidis." The same rule applies to non-Greek titles that contain a transliteration different from mine. Finally, in the rare instance when an author has published in both English and Greek using different names, I have provided the name transliterated from the Greek and then bracketed the alternative English spelling.

Moscow and Greek Communism, 1944–1949

I

INTRODUCTION: THE GREEK CIVIL WAR AND SOVIET FOREIGN POLICY

Despite the obvious importance of the Greek Civil War for the history of the postwar era, this is the first book on Soviet policy in Greece between 1944 and 1949. There have been numerous studies of British, Greek, and American policies of the period, but it will never be possible to explain the political developments in southeastern Europe adequately without establishing the means and objectives of Soviet conduct in Greece. It is said, however, that, as on many other issues of Soviet politics, the paucity of information precludes detailed investigation; when the "Greek question" is discussed, the analyst of Soviet policy usually relies only on general principles, with the consequence that the Greek Civil War is reduced to the status of an exception to the rule or a gloss on more important case studies. This approach creates a situation in which new information about the Soviet role in Greece is merely incorporated into overly simplistic, preexisting interpretations which maintain either that the Soviet Union was committed to the "communization" of Greece or that it remained completely uninvolved. Scholars predisposed to view Soviet activity as expansionist turn to the Greek case and, mirabile dictu, find their argument supported. Revisionist historians, concerned with defending their arguments that Stalin pragmatically accepted Greece's position in the West, turn to an exegesis of American and British documents to vindicate their suspicions.[1]

[1]This dichotomy is particularly evident when one compares more recent to earlier works. "Traditionalist" works, such as those by Edgar O'Ballance and Stephen G. Xydis, suffered

Such conclusions are particularly unfortunate because a detailed analysis of the evidence currently available indicates otherwise: those who have argued that the Soviets were involved in Greece were correct in their general assessment of Soviet behavior but incorrect in their characterization of Soviet methods; moreover, they greatly underestimated the complexity and mutability of Soviet behavior. There *is* now sufficient evidence on which to base an objective analysis of Soviet policy in Greece. In this book my first aim is to reconstruct that policy and to illuminate its pronounced shifts and turns in response to an environment and actors over which Stalin had only limited control. I argue that the Soviet record is mixed: Soviet efforts in Greece were moderately successful at first, then rapidly deteriorated into failure as Stalin was compelled to act to preserve other wartime gains that appeared threatened by the deterioration of political stability in the Balkans.

Another objective of this book is to demonstrate how Soviet policy severely limited the means and objectives of the Communist Party of Greece (KKE) in the most critical period of the Greek national drama. The KKE was a powerful political force in postwar Greece, but Soviet dictates led it away from policies with better prospects for success. Indeed, Soviet

---

not only from a dearth of Communist sources but from a predisposition to view Soviet policy as uniformly expansionist. They both argue *from* a viewpoint rather than *for* it, with the result that their suspicions about the Soviet Union receive confirmation. What distinguishes the two works, however, is that while Xydis' is a mine of information, O'Ballance argues on evidence he does not provide the reader; see Xydis, *Greece and the Great Powers, 1944–1947* (Thessaloniki: Institute for Balkan Studies, 1963), and O'Ballance, *The Greek Civil War, 1944–1949* (London: Faber & Faber, 1966). A more recent analysis in the "revisionist" vein also exhibits bias, but in the opposite direction; see Lawrence S. Wittner, *American Intervention in Greece, 1943–1949* (New York: Columbia University Press, 1982). Wittner does provide a great deal of formerly unexamined evidence, but his central argument suffers from the fact that he relies exclusively on English-language, primarily American, sources. The argument that the partisan struggle was destroyed by ideological divisions within the Greek Communist party is presented by Dominique Eudes in *The Kapetanios: Partisans and Civil War in Greece, 1943–1949* (New York: Monthly Review Press, 1972). The weakness of this work is also the bias with which the analysis begins; Eudes's work is often more polemical than scholarly. This weakness is compounded by the absence of citations, which makes it impossible to verify the evidence Eudes adduces in support of his case. Some recent case studies have begun to approach postwar Greece more objectively. The earlier phases of the Greek Civil War are carefully analyzed by John Iatrides in *Revolt in Athens: The Greek Communist "Second Round," 1944–1945* (Princeton, N.J.: Princeton University Press, 1972). An excellent Greek account is Vasil Kondis, *I Angloamerikaniki Politiki kai to Elliniko Provlima, 1945–1949* (Thessaloniki: Paratiritis, 1984). Although more problematic, Christopher M. Woodhouse's analysis, in *The Struggle for Greece, 1941–49* (London: Hart-Davis, MacGibbon, 1976), is still useful as a source of information.

policy appears to have played a not inconsiderable role in undermining the Greek Communist insurgency. The divergence between Soviet and Greek Communist interests devastated the KKE; for its attempt to conform to Stalin's desires resulted in an incoherent policy.

The most intriguing aspect of Soviet policy during this period is not its constancy but its variability, and it is this that I examine in greatest detail. Stalin initially used Greece to entice Churchill into the spheres-of-influence agreement that guaranteed him control of Romania. Subsequently, there was a shift to a policy of gradualism and political infiltration which attempted to create in Greece a strong pro-Soviet bloc capable of neutralizing any anti-Soviet initiatives. This change was made possible by and designed to capitalize on the collapse of British influence in Greece after the war, without alarming the Americans into supplanting the British commitment. This potentially promising policy subsequently deteriorated because of an incorrect assessment of the Greek domestic political context and an inability to control ideologically militant and independent Yugoslavia. To retain Soviet wartime gains in the Balkans, Stalin was forced to act to neutralize the Greek Communist insurgency and the militancy of the Yugoslavs.

Three sets of exogenous factors—strategic, regional, and local—provide a framework for my analysis of Soviet policy in Greece. *Strategic factors* are international systemic variables that are beyond Soviet control yet significantly affect Soviet policy decisions: the structure of the international system, a change in the major actors, and the polarity of the system. *Regional factors* are those subsystemic developments that have an impact on the Soviets' estimates of the success of their policy in a given geographic region. Particularly important are regional actors who, independent of any major power, are capable of crucially affecting the course of Soviet policy at the strategic level. *Local factors* are those events and developments within a country targeted by Soviet policy that have the capacity to alter Soviet calculations—especially domestic instability.

Conflict among the three sets of factors makes for hard choices for the Soviets. A policy that reflects an overriding concern for strategic factors, for example, may have to be put aside in response to the threat that uncontrolled regional or local forces may pose. Conversely, while domestic conditions in a state may indicate one course of action, a change in the strategic environment may pull policy in the opposite direction. The central dynamic of the book is the simple principle that, as strategic, regional, and local factors shifted in their importance, Soviet policy had to adapt by changing the order of priorities. By structuring the analysis in terms of such basic and general explanatory categories, I hope to achieve my final objective of providing a historical interpretation of Soviet foreign policy which transcends the significance of this particular case.

For the period of the Greek Civil War, we can characterize these exogenous factors quite precisely. There were several key strategic factors. In 1944 and early 1945, Stalin was still preoccupied with the struggle to defeat Hitler's Germany. After the end of the war, however, the new bipolar structure of the international system, in which the United States had replaced Great Britain as the leading Western power, became a major factor in Soviet calculations. The key regional factor was the threat to Soviet gains and interests posed by the independent course Josip Tito had charted in the Balkans. More recent analysis has revealed that Stalin was also concerned to preserve Albania's independence; for if it was absorbed by Yugoslavia, the possibility that all of the Balkans would slip from the Soviets' grasp increased substantially. Finally, the important contribution of local factors to the outcome of Soviet policy centers on the chaotic and dangerous situation within Greece, which pushed all parties toward higher levels of violence. As the level of domestic instability rose, the need for a more forceful Greek Communist response jeopardized gradualist, politically based policy actions.

The uncontrolled shifting of these exogenous variables is the basis for this book's three key propositions, each of which reflects a different phase of Soviet conduct in Greece. The first proposition is that because the defeat of Hitler and the securing of Soviet borders from any future attack were primary considerations during the war, the Soviet Union then had little interest in Greece, except insofar as it might be used to further such objectives. My argument, therefore, is that from mid-1944 to mid-1945 the central goal of the Soviet Union with respect to Greece was to use it in exchange for a guarantee of control of Romania. The May 1944 mutiny in the Middle East served as an excellent test of the value of Greece to the British and paved the way for the October 1944 percentages agreement in Moscow. In keeping with strategic and tactical principles of policy, the Soviets, to avoid jeopardizing their control of Romania, encouraged the KKE to enter the Greek government. The KKE therefore attempted the December 1944 uprising on its own initiative (with possible encouragement from Tito). Stalin ignored the uprising to secure higher Soviet interests. The policy was a success for Stalin, a disaster for the KKE.

My second proposition is that immediately after the war, in Greece and in other areas, Stalin adopted a policy of cautious and gradual political infiltration to capitalize on the collapse of British influence and the initial American hesitation to undertake commitments. The policy was intentionally gradual to avoid activating an American response. From mid-1945 to late 1946, the Soviets tried the full array of tactics at their disposal to infiltrate Greece by political means with the objective of solidifying a pro-Soviet presence. At the same time, the Soviets showed an interest in reconstructing KKE military forces, to be held in reserve for a future, apparently unspecified opportunity. Once again, the option of civil war did not figure in Stalin's immediate plans. This phase initially appeared promising for the achievement of Soviet objectives but ended in failure. Soviet policy failed this time because of the unsuitability of internal conditions in Greece, the independent actions of the KKE and its general secretary, the rising influence of the Yugoslavs, and ultimately, the American commitment to Greece.

The third proposition is that Soviet policy shifted once more when the challenge to Stalin's total control of international communism forced him to revise his perception of Soviet security interests and to initiate a course of action that progressively drew the Soviets into the civil war as they strove to control the tempo of events in the Balkans and protect their interests against independent factions, especially those associated with Tito. The potential threat to Soviet global and regional policies posed by an ideologically militant Yugoslavia through its support of civil war in Greece, as well as the threat of a competing Communist center, forced Stalin to reign Tito in. As Stalin gradually reestablished control over the Balkans, Soviet attention turned to using the civil war in Greece and the issue of Macedonian autonomy as a weapon against Tito. This policy in turn gave way in the face of a clear prospect of a Western invasion of Albania; the insurgency had to be terminated. In a final twist, however, Soviet leaders, apparently perceiving an American shift toward a negotiated solution, ordered the insurgency to continue in order to strengthen their hand at the bargaining table. Stalin had come around again to his policy (disrupted by the Yugoslav problem) of attempting to preserve, by means of a negotiated settlement, a pro-Soviet presence in Greece.

This brief overview suggests that Soviet conduct in Greece can be characterized as an example of "prudent expansionism."[2] Stalin's policy

---

[2]The sense of this term is captured in Adam Ulam's assertion that the "Soviet Union was bent upon expanding her sphere of influence but without incurring the risk of war"; see Ulam, *Expansion and Coexistence: The History of Soviet Foreign Policy, 1917–67* (New York: Praeger, 1971), p. 404. Similarly, Zbigniew Brzezinski has argued that as long as Stalin was assured of domestic stability and the prospect of revolutions elsewhere, he was willing to tolerate diversity in Eastern Europe and a rather vague and distant foreign policy in the West. That attitude certainly allowed Soviet policy to be more flexible and able to capitalize on opportunities as they arose; see Brzezinski, *The Soviet Bloc: Unity and Conflict* (Cambridge: Harvard University Press, 1967), pp. 49–51. It changed dramatically within two years of the end of the war.

was prudent in that it was mindful of the existing balance of power, sought to preserve wartime gains, and implicitly recognized the need to operate within the existing state system. These considerations were reflected in the policy's emphasis on gradualist politically oriented, as opposed to militarily based, options. It was expansionist in that it sought to acquire a belt of perimeter states, to neutralize more remote areas of interest, to occupy power vacuums to further the security of the Stalinist state, and to hold military forces in reserve in peripheral regions. Characterizing Soviet policy as prudently expansionist is also useful because it neatly combines the key elements of limited control and mutability of policy. For example, Stalin pursued a prudent and cautious policy to avoid galvanizing Western response, but the policy was so cautious and gradual that it effectively gave the initiative to regional and local forces, which brought about the collapse of Soviet efforts and the need to adapt to new conditions. Prudent expansionism reflected prime concern for strategic factors, which explains why it unraveled under the pressure of regional instability in the postwar Balkans.

There is another salient dimension of postwar Communist politics in the Balkans—the alleged conflicts within the Soviet Politburo and the Greek Communist leadership—that bears on this analysis. In the last substantive chapter, I consider and reject a hypothesis about the extent to which domestic elite conflict affected policy: divisions within the Soviet leadership, possibly reflected in the KKE and its military arm, the Democratic Army of Greece, significantly affected the performance of the Greek Communists, thereby contributing to their defeat. For Greek communism in the 1940s, Stalin was the only Soviet personality of significance.

2

CONSOLIDATING WARTIME GAINS, 1944–1945

During the final years of World War II, Soviet policy manifested little interest in Greece except insofar as events there could contribute to the principal objectives of defeating Nazi Germany, establishing a secure basis for the future defense of Soviet territory, and providing the potential for future projection of political influence in Western Europe. There is little doubt that strategic factors were dominant. With victory over the Axis powers still incomplete, it was impossible to begin reconstruction of the postwar world, but even so, once the prospect of Allied victory appeared likely, Stalin had to begin planning for the pursuit of his objectives: successful termination of the war, adequate security guarantees against any future attack from the West, and bases of political power for use in the postwar era.

Stalin sought fulfillment of these objectives through a dual policy. In relations among the Great Powers, the Soviets strove persistently to get the Anglo-American forces to establish a second front.[1] In relations with Communist organizations in the occupied territories, the Soviets mandated resistance à outrance to weaken German defenses further. The German push deeper into Soviet territory in 1942 had forced Stalin's distrust of guerrilla resistance to give way to a more sanguine appraisal of what partisan initiatives behind German lines could accomplish, and the Soviets

[1] On the question of the second front, see William H. McNeill, *America, Britain & Russia: Their Co-operation and Conflict, 1941–1946* (London: Oxford University Press, 1953).

had somewhat hesitantly endorsed Tito's policy of armed resistance and partisan warfare.[2] The Soviet's dual policy could and did produce complications, as Great Power and local Communist interests were often in direct conflict. Because the Great Powers would bear the greatest part of the burden in fighting the war, simple logic dictated that so long as the war continued, the Soviets would support British and American interests at the expense of local Communist objectives. Once the progress of the war indicated the eventual defeat of Axis forces, however, postwar political objectives grew in importance and increasingly absorbed the attention of all the members of the wartime coalition. Stalin could turn his attention to the creation of a belt of subservient states to serve as a buffer against future attacks.

Vojtech Mastny has perceptively noted the manner in which the Soviets sought to preserve bases of political power for the postwar era: from the end of 1943, the Soviets attempted to establish conditions within Europe whereby they would be in a position to extend their political influence beyond the limits of actual physical conquest.[3] The subtle connection between this objective of Soviet policy and that of winning the war has often been overlooked. Military logic dictated that Allied interests take precedence over indigenous Communist interests, but if Stalin wished to create a basis for extending his political influence in Europe, he had to find a way to preserve manipulatable Communist structures after the liberation. The solution was a policy that sought to extend Soviet power through local Communist organizations in a manner that avoided provoking a rupture in the alliance. A necessary corollary was that the Communist parties not become powerful enough to pursue their own interests.[4]

The Greek case is ideal for illustrating the specific form this policy acquired. Close examination of the relations of the Communist Party of Greece (KKE) with the Soviet Union reveals how Stalin used the Greek Communists to achieve all his major objectives. Specifically, the Soviet leader consistently supported British policy at the expense of the KKE to avoid jeopardizing the course of the war; he consented to sacrifice potential Communist ascendancy in Greece in exchange for a free hand in

[2]Vojtech Mastny, *Russia's Road to the Cold War: Diplomacy, Warfare, and the Politics of Communism, 1941–1945* (New York: Columbia University Press, 1979), pp. 64, 67. While Mastny mentions Soviet misgivings about adopting the Yugoslav model, Elisabeth Barker states that the Soviets "wholeheartedly" adopted the Yugoslav method of partisan warfare; see Barker, *Macedonia: Its Place in Balkan Power Politics* (reprint, Westport, Conn.: Greenwood, 1980), p. 84.

[3]Mastny, p. 133.

[4]Ibid., p. 144.

Romania; and finally, when the KKE could no longer pursue infiltration policies in its quest for power and was forced to opt for military confrontation, Stalin provided no assistance, thereby allowing the Greek Communists to be defeated and their independent power base destroyed. These results, and the problems they created for future Soviet policy, bear closer examination.

Postwar Soviet strategic interests were initially characterized by a marked reticence about entering into commitments that would constrain Soviet alternatives.[5] In particular, Stalin avoided any scheme that provided for joint Great Power responsibility or the federation of European states. At the Moscow Foreign Ministers' Conference in October 1943, Vyacheslav Molotov opposed the draft declaration for joint three-power responsibility for Europe as a whole, arguing that the declaration was superfluous, as his government had never expressed a preference for separate areas of responsibility.[6] In a similar instance at the Moscow Conference, Molotov and Deputy Foreign Minister Andrei Vyshinskii objected to the wording of an American-sponsored declaration on general security. A move that clearly implied a greater freedom of independent activity was the deletion of the phrase obligating the signatories to act together in occupying enemy territory and the territory of occupied states.[7] The Soviets evidently wanted to keep their postwar options open.

Other activity began to provide a clearer picture of the Soviets' conception of what constituted an adequate security border. In a March 1943 conversation with British foreign secretary Anthony Eden, the Soviet ambassador to London, Ivan Maiskii, related the following points of Soviet interest in Europe: (1) the Baltic states must be indisputably recognized as a part of the USSR; (2) the idea of a Balkan federation was admissible if necessary to avoid disagreeing entirely with the U.S. secretary of state; (3) any federation in Europe must, on Soviet insistence, exclude Romania; and (4) the Soviet Union desired bases and mutual assistance pacts in Finland and Romania. When Eden dined with Roosevelt several days later, the president was understanding of Soviet demands in Finland. Roosevelt also did not view the Polish situation as presenting any problem, nor did he take exception to the Russian claim to the Baltic

---

[5]Ibid., p. 98.

[6]Britain, Public Records Office, Foreign Office Files (hereafter FO), 371-37031, record of 12th meeting, October 30, 1943; as summarized in Elisabeth Barker, "Greece in the Framework of Anglo-Soviet Relations, 1941–1947," in *Greece: From Resistance to Civil War,* ed. Marion Sarafis (Nottingham: Spokesman, 1980), p. 19.

[7]U.S. Department of State, *Foreign Relations of the United States* (hereafter *FRUS*), *1943,* vol. I (Washington: USGPO, 1965), pp. 596–99.

states, believing that no one would be in a position to turn the Soviets out.[8]

After the Teheran Conference in November–December 1943, at which the Polish question was rather crudely "resolved," the country not satisfactorily accounted for under Great Power auspices was Romania. The Western Allies had acquiesced on the Baltic states; Poland was taken care of for the time being; and there were no insuperable difficulties on Finland. Stalin had gained Western acceptance of his conception of an East European sphere of influence, but Romania was not yet specifically included. The Soviet insistence on excluding Romania from any federative scheme indicated the importance of the country in Soviet estimation.[9] Stalin's eagerness to master Romania should not, however, obscure his greater desire to secure Western acceptance of the Soviet conception of security arrangements throughout Eastern Europe. When in mid-1944 the British demonstrated their desire to retain Greece, the Soviet leader saw his opportunity to kill two birds with one stone. The spheres-of-influence agreement that ultimately emerged served not merely as a guarantee of British acquiescence in Soviet control of Romania but as a means of eliciting Western consent to broader Soviet objectives in southeastern Europe.

Soviet attitudes toward the Balkans underwent significant changes as the war progressed. Whereas at the Moscow Conference, Molotov had demanded Turkey's entry into the war on the side of the Allies,[10] by the time the Teheran Conference convened, the Soviet position had undergone a complete reversal: in Molotov's view, a Mediterranean landing would endanger the landing in northern France; Stalin no longer favored Turkish entry into the war.[11] The Yugoslav Partisans' declaration on November 29, 1943, that their political organization, the Antifascist Council for the National Liberation of Yugoslavia (AVNOJ), was to be the "Supreme Representative of the nations of Yugoslavia" caught Stalin by

[8]FO 371-36991 N1605, March 10, and N1748, March 16, 1943.

[9]The Soviets were apparently so eager to control Romania that they made little effort to disguise their intentions. The British ambassador to Turkey recounted a conversation in November 1944, in which his Soviet counterpart, Sergei Vinogradov, declared: "You want to maintain your influence in Greece, . . . we want to keep Roumania in our orbit." Vinogradov went on to dismiss the rest of Europe, except for the additional comment, "Turkey will be left in complete tranquillity." Judging by later Soviet treatment of Turkey, one can legitimately wonder whether the Soviet ambassador's assurances about Greece did not also undergo modification after the end of the war: FO 371-44074 R19589, November 29, 1944.

[10]Record of meeting, October 20, 1943, FRUS, 1943, 1:583–86.

[11]Mastny, pp. 124–25.

surprise.[12] If the Yugoslavs were pursuing their own policies in the Balkans, the Soviets clearly needed some sort of Balkan agreement in order to control the emerging autonomous politicomilitary forces in the region.

The Emergence of Greece as a Major Soviet Concern

Despite this increased activity regarding the Balkans, the Soviets tended to neglect Greece and remained relatively ignorant of the Greek political context. There were several reasons for this. First, the appeals Moscow broadcast for unity and struggle against the invader were overwhelmingly pro-Slavic in their orientation and thus failed to stir the Greek people into action. Second, contacts between the Greek Communists and the Comintern were severed during the German occupation, and few attempts were made to reestablish communications.[13] The KKE was consequently left to its own devices, with only indirect contacts to Moscow as a guide. Finally, the Soviets viewed the Communist-dominated Greek Popular Liberation Army (ELAS) as a resistance organization for the prosecution of the war and discouraged the pursuit of anything resembling "revolutionary" goals so as to avoid unduly alarming the British. The latter concern is evident from the Soviet response to the "first round" of the Greek Civil War, which began in the autumn of 1943. To understand why this first round caused complications for Soviet policy, one must briefly examine the prior evolution of the Greek Communist resistance.

The Communists had succeeded in creating the largest and most effective resistance organization within Greece during the course of the war. Once the Germans occupied Greece in 1941, it became necessary to create a viable resistance organization, and the KKE was best suited for the task because its experience with oppression under the Metaxas dictatorship had provided excellent training in clandestine organization and activity. Accordingly, the KKE was the dominant force behind the creation of the National Liberation Front (EAM) on September 27, 1941. That EAM was under the complete control of the KKE is by now well established and requires little elaboration.[14] Supposedly EAM gave expression to the

[12]Barker, *Macedonia,* p. 95; Vladimir Dedijer, *Tito* (reprint, New York: Arno, 1972), p. 209.

[13]Foivos Oikonomidis, *Oi Prostates: I Alithini Istoria* (Athens: Kaktos, 1984), pp. 14–15, 17.

[14]See John C. Loulis, *The Greek Communist Party, 1940–1944* (London: Croom Helm, 1982), pp. 39–58.

Greek people's desire for national liberation, which allowed it to serve as a political front for the KKE; the Communists could act through EAM and appear to represent the great majority of the Greek people. In fact, when using EAM, the KKE dropped references to "communism" or "revolution" and reverted to espousing "unity" and the "national liberation struggle."[15] For the KKE the arrangement was ideal, for it is quite apparent that the majority of the Greek people did indeed indentify with the national liberation aims of EAM. The Greek public was not, however, aware of the extent of Communist control of EAM, as an Office of Strategic Services (OSS) report attests: "While it is certainly true that the larger portion of EAM supporters are *not* Communists and do *not* desire a Communist dictatorship but rather a free, democratic, somewhat leftist republic, it nevertheless remains true that this large body of opinion is not in a position to control the Communist direction of EAM."[16]

But a political front was not the real strength of the KKE; it was ELAS that formed the core of Communist power. Although ELAS was small at its inception in June 1942, through the efforts of the Communists it rapidly became the largest resistance organization in Greece.[17] By 1943, as later discussion of the first round will indicate, ELAS was large enough for the KKE to contemplate the elimination of all rivals. With an independent base of military power, an effective mouthpiece for the expression of popular sentiment, and an efficient clandestine organization throughout Greece, the KKE was in an excellent position to pursue its own interests.

One final attribute of the KKE is of crucial importance to this study: regardless of circumstances, the Greek Communist leadership remained overwhelmingly faithful to the Soviet Union and respectful of its position as the homeland of Communist revolution.[18] This pro-Soviet orientation had its basis in the KKE's fidelity to the ideology of Marxism-Leninism as developed under Stalin. The Greek Communists looked to Russia for guidance and advice, as is evidenced by their continuous attempts to reestablish direct radio contact during the war and their requests for more

[15]Ibid., pp. 41–43.

[16]U.S. National Archives, Office of Strategic Services Reports, Record Group 226, (hereafter OSS), 109050, December 19, 1944; emphasis in original.

[17]Dominique Eudes, *The Kapetanios: Partisans and Civil War in Greece, 1943–1949* (New York: Monthly Review Press, 1972), p. 5.

[18]John O. Iatrides concludes likewise; see his *Revolt in Athens: The Greek Communist "Second Round," 1944–1945* (Princeton, N.J.: Princeton University Press, 1972), p. 21. For a documentary survey of the relations between the Greek Communist party and the Soviet Union in the interwar years, see Andrew L. Zapantis, *Greek-Soviet Relations, 1917–1941* (New York: Columbia University Press, 1982), pp. 42–43.

Greek-language broadcasts from the Soviet Union.[19] Everything Russian was idolized by the KKE; ELAS general Stefanos Sarafis has described the adulation accorded the Russian Military Mission's members when they arrived in the mountains of Greece.[20] More important, the fidelity of the Greek Communists to the Soviet Union led them to accept Soviet actions even when they damaged KKE interests. On January 31, 1945, after most of the fighting of the "second round" of the Greek Civil War was over and no sign of Soviet support was forthcoming, the head of EAM in Thessaloniki argued, "EAM knows that Russia disapproves of British policy in Greece, but Russia is not expressing her disapproval because she needs Britain for other purposes."[21] Rationalization on behalf of Soviet interests was to prove the Achilles' heel of the KKE; for Stalin would use this ideological fidelity to secure Greek Communist conformity to his policies.

Two interconnected rivalries dominated the Greek political context. The first was the competition between the London-supported Greek government-in-exile in Cairo and the forces of EAM/ELAS, and it centered on the decades-old constitutional question that plagued Greek politics and was responsible for much of the extreme polarization of political positions. While EAM was adamant that the Greek monarchy should be abolished, the monarchists in the Cairo government (chiefly the Populist party) clung to King George, who stubbornly refused to consider a plebiscite on his return to Greece. Churchill's strong support of the monarchy and his antipathy toward EAM/ELAS forces bolstered rightist elements in Greece and increased the polarization and mistrust among political parties. Thus, as the Cairo government retained its promonarchy position thanks to British influence, the forces of EAM/ELAS opposed it with equal fervor. Each side had in view the political future of Greece, but the result was only to increase polarization and distrust. This critical aspect of the Greek question is too complex to examine here; for it is of greater relevance to Anglo-American, than Soviet, policy.[22] What is necessary to mention, however, is this problem's potential effect on Soviet intentions.

The Greek government-in-exile had the advantage of being the legitimate government of Greece as a result of the recognition it received from the Great Powers. Its major problem was that it had no representation in

[19]U.S. National Archives, Department of State Records, Record Group 59 (hereafter DSR), 868.00/1-2245, no. 427.

[20]Stefanos Sarafis, *ELAS: Greek Resistance Army* (London: Merlin, 1980), pp. 351–62.

[21]OSS L52536, February 5, 1945.

[22]See Iatrides, *Revolt in Athens*; also worthwhile are Christopher M. Woodhouse, *The Struggle for Greece, 1941–1949* (London: Hart-Davis, MacGibbon, 1976), and Loulis.

"free Greece" and commanded an army stationed in the Middle East and thoroughly penetrated by political factions. The KKE, through EAM/ELAS, had acquired prestige as the most powerful representative of liberated Greece and a dependable power base but had no official representation in the legitimate government. KKE general secretary Giorgis Siantos had succeeded in gaining Allied recognition for ELAS as a resistance movement in July 1943, but not solely because of the KKE's powerful position; the British Special Operations Executive had encouraged recognition because it viewed ELAS as a useful instrument for short-term military objectives.[23]

The second rivalry was the competition among the resistance groups. The two most important for present purposes were the National Republican Greek League (EDES) and National and Social Liberation (EKKA).[24] Although ELAS was by far the largest resistance army, the presence of the others made it impossible for ELAS to claim sole responsibility for the national liberation struggle. Furthermore, once the British began strengthening EDES and EKKA in response to the KKE's attempt to destroy them in late 1943, they could only pose a greater threat to ELAS.

These tensions in the political context impelled the KKE leaders toward two objectives: elimination of rivals in order to claim all of liberated Greece and the establishment of a rival government, thereby forcing the British to accept a Communist-dominated popular government in free Greece. This path, if pursued, could only provoke a crisis in British-Soviet relations. Besides creating deep divisions between Soviet and British interests in the prosecution of the war, it would mean that the Greek Communists would establish themselves independent of Soviet control.

In mid-October, ELAS apparently decided the time was ripe for elimination of rival resistance organizations. The principal target was EDES, under the command of Napoleon Zervas.[25] Siantos, considered to be the archi-

[23]Woodhouse, *Struggle for Greece*, p. 42. KKE Politburo member Andreas Tzimas also asserted that Soviet diplomacy had indirectly helped to bring about the July 1943 agreement.

[24]Other resistance groups operating in northern Greece during the war had little bearing on Soviet policy (with the exception of the Slavo-Macedonian case) and are not considered here.

[25]Possibly the necessity of eliminating opposition resistance groups had to do with developments in the plans for seizing power in Greece. KKE Politburo member Vasilis Bartziotas later admitted that plans for the "armed struggle" had been worked out by ELAS Command and the Communist Organization of Athens in the fall of 1943 and early 1944; see Bartziotas, "I Politiki mas ton Stelechon sto KKE ta Teleftaia Deka Chronia," in *Deka Chronia Palis* (reprint, Athens: Poreia, 1978), p. 49. Although no evidence links the attack on EDES with the plans for seizing Athens, the close coincidence in their dates suggests some coordination of actions may have taken place.

tect of this first round, underestimated both the strength of EDES and the strong British support that Zervas received.[26] The result was prolonged civil war that lasted into 1944.

The Soviet response was initially silent acquiescence to British policy. When Eden briefly related the situation in Greece to Molotov at the Foreign Ministers' Conference, Molotov made no apparent objection.[27] On January 3, 1944, the Soviet government clarified its position when it consented to join with Britain and the United States in supporting a broadcast appeal for national unity in Greece.[28] Stalin was displeased with the Greek Communists in two ways: he was concerned that their action could destroy his good relations with the British, and their show of independence was just what led him to distrust guerrilla movements in the first place.

A further consequence of the first round of the Greek Civil War was that the British decisively shifted their support toward EDES. The utility of Allied recognition for ELAS was greatly diminished, if not destroyed, since the British, as sole representatives of the Great Powers in Greece, were now opposed to the Greek Communists. As a result, the KKE found it more tempting to pursue an independent path and establish its own government, thereby challenging the legitimacy of the Greek government-in-exile. It is quite plausible that the negative Soviet attitude during the campaign against EDES had the effect of postponing such a decision. But within three months of the Soviet appeal for unity in the Greek resistance movement, the situation would arise once again.

Summer 1944: The KKE as a Threat to Soviet-British Negotiations on Greece

In March 1944, the KKE took the step of forming the Political Committee of National Liberation (PEEA). Since the date of the Founding Charter (given as March 10, 1944) came less than two weeks after the Plaka Agreement,[29] which ended the first round, it appears the KKE had switched tactics from open military confrontation to forcing the government-in-exile to grant EAM representation in the Cairo government. In keeping with EAM tactics, the PEEA Founding Charter stressed nationalist

[26]Woodhouse, *Struggle for Greece*, p. 56.
[27]Barker, "Greece in the Framework of Anglo-Soviet Relations," p. 19.
[28]FO 371-43336 N6534, October 16, 1944.
[29]"Idritiki Praxi," in *Keimena tis Ethnikis Antistasis* (hereafter *KEA*) (Athens: Sygchroni Epochi, 1981), vol. 2, pp. 15–17.

goals. It declared that PEEA's fundamental goal was "to coordinate and conduct, with all the means and all of the forces in Greece and from the side of our Allies, the struggle against the occupiers."[30] In its "Declaration to the Greek People," PEEA further reinforced these aims by declaring that it would seek to ensure the freedom of religion and private property.[31] There was no mention of PEEA as a "government"; instead, the Founding Charter stressed that the organization would carry out the task of "administration" in the liberated areas of Greece, and PEEA was composed of "secretaries," not "ministers."[32]

Nonetheless, the Founding Charter contains phrases clearly threatening to the government-in-exile. A major PEEA objective was "the formation of a government of general, national coalition."[33] The statement that there was an "obvious need for a responsible *political* organ in free Greece, which would symbolize the national unity," clearly implied that PEEA, if it so desired, could take on political functions. Even more significant was the phrase which declared that PEEA, as a central political organ, would "direct the administrative organs that had been spontaneously created."[34] This last phrase indicated that although PEEA's duties were still unspecified, they certainly extended beyond mere administration. The implications were clear: the KKE, through PEEA, could attempt to force its way into the government-in-exile and gain a predominant position; or, it could go its own way and declare itself the legitimate government of Greece.

The reasons the Greek Communists chose to pursue such a course of action help clarify the Soviet response. First, the initial round of the Civil War had ended in failure, with rival resistance organizations not eliminated, indicating the need for a change of tactics. Second, the British stand on the return of King George to Greece had hardened during the first few months of 1944, which could only have alarmed the KKE. In November–December 1943, Churchill and Eden had become convinced the king should not return to Greece immediately after liberation but should appoint a regent. King George, however, bolstered by some unexpected support from Roosevelt,[35] refused to budge and indicated on March 10, 1943, that his intention to return remained unchanged. Since the British Foreign Office had ceased exerting pressure on the king, Churchill gradually drifted back

---

[30]Ibid., p. 15.
[31]"Diangelma tis PEEA pros ton Elliniko Lao," *KEA* 2:18.
[32]"Idritiki Praxi," *KEA* 2:16.
[33]Ibid.
[34]"Diangelma tis PEEA pros ton Elliniko Lao," *KEA* 2:17; emphasis added.
[35]Lawrence S. Wittner, *American Intervention in Greece, 1943–1949* (New York: Columbia University Press, 1982), pp. 11–12.

to supporting the monarch's position.[36] Leaders of the KKE must have realized that to save the situation, they had to establish influence with the government-in-exile; hence the creation of PEEA. Last, KKE leaders must have been encouraged by Tito's establishment of AVNOJ as a government. No doubt the Greek Communists took this move as acceptable to Moscow, and they must have thought themselves in good company taking a similar step.

These developments could only have evoked Soviet concern. In fact, Tito had not given the Soviet regime notice of his intention to form the AVNOJ government,[37] a move bound to disturb the British. Coming so soon afterward, the creation of PEEA heightened British alarm just when the second front, so important to Stalin, was about to become a reality. Stalin thus felt it necessary to transmit his displeasure to the Greek Communists: on March 25, 1944, he sent King George a congratulatory telegram in honor of Greek Independence Day. The same day, the Soviets dispatched another telegram to Siantos, informing the KKE of the Soviet Union's recognition of the Greek government in Cairo.[38] KKE Politburo member Iannis Ioannidis recalled the chilling effect this clear sign of Stalin's disapproval had on the Greek Communists. The fact that PEEA, formed barely two weeks earlier, was not even mentioned in the Soviet telegram was especially disappointing.[39] Once again the Soviets had cut short its independent initiatives.

The founding of PEEA was also important to the evolution of events in the Greek armed forces in the Middle East. After the German occupation of Greece, the Greek armed forces had been transferred to the Middle East, where they remained with little to do, excellent targets for political agitation. Political organizations spanning the Greek political spectrum emerged within the armed forces. The most important of the leftist organizations were the Antifascist Army Organization (ASO) and the National Liberation Military Democratic Organization. The announcement of PEEA's formation touched off a great deal of activity in these and other

[36]Loulis, pp. 96–97.

[37]Dedijer, p. 209.

[38]Loulis, p. 102; Iannis Ioannidis, *Anamniseis: Provlimata tis Politikis tou KKE stin Ethniki Antistasi, 1940–1945* (Athens: Themelio, 1979), pp. 244–45. Ioannidis' memoirs were originally presented in the newspaper *Avgi* as a series of interviews with Alekos Papapanagiotou. Later in the interviews (pp. 246–47), Ioannidis failed to remember whether Tito had also sent a congratulatory telegram supporting the formation of PEEA; in an appended note (pp. 526–27n), Papapanagiotou cites Tito's congratulatory telegram, as published in *Rizospastis*, March 30, 1944.

[39]Ioannidis, p. 244.

organizations during the month of March. The key factor in igniting mutiny, however, was the king's refusal to follow Prime Minister Emmanuil Tsouderos's advice and appoint a regent.[40] After that, Republican and leftist elements within the armed forces united around their common antipathy to the king. A committee of officers soon confronted Tsouderos with a memorandum demanding the formation of a new government with PEEA as its basis.[41] Tsouderos had no alternative but to arrest them. Although they were later released, the repercussions could not be avoided; on April 7, 1944, mutiny broke out in the Greek fleet.

The British viewed these developments with grave concern. A mutiny inspired by leftist sentiments and aspiring to install a pro-EAM government was intolerable to Churchill. At his direction, British troops and Greek forces still loyal to the Cairo government forcibly put down the mutiny in the closing days of April. There is no conclusive evidence to indicate Soviet involvement in the mutiny,[42] and given Soviet policy in Greece up to this point, there is no reason to suspect Soviet instigation. To have become involved in such a venture would have provoked a sharp British response. There is sufficient evidence, however, to indicate that the Soviets used the mutiny to prod the British into an agreement that would give them the guarantees they needed on Romania. Furthermore, from the perspective of long-term (i.e., postwar) Soviet policy, the mutiny actually produced beneficial results. These two points merit closer examination.

The outbreak of the mutiny in the Greek armed forces prompted the Soviets to drop their attitude of disinterest. United States ambassador Lincoln MacVeagh tended to attribute the growing Soviet interest in Greece to the Red Army's victorious push through southern Europe. He was struck by the contrast between Russian professions of ignorance of Greek affairs in January and their sudden knowledgeability during the mutiny. According to MacVeagh, the Soviets had "come a long way with their victories and the appetite for influence which these have caused";[43]

---

[40]Iatrides, *Revolt in Athens*, p. 53.

[41]There appears to be some confusion about the composition of the committee of officers and the date it was presented to Tsouderos. Iatrides, ibid., p. 52, states that a committee of Republican officers presented the memorandum to Tsouderos on March 31, while Loulis, p. 117, maintains that the committee was Communist led and presented their demands on April 3.

[42]Iatrides, *Revolt in Athens*, p. 53, reaches this conclusion.

[43]Lincoln MacVeagh, *Ambassador MacVeagh Reports: Greece, 1933–1947* (hereafter *MacVeagh Diaries*), ed. John O. Iatrides (Princeton, N.J.: Princeton University Press, 1980), pp. 506–7, 494.

events appear to support his analysis. When, on April 11, the British and Greeks attempted to get from the Allies a joint statement on the mutiny "to allay Greek political excitement," Soviet ambassador Nikolai Novikov surprisingly disagreed with British policy, arguing that all the Greeks wanted was to change their government. At the same time, the Moscow press began openly to attack the actions of Tsouderos and the British.[44] Nor was criticism of British handling of the mutiny all that occupied Stalin's attention. MacVeagh's diaries also reflect the Soviet preoccupation with Romania. Specifically, on April 8, Novikov called upon the American ambassador "urgently" to bring a copy of the Soviet's armistice terms for Romania. And on the day the Soviet ambassador criticized British policy (April 11), MacVeagh wrote that Novikov had come "principally to talk about the Romanian affair."[45]

The Soviets' refusal to support British policy and their eager interest in Romanian affairs indicated to the worried British that something more was needed to draw the Soviets back into line. On April 16, Churchill responded to the Soviet statements in a letter to Molotov. He stated his determination to put down the mutiny in the Greek armed forces and added that he was sure the Soviets would not allow such things to occur in armies or forces under their control. The British prime minister closed the letter by referring to the Romanian case, in which the British considered the Soviets the dominating power.[46] Molotov replied on April 22, stating that the Tass news agency had been instructed to verify its information more fully. In the same reply, Molotov (echoing Novikov's April 11 call on MacVeagh), turned to Romania and wrote that the time had come to increase pressure from all sides so that the Romanians would "abandon their hopeless and criminal position." Elisabeth Barker has noted that this was the first instance in which Molotov seemed to link Greece and Romania.[47] After Churchill confidently assured Molotov on April 25 that the Greek mutiny was well in hand, the Soviet foreign minister replied on April 28 that the Soviet Union could not accept any responsibility for British action in Greece. As in the previous letter, Molotov again turned to Romania and complained that the British still had not informed the Soviet

[44]Ibid.; see also Loulis, p. 121.

[45]*MacVeagh Diaries*, pp. 487, 491, 494; see also pp. 490–91, 494–95.

[46]FO 371-437292 R6133, in Loulis, pp. 121–22. Barker, citing a different British government document (PREM 3 211/16, Churchill addition to FO draft of message to Molotov, April 16, 1944), does not mention that Romania is specifically referred to; see Barker, "Greece in the Framework of Anglo-Soviet Relations," p. 22.

[47]PREM 3 211/16, Molotov message T.193/4, April 22, 1944; in Barker, "Greece in the Framework of Anglo-Soviet Relations," p. 22.

Union of the steps that would be taken to put greater pressure on the Romanians.[48]

The decided shift in Soviet attitude toward Greece during the month of April and the British response to the mutiny indicate that developments in Greece had provided the Soviet Union with a choice of strategies. If British resolve was high and the mutiny effectively dealt with, the Soviets could plead ignorance of Greek affairs and discreetly back away from confrontation. If, however, the British could not contain the situation, the Soviets had the option of exploring the possibilities of supporting the Greek Communist position. The mutiny in the Middle East thus became a critical test of British resolve. Since the British successfully demonstrated their resolve, the Soviets did plead ignorance and began, as Molotov's letters indicate, to link the future status of Greece with Romania. In general, the Soviets wound up with a better bargain than they had hoped for; for not only had British action created the opportunity for a spheres-of-influence agreement, but it had also created conditions most beneficial to the Soviet's long-term policy of political infiltration.

Several consequences of the mutiny were of potential significance to the Soviets. First, the events dramatically revealed the Soviet potential for capitalizing on unrest in the Balkans. This could be tapped by combining the victorious Red Army advance into the Balkans with Russia's position as the center of revolution, as MacVeagh pointed out in a letter to Roosevelt on May 15. The American ambassador, paraphrasing the opinion of the U.S. consul general in Istanbul on the various Communist-led resistance groups in the Balkans, noted that there "can be felt in Istanbul a powerful Russian surge into the Balkan area at present—'but underneath.'" Later in the letter, MacVeagh commented on recent unrest in the Middle East: "Beneath all its traditional Greek trappings, the revolt was inspired and maintained by an ideology especially associated with Russia, and . . . while it lasted Russian sympathy with it was openly shown, *despite its dangerous implications for the Allied cause.*"[49] Hence the Soviets could tap their prestige as a military power and ideological homeland to activate elements faithful to communism. Although the vigorous British response forced the Soviets to back down and opt for an understanding on Romania, Stalin knew that he had a tremendous weapon at his disposal. In fact, as the course of events in Greece reveal, he was able to use the Greek Communists' fidelity to Soviet Communist ideology in such

[48]PREM 3 211/16, Molotov message, T.1004/4, April 28, 1944; in ibid., pp. 22–23.
[49]*MacVeagh Diaries*, pp. 517, 519; emphasis added.

a way that the KKE sacrificed its own interests for those of the Soviet state.

The reality of Greek politics was clear: Churchill was not going to tolerate a strong or influential pro-Communist element in Greece. The mutiny in the Middle East served as an ample demonstration and clearly implied that in any attempted negotiations, the Communists would be forced into an insignificant role. The only logical alternative for the KKE was to go its own way by defying the British and making suppression too costly for them.[50] In taking an independent course, the KKE did not, surprisingly, believe itself to be contradicting the wishes of Moscow. Local Communist elites generally exhibited a form of cognitive dissonance in pursuing their particular interests while simultaneously believing in their absolute fidelity to the Soviet Union. The divergence was especially pronounced because the rupture of communications with Moscow compelled Communist leaders to deduce Soviet interests in concrete circumstances with only general principles as a guide. Local Communists relied on their conviction that the best way to "please Moscow" in the absence of information was to pursue the goal of revolution. Stalin was consequently faced with resistance organizations that saw themselves as obedient yet were extremely difficult to control. This was certainly the case with Tito's Partisans, and there is no reason to suspect that KKE leaders were any different.

But with the emerging agreement with Britain at a critical juncture, it was imperative to transmit to the Greek Communists the message that aggressive action would jeopardize Soviet policy. Lacking any strong means of intervention (and unwilling to use them lest they arouse the suspicions of the British), Stalin had recourse only to his authority as head of the revolutionary movement to alter KKE policies. Thus the Soviets intervened with their powerful psychological leverage and pushed the KKE along the path of cooperation. By doing so, they were able to get a free hand in Romania and still retain the KKE as a potential source of political leverage in postwar Greece.

A second beneficial consequence of the mutiny was, as John Iatrides points out, the disintegration of the Greek forces in the Middle East.[51] This was potentially useful for the Soviets because it left the Greek government-in-exile in a vulnerable position; when the time should come for

---

[50]This is the central argument made by Tito's subordinate, Svetozar Vukmanović-Tempo, *How and Why the People's Liberation Struggle of Greece Met with Defeat* (reprint, London: Merlin, 1985).

[51]Iatrides, *Revolt in Athens*, p. 54.

the British to pull out of Greece, concessions could be extracted from the Greek government through the threat of Communist-led civil strife it would be powerless to control. The one consequence injurious to long-term Soviet interests was the increased polarization of the Greek political context. If mutual hostility rose to such a level that all forms of conciliation became impossible, the Soviets ran the risk of losing their influence.

The events of April had sufficiently alarmed the British and the Greek government-in-exile to lead them to begin negotiations to form a government of national unity. Tsouderos had resigned and, after Sofoklis Venizelos had proven ineffective, George Papandreou became prime minister. KKE/EAM had shown its capacity to cause unrest; now it was time to see if the military superiority and prestige of representing liberated Greece could be translated into political gains.

On May 17, politicians from virtually every party in Greece (twenty-eight delegates in all), converged on Lebanon for a four-day conference that would ultimately produce a government of national unity.[52] The British backed Papandreou and hoped that an agreement could be achieved that would bring EAM into the government and simultaneously render it innocuous. The KKE had no such intentions. Memoirs of key actors as well as government documents clearly indicate that the KKE would try to gain a predominant influence in the government of national unity. Sarafis briefly mentioned the objectives of the PEEA delegation (Socialists Alexander Svolos, Angelos Angelopoulos, Nikolaos Askoutsis, Dimitris Stratis; Communists Miltiadis Porfyrogenis, Politburo member Petros Rousos, and Sarafis): (1) the PEEA delegates were to ask for 50 percent of the ministries in the new government; (2) they were to specify which ministries were to be included; and (3) they were to request to transfer part of the government to free Greece. Ioannidis, who is more specific on these points, has stated that the delegation was to demand half of the ministries plus one, in order to have a majority. In addition, of the specific ministries to be obtained, Ioannidis mentions only the Ministry of Defense, but KKE cables intercepted by the British indicate that the Ministry of Interior and the War Office were to be requested.[53] On the third demand, transferring part of the government to free Greece, Ioannidis concurs with Sarafis.[54] These instructions, if fulfilled, amounted to the transformation of PEEA into the legitimate government of Greece.

---

[52]Ibid., p. 61.

[53]Sarafis, p. 331; Ioannidis, pp. 220, 221; FO 371-43732 R8429, in Loulis, p. 127. This discussion of PEEA demands follows that presented by Loulis, p. 127.

[54]Ioannidis, p. 221.

But the other delegates, especially Papandreou, were not about to let this transpire. Papandreou put the PEEA delegation on the defensive by playing on the other delegates' belief that the Communists knew of the mutiny and by skillfully exploiting the news that Colonel Dimitrios Psarros, military leader of EKKA, had been captured and killed by ELAS troops. The pressure on the PEEA delegates succeeded in forcing them to make concessions far beyond their initial instructions. The key factor was in the composition of the PEEA delegation: there were not enough Communists on it to stand firm, and a rupture between PEEA Socialists and Communists would pull the facade off the KKE's political front organization. (It is not clear, however, why the PEEA delegation felt compelled to reach a bad agreement rather than have the conference end in failure.) In the end, the PEEA delegation succeeded in getting only five unspecified ministries for EAM out of a total of twenty, and the government would remain in the Middle East. This solution was a setback for the KKE. In different circumstances such an agreement might perhaps have created a framework for cooperation among the various political parties, but the extreme polarization between the two most important actors (Papandreou backed by the British on the one hand, the KKE on the other) determined that in this agreement the victorious side would retain the power and influence while the loser was consigned to an empty role, ensnared in a web of political commitments. Papandreou was the victor; the KKE, the beneficiary of the first of a series of commitments that robbed them of their capacity for independent action. It is not surprising, therefore, that the KKE response to the Lebanon Charter was less than enthusiastic.

The day after the conclusion of the Lebanon Conference, KKE general secretary Siantos launched an attack on EDES and Papandreou: EDES for collaborating with the Germans, Papandreou for trying to disband ELAS.[55] The concern for the preservation of ELAS is of greatest significance; for it represents a growing appreciation of the most important part of the KKE: its army. One of the principal points of the Lebanon agreement was a clause that specified all guerrilla bands in free Greece be unified under the command of a single government. The guerrilla principle of organization was regarded as a transitional phase, and the government would take the initiative in determining when the transition was to occur.[56] If PEEA representation in the new government were only 25 percent, the KKE would lose effective control of its army. This was unacceptable to the KKE,

[55]Loulis, p. 133.
[56]Christopher M. Woodhouse, *Apple of Discord: A Survey of Greek Politics in Their International Setting* (London: Hutchinson, 1948), pp. 305–6.

and Siantos' speech represents the growing realization that if the KKE was to achieve a predominant position in Greek politics, it would have to do so by pursuing an independent path and relying on ELAS to an ever greater degree.

Indications that the KKE was seriously considering breaking away and declaring PEEA to be the government are revealed in the decisions of the KKE and its various organizations. In a PEEA decree that appeared in the EAM newspaper *Eleftheri Ellada* on May 28, Politburo member Thanasis Chatzis stated, "PEEA constitutes a supreme form of national unity and is *the only government* in Greece which expresses the wishes of the people."[57] This was the first time PEEA was described as a "government" and not an administrative body. In a May 27 decree of the National Council (the larger administrative body that controlled PEEA), the trend in favor of making PEEA a government also appears. Article 3 of the decree stated, "The National Council is the supreme organ of Popular Sovereignty," and article 9 declared, "PEEA represents the fighting Nation abroad [and] commands the National Army—ELAS."[58] Thus there was a double shift in KKE strategy: a move to declare PEEA to be the legitimate government combined with an effort to establish ELAS as the Greek national army. Having found out that an attempt to gain legitimacy from the British while at the same time retaining a commanding role in Greek politics was doomed to failure, the KKE appeared to be cutting its losses and trying to establish a claim to legitimacy on its own.

The KKE also attempted to make it seem as if the major reason for their refusal to join the government-in-exile was the constitutional question (i.e., the return of the monarchy), but as John Loulis points out, this was more appearance than reality. In the first place, when Papandreou clarified his position on June 12, stating that the king's return would have to await the decision of the people, the KKE stand did not change.[59] In the second place, KKE concern with the rival resistance organization EDES revealed the actual KKE interest in preserving the powerful position of ELAS. As continuous military clashes took place between ELAS and EDES, the KKE in mid-June began to develop the argument that EDES was solely responsible. By the end of June the KKE, through PEEA, decided to counterattack against Zervas' EDES, "with the object of disbanding his force."[60] This decision revealed that the KKE's actual concern was to

[57]As cited in *KEA* 2:157; emphasis added.
[58]"Ethniko Symvoulio: Psifizma A," *KEA* 2:159, 160.
[59]Loulis, p. 135–36.
[60]Sarafis, p. 341.

eliminate its rivals, thereby strengthening its position via à vis the Cairo government.

This tactic continued until July 2, when the EAM Central Committee published a communiqué attacking Zervas for supposedly initiating attacks against ELAS—and not merely attacking it but aspiring to dissolve it as well. The communiqué then proceeded to list its "final terms" for the Lebanon "negotiations." Some of the more important demands were: (1) ELAS should not be altered in character or structure until after the liberation. (2) The commander-in-chief of the Greek armed forces should be approved by EAM; his subordinate should be an ELAS officer; and if the commander-in-chief was not in Greece, the post of guerrilla commander should be given to an ELAS officer. (3) EAM should receive six ministries out of a total of fifteen and one deputy ministry (the Deputy Ministry of Defense, and ministries of Justice and Interior were specifically to go to EAM). (4) Part of the government was to be transferred to liberated Greece.[61] More than anything else, this list indicated that the KKE would not accept the Lebanon accord, was trying to wrap itself in a cloak of legitimacy, and was relying to an ever-greater degree on its military base to achieve its ends. Acceptance of these demands would have been a significant victory for the KKE and put it in a position to dictate terms.

Papandreou, however, rejected the KKE's terms and thereby forced the British to decide whether, in the event of a complete rupture, they would continue to support the Cairo government. Churchill ultimately decided that in a total deadlock the British would support Papandreou and condemn the Communists. On July 11 the EAM Central Committee released a communiqué that contained a blistering attack on Papandreou and Zervas. In addition, it stated that PEEA was "the only government" of the people.[62] The situation appeared headed for a crisis, and it seemed that the Communists had helped it along: the Greek prime minister was denounced as a national traitor; ELAS was to be sent into action against EDES; and PEEA was now being considered the "true" government of Greece. Clearly, KKE/EAM had all but abandoned the Lebanon agreement.

And yet, not only did confrontation *not* occur, but within one month the Greek Communists had conceded on all points and entered the government of national unity. A plausible explanation of this startlingly rapid reversal from confrontation to concession is that Stalin secured a change in Greek Communist policy in order to preserve a spheres-of-influence

[61]For the specific demands, see *KEA* 1:75–77. The KKE's efforts to reinterpret the finalized agreement as merely one phase of negotiations are covered in Loulis, pp. 132–38.
[62]*KEA* 1:78–81.

agreement with the British which guaranteed Soviet control of Romania. An examination of Anglo-Soviet exchanges during the summer of 1944 supports this position.

Restraining the KKE to Preserve Allied Agreement

Although the mutiny of the Greek armed forces in the Middle East served to spark initial British interest, exchanges in May and June 1944 finally crystallized the spheres-of-influence agreement.[63] Since late April, Molotov had become more insistent about Romanian affairs. The Soviet foreign minister's "nasty messages" concerned British intelligence operations in Romania.[64] A British mission had arrived there four months earlier with full Soviet knowledge,[65] yet it did not immediately create serious diplomatic friction, despite Romania's importance for Soviet policy. The Soviets evidently were waiting until they were in a position strong enough to push for complete control of Romanian affairs, which the April mutiny, combined with the continued advance of the Red Army in Europe, provided them. Molotov's criticism of the British presence in Romania was a convenient means of pressing the British on the question of Balkan affairs. This prompted Churchill to ask Eden on May 4 for a paper on the "brute issues" between Britain and the Soviet Union in Italy, Romania, Yugoslavia, and "above all," Greece.[66] The next day, Foreign Secretary Eden discussed the matter with Soviet ambassador Fedor Gusev. Eden suggested the Soviets take the initiative in getting Romania out of the war and the British in return receive Soviet support for their policy in Greece.[67]

On May 18, Gusev returned to the Foreign Office and stated that the Soviets were prepared to accept such an agreement but wished to know if the United States had been consulted.[68] Stalin's reluctance to go ahead

---

[63]Various official sources record Soviet movements in Romania before May 1944, but the *explicit* linkage of Romania to Greece does not appear before early May.

[64]*MacVeagh Diaries*, p. 515.

[65]Barker, "Greece in the Framework of Anglo-Soviet Relations," p. 23.

[66]Winston S. Churchill, *Triumph and Tragedy* (Boston: Houghton Mifflin, 1953), pp. 72–73.

[67]Bruce R. Kuniholm, *The Origins of the Cold War in the Near East: Great Power Conflict and Diplomacy in Iran, Turkey, and Greece* (Princeton, N.J.: Princeton University Press, 1980), p. 101.

[68]Churchill, *Triumph and Tragedy*, p. 73.

with the agreement until he heard from the Americans was an indication of the sensitivity of the issue as well as the value he placed on maintaining Allied unity. Since the Americans were initially reluctant to accept this arrangement for fear of its creating a permanent division of the Balkans, the agreement was allowed to languish until mid-June. Hence, during this period, Stalin had no incentive to restrain the Greek Communists. He may actually have reasoned that the continued advance of the Red Army into the Balkans combined with internal unrest in Greece might succeed in bringing U.S. policymakers down from the heights of postwar idealism to the low but solid ground of realpolitik.

Churchill persisted and, in his June 11 letter to Roosevelt, recommended that his proposal be valid for a period of only three months. The president finally agreed on June 13, and the next day Churchill instructed Eden to inform Molotov of American acceptance.[69] Thus, by late June 1944, the Soviets had every reason to believe that the temporary division of the Balkans would take place, freeing them to take the lead in Romania.

Stalin now had some incentive to bring the KKE into line with his policy, but he wanted to be sure. When Churchill personally cabled him the news of American acceptance on July 11 (the same day the KKE's attack on Papandreou and the Lebanon agreement reached its zenith), Stalin wired back on July 15 that he preferred to hear from the Americans directly. Churchill, upon receipt of Stalin's telegram, became convinced the entire arrangement had fallen through and concluded that he was "unable to reach any final agreement about dividing responsibilities in the Balkan peninsula." The British prime minister then reasoned that the Soviet Military Mission sent into Greece in late July constituted a violation of a "gentleman's agreement" and was therefore an act of bad faith.[70]

Other events at the time indicate that Churchill's pessimistic assessment may not have been correct. In fact, on July 11 the State Department sent a memorandum to the Soviet Embassy indicating American assent to the plan.[71] Since Stalin probably would not have received this direct notification of American acceptance until *after* his July 15 telegram to Churchill, it is more reasonable to assume that he simply considered the agreement finalized on the basis of the British notifcation in late June and began acting accordingly.

The agreement gave Stalin the opportunity he had sought for months:

[69]Ibid., pp. 76–77.
[70]Ibid., pp. 81, 80–81.
[71]Kuniholm, pp. 103–4.

Romania, the only loose end in the Soviets' security belt, was being offered to him by both the British and Americans. But the increasingly militant policy of the KKE, of which Stalin was aware through Novikov in Cairo (and Soviet agents in Athens),[72] made it imperative that the Greek Communists be brought into line, lest their actions jeopardize Allied harmony. It was essential to let the KKE know Moscow considered a confrontational policy counterproductive.

In late June and early July 1944, with indirect knowledge of American assent to the plan, the Soviets were content to convey their directives through diplomatic channels. Hence, in early July, Ambassador Novikov reportedly advised Svolos, head of the PEEA delegation in Cairo, that EAM should join the Greek government in Cairo.[73] In addition, Rousos, the KKE representative in Cairo, was informed by the Soviet attaché in Cairo during the end of June that the Soviet ambassador conveyed his personal view that (1) the Lebanon agreement corresponded to existing circumstances; (2) the attitude of the PEEA delegation was correct; (3) PEEA should enter the government; and (4) the delegation should make sure that this opinion was transmitted to the mountains.[74]

Once Stalin received *direct* confirmation of American willingness to accept a British-Soviet agreement on the Balkans, it became essential to ensure KKE compliance. Although the evidence is still scant, a plausible hypothesis is that Stalin felt compliance could be guaranteed only by the dispatch of a military mission to the partisan strongholds in the mountains of Greece, to present the KKE with direct instructions to adopt a more conciliatory policy. The Russian Military Mission arrived at ELAS head-

---

[72]DSR 868.00/10-2444. Iatrides, *Revolt in Athens,* p. 76 n, also refers to the same document.

[73]DSR 868.01/7-2844. William H. McNeill reports that in 1946, Svolos informed him that the decision to join Papandreou's government without further negotiation was due to the instruction his Communist colleagues received from the Russian minister in Cairo; see McNeill, "The View from Greece," in *Witnesses to the Origins of the Cold War,* ed. Thomas T. Hammond (Seattle: University of Washington Press, 1982), p. 108 n. Soviet instructions to the KKE are also confirmed by the testimony of Miltiadis Porfyrogenis, who, in a conversation related by Giorgis Vontitsos-Gousias, stated that the Soviets told Petros Rousos to accept the Lebanon agreement. In a related vein, Porfyrogenis added that the Soviet Military Mission to the mountains of Greece in summer 1944 had as its main objective to secure KKE consent to the Lebanon agreement: Vontitsos-Gousias, *Oi Aities gia tis Ittes, ti Diaspasi tou KKE kai tis Ellinikis Aristeras* (Athens: Na Iperetoume to Lao, 1977), vol. 2, pp. 142–45.

[74]*KKE: Episima Keimena, 1940–1945* (N.p.: KKE Esoterikou, 1973), p. 629; in Loulis, p. 141. Pavlos Nefeloudis confirms that this was the information the KKE received from the Soviets in Cairo: Nefeloudis, *Stis Piges tis Kakodaimonias: Ta Vathitera Aitia tis Diaspasis tou KKE, 1918–1968,* 5th ed. (Athens: Gutenberg, 1974), p. 236.

quarters on July 28 and received a joyful welcome from Greek Communists. The Soviets were held in high regard by ELAS, and the head of the mission, Lieutenant-Colonel Grigorii Popov, served as a symbol for KKE admiration. William McNeill echoed this impression when he wrote of his first encounter with Popov: "When I had occasion to compliment him on his excellent command of spoken English, he [Popov] remarked that his first language was Chinese! He claimed, also, to have been a member of the first parachute class trained by (the) Red Army sometime in the early 1930s, and was, altogether, an impressive representative of the USSR: athletic, bold, secretive and self-controlled, as well as being extremely well-educated."[75]

Several other sources, however, cast doubt on this picture of Popov as a symbol of the great Red Army and even suggest that he was not the real source of authority in the Russian Mission. Christopher Woodhouse has remarked that although Popov seemed a nice representative, he (Woodhouse) had gained the impression that Popov performed the task of getting individuals to relax and drop their guard, after which the second-in-command, Lieutenant-Colonel Nikolai P. Chernichev, would "go around to everyone and get what he needed."[76] This characterization of Popov as a mere front is strengthened by an OSS report that describes an interview with the head of the Russian Mission: "Col. Popov . . . impressed source—by the nature of his questions—as being very stupid or pretending to be so. Source is inclined to believe stupidity was not feigned."[77] As indicated below, it was indeed Chernichev who admonished the EAM leadership for their failure to accept the Lebanon agreement.

Whatever may have been the true lines of authority within the mission, its arrival had surprised and alarmed the British. Molotov responded as if the British were overreacting. The Soviet foreign minister maintained that his government had not sent a mission, but only "a few officers" drawn from the mission in Yugoslavia to get information on Greek partisans. Furthermore, he added, "These officers had been instructed not to meddle in any way in political matters."[78] Available evidence does indicate,

[75]McNeill, "View from Greece," p. 111. According to FO 371-43772 R12514, August 12, 1944, the Russian Military Mission to Greece was composed of Lieutenant-Colonel Popoff [Grigorii Popov], Lieutenant-Colonel Tzernikov [Nikolai P. Chernichev], Lieutenant-Colonel Troyan [Troian?], Major Ivanoff [Ivanov], Major Romanoff [Romanov], First Lieutenant Turin, First Lieutenant Ivasikov, and Second Lieutenant Crasin [Krasin?]. Unfortunately, neither the proper spelling nor initials were provided in the documents.

[76]Woodhouse mentioned this in a conversation with the writer in June 1984.

[77]OSS L50498, December 8, 1944.

[78]FO 371-43772 R12990, August 21, 1944.

however, that they went a long way toward dashing the KKE's hopes of any support.

Officials of KKE/ELAS found it frustratingly difficult to extract from their Soviet guests any indication of whether they would supply the Greek Communist partisans. Ioannidis has related that it was Chernichev's "grimace" of dismay when told of KKE willingness to fight the British that was an important factor in convincing the KKE to accept the terms of the Lebanon accord.[79] Other documents tend to support the contention that the mission's aim was to retrain the Greek Communists: on January 13, 1945, the KKE Central Committee "received a communication . . . informing them that [the] Russians categorically disapprove of their policy and actions and *reiterating [the] directive given PEEA by Popoff [sic] after the split that the KKE should remain loyal to [the] State and participate in the National Government.*" Two days later, Evripidis Bakirtzis stated that KKE policy in resorting to force during the December 1944 second round had been "inexcusable since Popoff [sic] had clearly explained the Russian attitude" to him when he was vice-president of PEEA.[80] Another OSS report echoed this negative line by concluding that "the Russian Mission to Greece told EAM to agree to any demands of the National Government."[81]

Still other evidence points to the conclusion that the KKE was similarly let down on the all-important question of military assistance: the Russian Mission gave the impression that Moscow would provide no arms to ELAS.[82] According to Sarafis, in his memoirs, "On the question of the Red Army undertaking our supply they [the Russian Mission] made no promises, as they had no instructions about this, but said they would send word of our needs to Moscow by radio, and Moscow would decide. They asked for a list of our requirements and this was handed to them within two days. However, to the end we received no aid."[83] There were un-

---

[79]Ioannidis, pp. 250–51. Porfyrogenis provides a similar account, recalling that the Russian mission met with Siantos and Ioannidis and asked the two "KKE members if, in not accepting the Lebanon agreement, they intended on clashing with the British? [When] Iannis Ioannidis replied that [they] would do so if necessary, the Soviet delegation told them that such an action would cause enormous damage to the allied struggle . . . and prudently advised them to accept Papandreou's terms and the Lebanon agreement": Vontitsos-Gousias, *Aities gia tis Ittes, ti Diaspasi* 2:144.

[80]OSS L53690, February 12, 1945. According to Eudes, p. 147, Chernichev told Bakirtzis that refusal to ratify the Lebanon agreement was "illogical"; emphasis added.

[81]OSS L45704, September 9, 1944; Vontitsos-Gousias, *Aities gia tis Ittes, ti Disaspasi* 2:144–45.

[82]Vontitsos-Gousias, *Aities gia tis Ittes, ti Diaspasi* 2:144–45; Eudes, p. 146.

[83]Sarafis, pp. 364–65. The Russian Military Mission evidently did not constitute all the Russians in Greece at the time. On occasion, a Russian plane or pilot would have to make a

doubtedly a variety of internal factors affecting KKE policy at this crucial juncture, not the least of which were difficulties in managing relations with the other parties in EAM. What this fragmentary evidence on the Russian Military Mission indicates, however, is Stalin's effort to dampen Greek Communist hopes for military and political support, thereby causing them to reconsider their aggressive stand toward the Greek government.

Hence, when events in Greece during the summer of 1944 are combined with various exchanges among the Great Powers, a great deal of plausibility is lent to the hypothesis that Stalin acted as if the division of the Balkans was in force and that his dispatch of the mission to Greece actually reflected Soviet assent to at least three months of *good* faith; for the mission's aim (at least its immediate aim) was to discourage independent Greek Communist activity and to ensure conformity with Anglo-Soviet policy. Churchill had therefore been incorrect in his assessment of the purpose of the Soviet Military Mission. He was in good company, however, for so had the KKE leadership.

Once the Soviets had conveyed to the KKE (both in Cairo and the mountains) that they wished to see Greek Communists accept the Lebanon agreement, the leadership of the party faced a difficult choice: either abide by the precepts of ideology and accept the Soviet position or rely on their own military strength and pursue an independent path of open confrontation. Despite discord within the KKE leadership,[84] ideology prevailed over interest, and on August 1, PEEA agreed to accept the Lebanon Charter on only one condition: that Papandreou be removed as prime minister. In the face of the sudden collapse of KKE intransigence, Papandreou, with

---

forced landing in Greece, but what is interesting is that on at least one occasion, according to Soviet sources, the Russian had a quite extensive visit to ELAS-occupied territory: "In September 1944, in the process of carrying out a military mission, it was necessary for Captain A. I. Koldunov of the 228th fighter aircraft division, a Hero of the Soviet Union, to make a forced landing on Greek territory. The Greek partisans gave him a warm reception, provided an automobile [and] translator, and took him to the staff of the partisan regiment. On passing through populated areas, the translator would loudly declare to the inhabitants 'here comes the liberator of Greece.' The people carried the Soviet officer on their hands and vigorously greeted him. Red flags were hanging everywhere. On returning to his division, Koldunov took a letter of gratitude from the Greek partisans to the Soviet command": M. I. Semiriaga, *Bor'ba narodov tsentral'noi i iugo-vostochnoi evropy protiv nemetsko-fashistskogo gneta* (Moscow: Nauka, 1985), p. 247. In a curious twist, it appears that this young Soviet officer is Aleksandr Ivanovich Koldunov, the USSR deputy minister of defense and commander-in-chief of USSR Air Defense Forces who was sacked by Mikhail Gorbachev in June 1987, after West German Mathias Rust succeeded in penetrating Soviet air space with a private plane and landing it in Red Square.

[84]Eudes, p. 148.

full British support, stood his ground. On August 15 the KKE accepted the terms of the Lebanon agreement without making a single demand. This completed what amounted to a spectacular reversal of policy from adamant refusal to complete acquiescence in less than one month.

When one looks for other circumstances that could have pressured the KKE to accept a clearly unsatisfactory political agreement, it becomes readily apparent that there were no major obstacles to the pursuit of a militant policy. The KKE had laid all the groundwork for a serious attempt to gain power: ELAS was the most powerful resistance army in Greece; PEEA was being groomed to take over as the government; and EAM assured the Communists a great deal of popular support. The only thing preventing an open break was the Greek Communists' obedience to Moscow. The ideology that had provided the KKE with its organizational strength now proved to be its nemesis. The decision to join the government of national unity was one more step in the KKE's progressive ensnarement in a web of agreements designed to render it powerless. Soviet advice implied that the KKE should pursue political, as opposed to military, policies in the future. The net result disoriented party leaders and distanced them from their source of strength—ELAS. As events subsequently unfolded, Soviet influence was decisive because when the optimum time for military confrontation arose, the KKE was pursuing politically oriented policies. Their best chance to assert their independence slipped away from the KKE leaders.

While the KKE lost ground, the Soviets gained a great deal. In the first place, they obtained a free hand in Romania, a country of vastly greater strategic importance for the defense of the Soviet Union than Greece. Second, they had managed to do this in the spirit of Allied unity, thereby avoiding any possible complications in defeating the Germans. Third, the Russian Mission was in an excellent position to gather information on the structure and performance of the various KKE-dominated organizations. This information could be used in assessing the potentialities that Stalin could exploit in the future.

Unfortunately for the KKE, the Soviet Military Mission had one story for the Greek guerrillas and another one for their reports. Sarafis describes the Red Army officers as being very impressed by the morale of the people. The Russians "were equally amazed by the organization of the guerrilla army and the work it did under conditions of extreme deprivation. They had never imagined that an occupation could be so insubstantial. Again and again they told me of their admiration for the people and for our army." But the Russian officers told a different story to the British. Despite Sarafis' enthusiasm and the fact that Popov received full information about ELAS "organization, strength, the functioning of its staff, its intelligence service and military activities,"[85] the head of the mission remained "profoundly skeptical" of anything ELAS told him, while a junior member of the mission observed to a British officer in Macedonia "that although Russia had no interest in Greece, he was very much puzzled by one thing—why had the British put up with this rabble for so long?"[86] Although it is impossible to tell which version the Soviets actually believed, it is reasonable to assume that the Red Army officers had serious reservations about the potential of ELAS, which they related to Moscow. These reservations most likely reinforced Stalin's distrust of guerrilla movements and contributed to the growing skepticism about the role of Communist military power in areas within the Western sphere of influence during the war.

As events moved toward liberation, the KKE followed Soviet counsel and attempted to pursue a path of political conciliation and infiltration. The Caserta Agreement, signed on September 26, 1944, was a direct outcome of this shift in policy. The terms of the agreement indicate the extent of the shift to a policy of conciliation; for example: (1) all guerrilla forces operating in Greece were to place themselves under the Greek government of national unity; (2) the Greek government would place these forces under the orders of Lieutenant General Ronald Scobie; (3) no action was to be taken in Athens except under the direct orders of General Scobie; and (4) all guerrilla forces were to put an end to past rivalries and form a national union.[87] That the Greek Communists, who had so recently appeared ready to go their own way, should have signed such an agreement is astonishing. By doing so, the KKE continued the progressive entrapment of its military power. Even more surprising is the fact that by the terms of the agreement, the British government took complete charge of Greek affairs. If the Soviet Union was opposed to this unprecedented document, it manifested no disapproval. Instead, as Iatrides points out, "The policies of the United States and the Soviet Union offered silent, though powerful, endorsement of this unique decision."[88]

Pursuit of the political path was to cost the KKE dearly. Doubts continued within the party about the wisdom of such a policy. The result was that the liberation of Greece arrived, and the KKE was left without an

[85]Sarafis, pp. 362–64, 148.

[86]FO 371-43772 R18966, November 21, 1944. According to British ambassador Reginald Leeper's cable, "Col. Popov observed with some distaste that they [EAM] would soon be wanting to paint slogans on the walls of his bedroom."

[87]Woodhouse, *Apple of Discord*, pp. 306–7.

[88]Iatrides, *Revolt in Athens*, p. 116.

effective policy. The moment of liberation was the optimal time to seize power because the British were at their weakest. British resident minister Harold Macmillan believed that had EAM attempted a coup d'etat at this time, it would have been successful.[89] But liberation came and went, and the KKE did not respond. A plausible explanation for this failure to act decisively is revealed in secret KKE/EAM cables intercepted by British intelligence. One cable from the KKE Central Committee to the EAM Central Committee, dated October 23, 1944 (the day the Greek government of national unity officially took office), complained, "our policy lacks direction, and if we had paid more attention to this we could have increased our influence over the masses."[90]

The Greek Communists were not the only ones who were experiencing difficulties. The Papandreou government was unable to carry out measures that would resuscitate the shattered Greek economy. Consequently, the political and economic situation in Greece deteriorated even further, with a corresponding deterioration of popular support for the government. In the midst of this highly volatile situation, Churchill added yet another problem. The British prime minister's insistence on supporting the return of the king kept the level of mutual hostility high, and the transport of staunchly promonarchist Greek troops into Greece in November, intended to reinforce the Papandreou government's position in Athens, caused the KKE to undergo an agonizing reappraisal of its position.

Churchill proceeded in this fashion as a direct result of the meetings he had with Stalin in Moscow. There, on October 9, the British prime minister proposed the now-famous "percentages agreement" on the Balkans. Interestingly, the course of the discussions tends to support the hypothesis that the question of the disposition of Romania and Greece had been settled earlier in the summer. In subsequent bargaining on October 10 and 11, the assignment of 90-percent influence in Romania to the Soviets and 90-percent influence in Greece to the British was never questioned by either side.[91] Most of the haggling over percentages reflected the Soviets' attempt to improve their position in Hungary and Bulgaria. The agreement did have two significant consequences. For the first time, Churchill felt that he had actually obtained Soviet consent to a free hand in Greece; the Soviets, armed with a renewed acceptance of their position in Romania, felt confident enough that they could exert their influence without British

[89]Ibid., p. 134; see also McNeill, "View from Greece," p. 105.
[90]DSR 868.00/1-2245, no. 427. Difficulties with the Yugoslavs over Macedonia (treated in chap. 4) also contributed to KKE indecisiveness.
[91]Kuniholm, pp. 109–20; Mastny, pp. 207–12.

objection. It took little foresight to realize that once Churchill felt he could operate in Greece with impunity, he would seek to impose his solution; yet, given the critical disposition of the Greek political context, British pressure was more than likely to precipitate a crisis. The Soviets would therefore have the first opportunity to hold up their end of the bargain.

Soviet Response to the Second Round

At the conclusion of the Moscow Conference, the Papandreou government acted quickly, with British support, to establish a military counterweight to the armed might of leftist organizations. In early November, it was decided that approximately eight thousand British troops should remain in Greece until the formation of a new national guard. Some days later, the Mountain Brigade of the Greek army arrived in Athens, followed by the arrival of the staunchly promonarchist Sacred Squadron on November 9, 1944. Iatrides is quite correct to stress the significance of these events;[92] for they alarmed the KKE and led to a decided shift in policy.

An October 23 telegram from the KKE Central Committee clearly shows the party leadership still trying to pursue a policy of political infiltration. Of the various policy recommendations, some of the more significant were: (1) Arrange for the EAM Central Committee to visit the British ambassador and then prepare a good reception for him. (2) Use the influential connections of the KKE to place some pro-EAM people "in official or semi-official government posts, in order to control the administration." (3) Make *Rizospastis,* the official paper of the KKE, into a professional paper. (4) Change the title of the General Confederation of Workers to the Confederation of Workers and Clerks in order to attract more nonlabor members.[93] These recommendations certainly do not reflect a policy designed for the forcible seizure of power. A November 6 telegram shows no change;[94] yet when the Sacred Squadron arrived in Greece three days later, there was a clear policy shift to keep KKE options open. Thus, on November 9, Siantos sent the following telegram to Thessaly-Sterea: "Reaction aims to create conditions favorable to a coup and dictatorship. Watch. ELAS should remain at their position until presuppositions for a normal development of the situation are secured. Will

[92]Iatrides, *Revolt in Athens,* pp. 152–66; his analysis makes use of the same cables.
[93]DSR 868.00/1-2245, no. 427.
[94]Ibid.

disband only when the forces from Egypt are disarmed and a new army is formed under the command of men cherishing the confidence of the fighting people. . . . Gendarmerie should be dissolved. See that a democratic front is created against the danger of monarchy."[95]

The reference to disbandment was a response to Papandreou's British-supported plan for demobilization: a new national guard to be created on November 20 and all guerrilla troops to be dissolved during the first ten days of December. As late November approached, the KKE balked at surrendering its arms. They appeared to have shifted to a new policy of formally abiding by the government's plan, yet remaining organizationally intact. On November 22, Siantos ordered all Communists and EAMites to "organize themselves securely within the National Guard." In two other telegrams (undated, but most likely issued near the end of November), the KKE ordered former reserve ELAS troops to enroll in "Official Veterans' Associations, but . . . in such a way that they will not lose their military cohesion and their fighting value *should the occasion arise after the demobilization of active ELAS* in accordance with the Party's policy regarding the evolution of the situation in the immediate future." That this was all to be done secretly is evident: "The Veterans' Associations connected with EAM must be formed on a military pattern, but camouflaged, i.e. in every small village there will be a Veterans' Group, corresponding to a Battle Group."[96]

KKE strategy was no longer political, yet neither was it purely military. It reflected an unrealistic attempt to keep the best of both: a policy that publicly conceded the dissolution of ELAS, yet privately retained it in a new form. It was a last feeble effort; for the cables of the final days reveal that anxiety about the loss of ELAS forced Siantos toward defensive preparations for civil war. On November 28, Siantos informed the party organizations of Macedonia, Thessaly, Epirus, Central Greece, and the Peloponnesus: "[The] Prime Minister insists on disbandment (of) ELAS and refused to disband Mountain Brigade and Sacred Company (sic). This is unacceptable. Situation critical. Watch and be ready to repulse any danger." This same day the EAM ministers in the Greek government withdrew their support of a compromise demobilization plan. The next day, Siantos informed the same party organizations that the "situation continues to be extremely critical. . . . Opposition ready to start war against us. Issue necessary orders and take suitable dispositions for any eventuality." One day later, ELAS major-general Emmanuil Mantakas cabled ELAS headquarters that it was necessary "to send explosives and mines for

[95]Ibid.
[96]Ibid.; emphasis in original.

probable fighting in built-up areas."[97] Hence, by the time hostilities broke out on December 3, the KKE had all but abandoned its policy of infiltration but not yet (according to documentary evidence available) opted decisively for a seizure of power.

In retrospect, the policies of the KKE from the time of the Russian Military Mission appear to have been decisively affected by Soviet advice. The lack of support for requests for arms, combined with the advice to enter the government of national unity, coming just as the KKE appeared to be moving toward open confrontation, resulted in ambiguous and indecisive policies at the critical moment of liberation, when the military option had the greatest chance of success.[98] With the return of government forces, the KKE began to realize that it was going to pay dearly for its ideological fidelity. With two irreconcilable sources of military power in Greece, each supporting persons aspiring to control the political process, the Greek Communists realized that demobilization meant the destruction of their independent power base. To try to rescue its hopes of political control, the KKE was compelled to use force at an inopportune time and with no support from the Great Powers.

One other possible influence on KKE policy is worth mentioning briefly. Yugoslav actions may have been critical in giving the Greek Communists the resolve to opt for civil war. This is the argument of George Kousoulas, who asserts that a telegram from Tito supporting a KKE move to take the capital arrived in ELAS headquarters on November 26.[99] If such a telegram was in fact received, no version has ever been published. The only documentary evidence that currently exists is a November 30 telegram from Stergios (possibly a pseudonym used by Andreas Tzimas, the KKE representative at Yugoslav Partisan headquarters), which states: "Saw Bulgarians and Tito. They advise we must insist on not repeat not being disarmed, no repeat no British interference."[100] In the absence of more decisive documentary evidence, this is difficult to interpret as a solid endorsement of civil war. A second problem with Kousoulas' argument is that he did not adequately take into account the situation in Macedonia. Iatrides shows that, contrary to any assumptions of "fraternal" Communist relations, the KKE had its hands full in Macedonia with an autonomist movement claiming support from Yugoslavia.[101]

[97]Ibid.

[98]The KKE's indecision at this crucial juncture is a point some accounts, such as Loulis', fail to consider.

[99]D. George Kousoulas, *Revolution and Defeat: The Story of the Greek Communist Party, 1918–1949* (London: Oxford University Press, 1965), p. 201.

[100]DSR 868.00/1-2345, no. 433.

[101]Iatrides, *Revolt in Athens,* pp. 156–57.

When the revolt actually began, the KKE received no support whatsoever from the Soviet Union. Churchill commented on the fact that Stalin was keeping his end of their bargain. The Soviet news media reflected Stalin's silence during the second round. A British Foreign Office memorandum of December 21, 1944, noted that there was no Soviet comment on the current civil war but that extensive Tass selections from the foreign press were definitely in favor of EAM.[102] Quite possibly Tass was pursuing a familiar tactic: impressing the Soviet reader with foreign support for a movement the USSR secretly approved of, while avoiding any commitment of Soviet prestige or interests to it. In this instance the tactic was easy because the foreign press was overwhelmingly pro-EAM. Two weeks later, the U.S. State Department received word that the Soviet Union continued its "objective" quotation of press correspondents, without expressing approval of left-wing activism in Greece.[103]

But Soviet refusal to endorse EAM's resort to force was not limited merely to the press, as the following sequence of events indicates. On December 10, 1944, KKE Politburo member Tzimas, recently arrived from Tito's headquarters, made a speech in Thessaloniki assuring Tito's moral support for the struggle. The next day, Tzimas met with Siantos and Politburo member Iannis Zevgos and reported that Tito expressed his sympathy but would go no further without Russian consent, for which he (Tito) was not prepared to ask. Tzimas also relayed Tito's advice to the KKE Central Committee to send delegates to Moscow; on December 15 it decided to send Politburo member Rousos. Things did not go well for him. When he presented himself to Russian authorities in Sofia on December 18, they immediately placed him under house arrest. Three days later, the Russian authorities escorted him to the Greek frontier, from whence he returned to Thessaloniki to inform the KKE of his reception.[104]

On December 30, the Soviets continued what amounted to a policy of

---

[102]FO 371-47863 N78, December 21, 1944.

[103]DSR 868.00/1-1045.

[104]OSS L53690, February 12, 1945. It should be pointed out here that Markos Vafeiadis (Markos) maintains that in the third week of December he received encouragement from Soviet representatives to carry on the fighting: *Anti*, September 4, 1976, pp. 32–33. If this is true, it alters the present analysis, implying instead that the Soviets actively encouraged the Greek Communists in their effort to seize power. But there are several questions that raise doubts about this information: Why did the Soviets convey the information via Thessaloniki, where Markos was stationed, when the fighting was taking place in Athens? Why have no other KKE leaders ever referred to this potentially significant point? It surely would have made a world of difference to the KKE to know it had actual Soviet endorsement of its actions.

discouraging the Greek Communists: they announced their intention to appoint a new ambassador to Athens, filling a post vacant since late July.[105] This manifest preference for a British-backed government over the KKE must have depressed the Greek Communists. By January 3, 1945, when the British launched a new offensive, ELAS command realized the futility of further fighting. On January 10, negotiations for a truce began. With ELAS clearly defeated and unable to bargain from strength, agreement was reached the next day on a truce effective January 14.

During early January 1945, the KKE continued to receive strong indications of Soviet disapproval. On January 13, the KKE Central Committee received a communication (already alluded to in the discussion of the Russian Military Mission) informing them that the Soviets "categorically" disapproved of their policy; several days later, Bakirtzis declared KKE/EAM policy to be "inexcusable" in light of the advice the Russians had given him the previous summer.[106] The Soviets apparently made sure that the Yugoslavs received an unambiguous statement of the Soviet desire for nonintervention. As OSS document stated that ELAS planned to retreat into Yugoslavia if defeated by the British, but "two Russian officers went to Yugoslavia and said that no ELAS [troops] were to be allowed to cross to Yugoslavia."[107] Although it is questionable that this order was fully carried out (as stated in the OSS document), it does serve to indicate the degree to which the Soviets wished to appear uninvolved.

Once the truce had been signed on January 15, there only remained the matter of a political solution. This was accomplished on February 12, when the Greek government and EAM formally signed the Varkiza Agreement. The terms of the agreement reflected the extent to which the KKE's position had been destroyed. There were provisions for a plebiscite on the constitutional question and elections for a constituent assembly, to

[105]Stephen George Xydis, *Greece and the Great Powers, 1944–1947* (Thessaloniki: Institute for Balkan Studies, 1963), pp. 63, 547 n; see also Christoforos A. Naltsas, *To Makedoniko Zitima kai i Sovietiki Politiki* (Thessaloniki: Institute for Balkan Studies, 1954), p. 369.

[106]OSS L53690, February 12, 1945. Italian political leaders have also provided some indirect evidence that Stalin opposed the civil war because it would damage Soviet interests. Palmiro Togliatti, head of the Italian Communists, sought to justify his own preference for a parliamentary policy by arguing that the military option was disadvantageous for Soviet policy in 1945: Paolo Spriano, *Stalin and the European Communists*, trans. Jon Rothschild (London: New Left, Verso, 1985), p. 289. Similarly, when Pietro Secchia asked Stalin in December 1947 whether it would not be good to press the class struggle, the Soviet dictator responded negatively, arguing that this was impossible at the time because it would lead to an insurrection, and insurrections were to be avoided; see Secchia, *Archivo Pietro Secchia, 1945–1973* (Milan: Feltrinelli, 1979), p. 426; as cited in Spriano, p. 289.

[107]OSS L52360, February 1, 1945.

be held within 1945; but the immediate dissolution of ELAS was ordered despite the fact that government troops (the Mountain Brigade) were not mentioned.[108] An amnesty for all political crimes during the second round was also included.

The second round was a devastating experience for the KKE: they lost their army, incurred Soviet displeasure, and succeeded in alienating the majority of the Greek population. All they retained were the organizational apparatus and large caches of hidden weapons. But Varkiza was only a stopgap; for it did nothing to ameliorate the deep political divisions nor provide for a government capable of controlling the anti-Communist backlash that soon engulfed the country. Within a year the old antagonisms would reemerge and Greece would be in the throes of its third civil war in as many years.

Stalin did not wait long to collect the debt Churchill now owed him. On January 20, General Cortlandt Schuyler informed the U.S. government that Romanian Communist party members Ana Pauker and Gheorghe Gheorghiu-Dej had, on their return from Moscow, held a secret party meeting at which they announced the decision to bring the Communists to power.[109] The Russians ordered the bulk of Romanian troops to the front, thus clearing the way for a seizure of power in the capital.[110] Finally, in late February 1945, Vyshinskii arrived in Bucharest and delivered an ultimatum to King Michael, demanding that he appoint the government the Communists desired.[111] On March 6, a Romanian government totally subservient to Moscow was appointed.

Soviet actions in Romania thus antedated the Yalta agreement, indicating that as far as Greece and Romania were concerned, Yalta had no influence on immediate Soviet policy. The Declaration on Liberated Europe, which stipulated that the Great Powers "concert [their policies] during the *temporary* period of instability in liberated Europe . . . in assisting the peoples liberated from the domination of Nazi Germany,"[112]

[108]Iatrides, *Revolt in Athens,* pp. 320–21.

[109]Mastny, p. 255.

[110]Henry L. Roberts, *Rumania* (New Haven, Conn.: Yale University Press, 1951), pp. 262–65.

[111]Mastny, p. 256; John Malcolm Mackintosh, *Strategy and Tactics of Soviet Foreign Policy* (London: Oxford University Press, 1963), p. 7.

[112]"Protocol of the Proceedings of the Crimea Conference, February 11, 1945," *FRUS: The Conferences at Malta and Yalta, 1945* (Washington, D.C.: USGPO, 1955), p. 977; emphasis added to stress the fact that the Declaration on Liberated Europe was not intended to have permanently obligated the signatories. It is often argued with respect to Greece that Yalta accomplished the division of Europe, after which the Soviet Union tended to affairs in its own sphere of influence. This analysis implicitly contests such a view; the next chapter does so more explicitly.

did, however, provide the Soviets with the juridical basis for future intervention. Molotov may have unintentionally let slip a clue to future Soviet policy in liberated Western European countries when he suggested adding the following phrase to the declaration: "and strong support will be given to those people in these countries who took an active part in the struggle against German occupation."[113] Were this incorporated into the final protocol, it would have considerably strengthened EAM's recourse to the Yalta accords. In any event, this strategy is examined in the next chapter.

What has emerged from the analysis is an image of Soviet policy as disinterested in Greek affairs except insofar as they may have assisted in defeating Nazi Germany and establishing a secure belt of states to prevent future attack. In particular, the Soviets took the opportunity caused by unrest in Greece to secure control of Romania under Allied auspices. To accomplish this they shunned the independent KKE initiatives and gave the British a free hand in Greece.

There are, however, two other important conclusions from this analysis. First, though it is true that the Soviets did not have a hand in the KKE's decision to attempt a military seizure of power, it is undeniable that Soviet activity decisively influenced events in Greece in the final year of the war. Successful use of the Greek Communists' fidelity to Soviet communism enabled Stalin to blunt what appeared to be an imminent KKE-initiated break with the Greek government.[114]

Second, although Stalin was obviously in no position to prevent the defeat of ELAS, he might have prevented its complete destruction; yet the evidence indicates his behavior actually *maximized* ELAS losses. Had his object been preservation of the nucleus of an ELAS military force, Stalin would quickly have let the KKE leadership know. Had it been strict adherence to his agreement with Churchill, he would have eschewed communication with the Greek Communists.[115] What he actually did was withhold Soviet opinion until *after* it was clear the Greek Communists were suffering a terrible defeat, *then* express Soviet disapproval. This

---

[113] "Bohlen Collection," in ibid., p. 863.

[114] Spriano, p. 189, notes that the "Communists felt a genuine love of country, which was linked to their love of the USSR—no other term is accurate—in a manner that none of them considered contradictory." Later, he cites Leon Blum's reflections on the relationship between Communists and the Soviet Union following the dissolution of the Comintern: "What we have failed to foresee . . . is that although it has recovered its freedom to make decisions, French Communism has not recovered its freedom of judgement. The relationship of hierarchical obedience has been broken. . . . But a psychic, emotional dependence subsists, anchored in habit and passion" (p. 202).

[115] Xydis, p. 62, for example, argues that Stalin did nothing to discourage the KKE from their action.

raises an intriguing question: Did Stalin allow the destruction of ELAS to take place because it removed the independent military base of the KKE, thereby making the Communist organization dependent upon outside (Soviet) support? If true, then the British in Greece performed a service similar to that which the Germans provided Stalin in Poland: elimination of local independent organizations that could prove troublesome if left in place.

It is tempting to conclude that Stalin intended the destruction of ELAS, but there is insufficient supporting evidence; indecision on Stalin's part as to the role of independent Communist military organizations in the postwar era could as easily account for the strange timing of Soviet statements. Furthermore, Soviet actions on the Varkiza Agreement clearly reflected an interest in retaining the KKE as a legal organization in Greece, and the Soviet media remained sympathetic and supportive of EAM/KKE demands. The most that can be said is that Stalin's unwillingness to tolerate independent power centers leaves two possibilities: either he wanted party organizations shorn of their militaries, or he still had not yet decided whether these forces could be useful and reliable adjuncts to any future Soviet policy. Developments in Greece immediately after the end of the World War—a cautious effort to preserve Greek Communist military forces for some future, unspecified occasion—support the latter conclusion.

Soviet Attitudes toward Other Communist-Led Resistance Movements

Even without resolving the question of Stalin's position on independent Communist military forces, a brief review of Soviet policy toward other Communist-led resistance movements clearly reveals that the Soviet leader wanted to have at his disposal manipulatable organizations for pursuing foreign policy objectives. One of the most significant consequences of the outbreak of World War II for international communism had been the rupture in lines of communication between the Comintern and the various European Communist parties, with two immediate results: first, though fanatically devoted to the Soviet Union, European Communist parties began to pursue their own interests, and second, the Soviet Union could rely on little more than its ideological preeminence to get the parties to conform to Soviet interests.

The case of Yugoslavia is the best known example of Stalin's tactics. In the early phases of the war, when Tito's Partisans were struggling against Draža Mihailović's *chetniks* for control of Yugoslavia, Stalin consistently tried to stifle any Partisan initiative that would strengthen Tito's military and political position in Yugoslavia. The major reason for this was Stalin's concern that a revolutionary situation adversely affect Great Power relations. Britain and America had yet to be brought into the war, and this goal could not be jeopardized. But Soviet policy in Yugoslavia also reflects a conscious desire to avoid having the Communists emerge independent after the war. The best way of accomplishing this was to hamper the growth of Tito's military forces. When the Yugoslav Communists repeatedly asked for military aid in 1942–43, none was forthcoming from the Soviet Union, although much was promised.[116] In addition, Stalin attempted to undermine the morale of the Yugoslavs by denigrating the fighting ability of the Partisans,[117] implying their contribution to the Allied cause was minimal.

Soviet policy was most obvious on the political level: Stalin consistently refused to break openly with the royal Yugoslav government and advised Tito to enter into a coalition. Even as the Soviets began to condemn Mihailović in July 1942, they still counseled Tito to achieve a negotiated settlement.[118] In November 1942, Moscow cabled the following directions to Tito:

> The creation of a national liberation committee of Yugoslavia is very necessary and of exceptional importance. You must not fail to give the committee an all-national Yugoslav and all-party anti-fascist character, both in personnel and in program of work. *Do not look upon the committee as a sort of government,* but as a political arm of the national liberation fight.
> *Do not put it in opposition to the Yugoslav government in London.* At the present stage, do not raise the question of abolition of the monarchy.[119]

The Soviet attitude reflected an interest in retaining the political power of the Yugoslav Partisans, tempered by a wish to blunt their independent initiatives.

But the success of Yugoslav Communists in dealing with their own difficulties without Soviet assistance ultimately paved the way for more

[116]Moša Pijade, *About the Legend That the Yugoslav Uprising Owed Its Existence to Soviet Assistance* (London: n.p., 1950). This was something that would repeat itself four years later, when the KKE requested assistance (chap. 4).

[117]Milovan Djilas, *Conversations with Stalin,* trans. Michael Petrovich (New York: Harcourt, Brace & World, 1962), p. 112.

[118]Loulis, p. 113n.

[119]Pijade, p. 20; emphasis in original.

independent policies. When in November 1943, Tito declared AVNOJ the legitimate government of Yugoslavia, he did so without Stalin's consent and took the Soviet dictator by surprise.[120] At the Teheran Conference, Stalin, concerned about the reaction of his two Western allies, refused to accept the decision. When the Allies did not object, Stalin acquiesced but continued to acknowledge the legitimacy of the king.[121] In June 1944, at British and Soviet suggestion, Tito met with Dr. Ivan Šubašić, representative of King Peter, to try to achieve some sort of joint government. Although agreement was ultimately achieved, it must have been disappointing to Stalin; for the agreement left Tito in sole command of the National Liberation Army, and AVNOJ was recognized as the sole authority in the country.[122] Whereas in Greece negotiation and compromise had ensnared the KKE and left the British with the upper hand, in Yugoslavia the absence of the British created a situation where political agreements favored Tito. Still, Stalin persisted in his attempts to compromise Tito's position. When Tito met with Stalin in Moscow in September 1944, the question of retaining the monarchy arose again. Tito flatly refused to accept King Peter, to which Stalin responded: "You need not restore him forever. Take him back temporarily, and then you can slip a knife into his back at a suitable moment."[123] Tito held firm and ultimately the final version of the Tito-Šubašić agreement, signed in December 1944 and accepted by the Allies at Yalta, reflected Tito's strong position: the monarchy issue was postponed and AVNOJ became the legitimate, though formally only temporary, government of Yugoslavia.

In the case of the Communist parties of France and Belgium, the situations were somewhat different, since in both countries the Communists had failed to seize power during the liberation. As in Greece, the real crisis came about over the question of the demobilization of the resistance military organizations. In France, De Gaulle's demand for the disbandment of the resistance forces provoked a sharp response from the Communist Party of France (PCF). The two Communist ministers in De Gaulle's government threatened to resign, effectively withdrawing Communist recognition of the government.[124] Evidence is scant, but sufficient to estab-

[120]Dedijer, p. 209.
[121]Walter R. Roberts, *Tito, Mihailović and the Allies* (New Brunswick, N.J.: Rutgers University Press, 1973), pp. 174–80.
[122]Dedijer, pp. 223–25.
[123]Ibid., p. 233.
[124]Gilbert Mathieu, "The French and Belgian Communist Parties in Relation to Soviet Objectives towards Western Europe in 1940 and 1944," Ph.D. diss., University of Wisconsin, 1971, pp. 148–49.

lish as plausible the argument that Soviet interests played a part in pushing the PCF onto the path of parliamentary collaboration. At this critical juncture (November 1944), Party Secretary Maurice Thorez returned from Moscow, and immediately the crisis abated. As Gilbert Mathieu suggests, "Thorez may have been the bearer of instructions from Moscow to end the dispute over the militia in exchange for the amnesty of all Communists who had been involved in 'irregular' activities in 1939–40."[125] Indeed, the PCF leader returned in a remarkably conciliatory mood, arguing that all armed groups (Communists included), should be dissolved to strengthen the liberation army under De Gaulle's command. Despite resistance within Communist ranks, Thorez had his way; the PCF collaborated with De Gaulle and threw its energies into establishing power in the new parliamentary democracy.[126]

By contrast, relations between the Belgian government and the Communist Party of Belgium (PCB) took a much more serious turn. The Communist ministers in the Belgian government did resign over the demobilization issue. On November 16, 1944, the PCB instructed its resistance groups not to surrender their weapons, as ordered by the government on November 13. Mathieu has argued that the Belgian situation was the result of a PCB failure to receive instruction from Moscow, which allowed the militant faction to gain the upper hand. In any event, a sudden change of tactics followed several days later, as the PCB became more conciliatory.[127] The change was apparently not sufficient to stop the momentum created by the crisis; protest demonstrations on November 25 erupted into civil violence and required the intervention of local gendarmerie. The parallels between the Greek case and the French and Belgian cases are significant: a demobilization crisis, threats by the local Communist parties to withdraw their support from the national government, a significant change of tactics in response to Soviet intervention.

In Italy the collapse of Mussolini's regime created a problem for the Communist party: it could either cooperate with non-Communist, anti-Hitler sections of society and continue the war effort or attempt to pursue an independent path. As in France and Belgium, the choice was reflected in a party split between the more and less militant factions (Italian national politics underwent the same split). Initially, the more radical faction pre-

[125]Ibid., p. 150.
[126]Spriano, p. 229–30. Spriano also points out the recollections of Charles Tillon, who maintains that in autumn 1944 the Soviets advised the French Communists not to oppose the demands of De Gaulle or the Allies; see Tillon, *On Chantait Rouge* (Paris, 1965[?]), p. 504; as cited in Spriano, p. 227.
[127]Mathieu, p. 152.

vailed, and the Communist Party of Italy (PCI) abstained from joining the government of Marshal Pietro Badoglio, despite the fact that the party's leader, Palmiro Togliatti, insisted on cooperation with the new Italian government.[128] The Soviets made their position unambiguous on March 14, 1944, when they officially recognized the Badoglio government.[129] Franz Borkenau argues that in order to bring the PCI back into line with Soviet policy, Togliatti returned from Russia and skillfully turned the party leadership toward the war against the Germans by joining the Badoglio government.[130] Consequently, by April the PCI had established itself firmly on the path of political infiltration rather than military action.

Although differences emerge in the policies of the Communist parties in Greece, Yugoslavia, France, Belgium, and Italy, several features common to all emerge from this brief comparison. Soviet policy in these countries was designed to place the Communists in an excellent position to exercise significant political power in the postwar era. To this end, Stalin sought to ensure that local Communist organizations in countries to be in the Western sphere of influence would share power in the parliamentary democracies to be established there. This policy combined conveniently with the Soviet leader's desire to retain control over these organizations, as the postwar political leaderships were loyal to Moscow. But a policy stressing political structures and activity also created an important ambiguity: there was no clear and consistent decision about the postwar utility of Communist military forces. Although Stalin encouraged the political path, at no time did he completely abandon the possibility of using the military organizations: his attitude was always that *at the present time,* such forces were unhelpful.

Perhaps the best that can be said is that Stalin was, for the moment, of two minds: on the one hand, his distrust of independent military forces impelled him to find ways to disband or render useless the military power local Communists had acquired during the war; on the other hand, he must have been tempted to find a way to preserve and exploit such powerful

---

[128]Franz Borkenau, *European Communism* (New York: Harper, 1953), p. 288.

[129]Roberto Battaglia, *The Story of the Italian Resistance* (London: Odhams, 1957), p. 107.

[130]Borkenau, *European Communism*, pp. 289–91. In support of this interpretation are the recollections of Eugenio Reale, who recounts that when he and Luigi Longo were on their way to the founding meeting of the Cominform in September 1947, Togliatti told them that if the policy of the PCI were criticized because it had been thrown out of power, they were to tell the delegates that the party could not turn Italy into another Greece and that its actions were in the Soviet interest; see Reale, *Nascita del Cominform* (Milan: Arnoldo Mondadori, 1958), p. 17.

domestic forces. This tension helps explain why the Soviet dictator never fully wrote off the military option, preferring to couch his rejection in terms of that option's inapplicability under existing conditions and leaving open the question of its possible future usefulness. The overriding importance of strategic factors in Soviet thinking at the time dictated that if such forces posed a threat to the war effort, they were to be neutralized. While in the rest of Western Europe, the Communist transition to parliamentary politics was carried out short of civil war (although often with a great deal of violence), in Greece, tensions erupted into civil war. The Varkiza Agreement amounted only to a respite in a longer social drama, as the Greek Communists began the reconstruction of their military base. Stalin would once again be faced with the problems of managing a Communist party at arm's length and of resolving the question of the utility of local Communist military force in pursuit of Soviet objectives. But since it would no longer be necessary to mollify Western sentiments for the sake of the war effort, Stalin would be free to consider those problems in an entirely different light.

3

POSTWAR SOVIET OBJECTIVES AND GREEK COMMUNIST GRADUALISM, 1945–1946

The agreement finally achieved at Varkiza in February 1945 neither resolved the deep conflicts within Greek society nor provided the basis for successful political compromise. Since Greece still had no elected government and the KKE/EAM forces received unusually lenient terms, it was obvious to all parties that only strong and effective Greek political leadership and concerted Allied support could prevent further hostilities. Both were lacking. Stalin, in particular, had his own agenda: consolidating his wartime gains and acquiring further concessions to secure his southern border. Any aggressive Soviet activity to achieve these goals in the Near East threatened, however, to increase Western presence in the region. Soviet policy had to be pursued at a level that precluded Western response and by means that did not suggest Soviet expansion. The most reasonable policy option in Greece, and the Near East generally, was gradual political infiltration with the aim of detaching the Western presence and creating internally unstable states in the eastern Mediterranean. Once this goal was achieved, the Soviets could proceed with more aggressive policies.

In the immediate postwar period, two areas were vital to the success of Stalin's objectives: Turkey and the Balkans. Modification of the Straits Convention and the acquisition of Turkish territory could provide the long-sought Soviet outlet to the Mediterranean, create a buffer against any future Turkish activity, and produce domestic turmoil within the Turkish government. In the Balkans, where Great Power differences and the uncomfortably independent attitude of the Yugoslavs created a very uncertain situation, protection of Bulgaria and especially Albania was a prime Soviet concern. Greece, by virtue of its location between these two highly sensitive Soviet objectives, became a third objective. In Greece the immediate Soviet intention was neither acquisition of territory nor protection of gains; it was creation of a weak, penetrable, and minimally stable state in competition with a strong and popular Communist party apparatus. This task required transforming the wartime military basis of the KKE into an effective political organization. The ideal would be a KKE unable to assume power immediately yet able to prevent any other domestic actors from acting independently. As British influence weakened and no American presence developed, the Communists could gradually penetrate and later overthrow the state mechanism.

The central strategic constraint on this policy of gradualism was the need to avoid antagonizing the British while simultaneously removing their influence from the Balkans. Conditions in 1945 appeared promising: the Americans manifested little interest in Greek internal affairs, and the British position throughout the world was deteriorating rapidly. Faced with American reticence to become involved, the British were forced to handle events on their own as the situation in Greece worsened. The Soviets, however, had already concluded that Britain would not be a power much longer. Stalin was therefore moving toward a future division of Europe between the United States and the Soviet Union, as Truman's fact-finding commission to the Balkans in late 1945 recognized. From discussions with Russian commanders in Bulgaria and Romania and their political commissars, commision head Mark F. Ethridge concluded that Greece and Turkey were the next objects of Soviet expansion. In the Soviets' view, somebody had to move into the regions from which the British were withdrawing. As Stephen Xydis noted, "In spite of any commitment the Soviets might have with regard to Britain, they expected to oust the British from Greece and 'organize,' . . . the entire Balkans." Indeed, several Russians had suggested a postwar split-up of the world into two spheres, with the Soviets controlling everything east of Italy.[1]

The Soviets' use of the KKE to advance their interests made it an important local constraint on policy. Insofar as the Greek Communist party could be firmly controlled and did not develop interests in conflict with Soviet ones, its use would not be a problem. In fact, the situation in early 1945 must have appeared favorable to the Soviets: the KKE had

[1]Stephen G. Xydis, *Greece and the Great Powers, 1944–1947* (Thessaloniki: Institute for Balkan Studies, 1963), pp. 153, 154.

been shorn of its army and was thus dependent on external support for any coercive policy; and Nikos Zachariadis, former head of the KKE and member of the Communist Party of the Soviet Union (CPSU),[2] had returned in June 1945 to guide the Greek Communists. A dependent party organization under the leadership of a staunchly pro-Soviet leader held out the promise of a successful implementation of Soviet policy.

Finally, there was another regional constraint on Soviet policy: the condition of the remaining Balkan countries. In these countries there was always the possibility of events beyond Soviet control that could destroy Soviet policy or even threaten gains already made. The Macedonian issue and the independent position of the Yugoslavs were paramount worries; for the tense border situation in the north of Greece roused Western concern about a further expansion of Soviet influence.

Despite the Soviets' initially favorable estimate of the Greek situation, by the time of the March 1946 elections, internal violence had escalated enough to provoke serious British and American concerns about the outbreak of civil war; and the KKE, having abstained from the elections, was virtually shut out of the political scene. One more year brought the beleaguered Greek government firm American support, with an American presence supplanting the British. Hence, although the Soviets encountered initial success in helping push successive Greek governments further to the left and into more accommodation with the KKE, their policy ultimately failed to produce results conducive to their interests.

One method of explaining the policy and its consequences is to place Soviet objectives in the context of Greek politics and the burdens such a policy imposed on Stalin's main instrument, the KKE. While the KKE easily grasped larger Soviet objectives, it apparently found Moscow's specific policy orders and indications of support incomplete and indecisive. In particular, Stalin was much clearer on the political aspects of KKE policy than on the crucial question of what to do with the resurgent military forces. This placed a severe burden on Zachariadis, who, in his efforts to remain faithful to Soviet interests, was forced to pursue a policy of compromise between the need to respond to local conditions and the desire to conform to Stalin's apparently fragmentary and tentative directives. While no doubt frustrating to the KKE leadership, this situation permitted them a degree of latitude in the determination of strategy, providing they remained within the broader limits of Soviet policy. The result was a dual policy of political activity and gradual preparation for

[2]Foivos Oikonomidis, interview with Alekos Papapanagiotou, *Anti*, June 19, 1981, p. 35; also mentioned to the writer in a discussion with Ole L. Smith, January 1984.

armed action, an outcome that provoked increasingly bitter and divisive opposition from more militant KKE factions. Stalin's exact position on the dual strategy is still unclear; he never explicitly criticized it and apparently did approve it after the fact.

The dual strategy may have been an ingenious political compromise between Soviet interests and local conditions, but it was unrealistic. The opposition faction of the KKE made a strong case that local conditions were so polarized any political activity was pointless and that the KKE would suffer a decisive defeat unless it could immediately seize power through armed struggle. Zachariadis succeeded in having his political line adopted, only to produce incoherence and disorganization in KKE activity. While the Greek Communist leader pursued his pro-Soviet policy of political infiltration, the KKE military leaders pursued a nationalist-oriented program of preparation for civil war. The net result of these two policies operating simultaneously was doubly destructive: the West was sure to take the increasing militancy in Greece as proof of a Soviet-sponsored drive toward the Aegean Sea, and the excessive delay in organizing a concerted military effort to seize power gave the Western Allies time to recognize the danger and begin reinforcing the Greek government. Thus the Soviets were left with a civil war that went against their interests, and the Greek Communists chose once again to resort to force after the optimal moment for striking had passed.

February–May 1945: KKE Retrenchment and Soviet Initiatives

During the early months of 1945, Stalin was still anxious to see the final defeat of Nazi Germany, but this concern did not prevent him from beginning to exert pressure in the Near East. Turkey was the object of Stalin's interest at this time for several reasons. First, through Turkey the Soviets could best realize their goal of an outlet to the Aegean. Second, because security considerations during the war had always forced the Soviets to divert forces to the Turkish border to ensure against attack, territorial concessions from the Turks could provide a small but strategic security buffer and simultaneously destabilize the Turkish government. Third, the time was opportune because the Soviet Red Army was the dominant force in the region, and Western presence was weak.

Stalin had at his disposal several means of bringing pressure to bear on the Turkish government. Besides open diplomatic exchanges and military activity in the region, there were territorial claims with which to put the Turkish government on the defensive. Here, the KKE could be extremely useful; based on Greece's geographic position, the KKE could make a claim for part of Turkish territory. Greece was thus not only a field of action in which Stalin could attempt to detach British influence but a source of pressure on the Turkish government to accept concessions.

During the first four months of 1945, the Greek Communists had few contacts with the Soviets, most likely because Stalin was more concerned with ending the war and consolidating his control over Romania. The KKE, however, already knew from the fighting in December 1944 what sort of policy the Soviets wanted them to pursue. In mid-December 1944 the KKE had received from Georgi Dimitrov a telegram in which the Bulgarian leader stated that the current international situation did not permit other Communist states to support the actions of the Greek Communists. Furthermore, he added, the Greek Communists should preserve their forces as much as possible and await a more auspicious moment for the realization of their "democratic program." Finally, he advised the KKE to use its popular organizations (EAM, the General Confederation of Labor, etc.) to "officially address the Unions and the British Labor Party, American mass organizations and Unions, and foreign public opinion in order to enlighten them concerning the aims and character of [the KKE's] struggle."[3] Thus, the Soviet message had come through: preserve your forces and engage in aggressive political activity to strengthen your cause.[4] Before this could be undertaken, however, the KKE had to do some serious reconstruction of its party organization.

The terms of the Varkiza Agreement were unusually lenient for a defeated party, but as Woodhouse has pointed out, KKE/EAM did not consider themselves a beaten army.[5] Indeed, with tenacious bargaining, they managed to get a partial amnesty for high-ranking EAM/ELAS officials (Siantos, Dimitris [Mitsos] Partsalidis, and most of the EAM Central Committee). While the amnesty did not apply to the EAM rank and file, it did at least provide the KKE with an essential basis for

[3]Interview with Dimitris [Mitsos] Partsalidis, *Avgi*, February 29, 1976.
[4]During the course of a dispute between the Albanian and Greek Communist parties in 1950, Partsalidis tried to deflect Enver Hoxha's criticism, that mistakes were made in accepting the Varkiza Agreement, by reminding Stalin of Dimitrov's advice to pursue a political strategy. Stalin replied that he had no knowledge of this action and that in any event, Dimitrov did not speak for the CPSU; see ibid. This curious volte-face most likely has to do with Soviet sensitivity to the position of Albania.
[5]Christopher M. Woodhouse, *The Struggle for Greece, 1941–1949* (London: Hart-Davis, MacGibbon, 1976), p. 136.

reconstructing the party apparatus. The free expression of political opinion guaranteed by Varkiza would also be enormously helpful in future
propaganda work.

In actuality, the KKE had begun to implement its policy even *before* the
signing of the Varkiza Agreement. In a telegram from the Peloponnese
Party Committee to KKE headquarters on January 19, 1945, the following
proposed plan of action was suggested in response to orders from the
Athens office of the KKE:

> Since the alliance of the British with the opposition, we are . . . asking for
> an Allied Committee to consist of the American, Russian, British and
> French representatives to undertake the solution of the Greek problem.
>
> Apart from the above, our organization in British held territory must
> continue to organize popular demonstrations for the assurance of popular
> liberties, backed by financial demands. . . . The intransigence of the Right
> based on unreserved British support might lead to a new conflict, in which
> case it is probable that the new campaigns will take the form of guerilla
> war, independent from city fighting. In all events our organization must
> start to sabotage the Plastiras mobilization. At the same time all measures
> must be taken to organize KKE "pirines" [cells] in Plastiras units to carry
> out intensive enlightenment work. We must take from our men those of
> mobilization age, who are not known as Communists, and place them in the
> new Army, after training them in their duties.[6]

This document clearly indicates that the KKE was planning an intensive
program of political activity and penetration of the Greek armed forces
before the Communists' protestations of a "white terror." Although it
reveals the beginning of a concerted effort to bring down the government
of Prime Minister Nikolaos Plastiras, there is little optimism that a third
round of civil war can be avoided. Even at this early date, the KKE (or at
least certain members) clearly recognized the likelihood of a new round of
fighting.

This possibility probably was another incentive to rebuild the KKE
organizational apparatus shattered in the second round, since without an
effective organization, the KKE could not possibly hope to control military operations. Thus the program to undermine the Plastiras government
coincided with rapid reconstruction of the KKE apparatus, mostly in
Athens, despite KKE assurances it had withdrawn from the Athens area.
A meeting of the Communist Organization of Athens (KOA) in mid-
January discussed organizational matters, putting primary emphasis on

[6]OSS L54716, March 11, 1945; see also FO 371-48256 R3348, February 17, 1945.

reconstruction of party cells, with the immediate aim of creating, "before the end of January, cells of at least three members in every district, factory, business, and office." In addition, the KOA decided it was necessary to rally rank-and-file morale, which had fallen after the December defeat. Thus propaganda should stress the "victorious advance of the Red Army—the USSR is winning the war singlehanded since their army is striking at the heart of Germany, while on the Western front the Allies are in retreat and the Germans may even throw them into the sea."[7]

The informant commented that despite these decisions, the KOA was in a state of partial dissolution and experiencing great difficulty rallying its forces. This pessimistic estimate of the Communists' recuperative powers proved premature, however, for the same source reported that during late January and early February 1945, the reconstruction of the KOA was proceeding rapidly. In fact, by February 20 the party organs were functioning again, and there were 127 active cells in the Athens area.[8]

A significant indicator that the KKE was seriously contemplating a parliamentary and infiltrative policy, regardless of forecasts of a new civil war, was the priority it placed on the reconstruction of the Athens party organization. The firmly established KKE presence in the north of Greece (where party organizations did not suffer from the demoralizing effects of the December defeat) did, afterall, make a more militant policy based in the mountains a distinct option. For the time being, however, the conciliatory policy prevailed, and Athens remained the focus of activity.

By March the KKE had apparently recovered enough strength to begin articulating its policy in public and diplomatic circles. Faithfully following Dimitrov's advice in December to seek out international opinion, an EAM delegation, which included Siantos (general secretary of the KKE) and Partsalidis (general secretary of EAM), visited Ambassador MacVeagh on March 10 and asked him, as a representative of one of the powers in the Yalta Conference, to support the immediate formation in Greece of a "representative government in the spirit of [the] Yalta Agreement."[9] Siantos based his request on the facts (according to him) that EAM had fulfilled its part of the Varkiza Agreement, while the government had undertaken to protect civil rights and the freedom of the press and form a truly national army but had failed on all counts. Siantos claimed EAMites were being attacked and excluded from the army, thereby making the army

[7]OSS L55163, March 13, 1945.
[8]OSS L55984, April 11, 1945.
[9]DSR 868.00/3-1045. Similar protests were made to British ambassador to Greece Reginald Leeper and the Greek government; see Woodhouse, *Struggle for Greece,* p. 144.

strictly a one-party body.[10] This particular visit is instructive; for it reveals some of the central components of future KKE policy in embryonic form: continual stress on the rightist terror, demand for Allied intervention, and repeated requests for a representative government.

The KKE used the amplification of a "rightist terror" to good effect, undoubtedly because there was a solid basis to the charges. MacVeagh acknowledged that rightist retaliation for ELAS offenses was unquestionably widespread and that police methods under the quisling Greek government and the Security Battalions were barbaric.[11] Woodhouse accurately points out that during this period the KKE had taken the terror issue and launched a propaganda campaign intended to give the impression that an indiscriminate campaign of terror was being launched against the Greek Communists.[12] The KKE was, however, equally culpable in the matter of terroristic practices. The U.S. ambassador concluded his report on communism and terrorism in Greece as follows:

> No one, I believe, could read my series of top secret dispatches . . . commenting on verbatim reports of conversations between British and Greek leaders and believe there is any danger of a "rightist terror" being now either instituted or countenanced by the authorities. On the other hand, I myself have talked at length with members of the Central Committee of EAM, and can testify that they personally evince not the slightest feeling that anything their followers have done to date has been unjustified by the aims of the "people's struggle."[13]

The conclusion appears to be that there were indeed serious rightist excesses in the immediate post-Varkiza period, but they were not on the scale depicted in the leftist press, nor was the Left as innocent as it depicted itself to be. Furthermore, rightist retaliation often resulted from government ineptitude rather than any well-thought-out plan, a fact not lost on the British. In late March, Macmillan complained to U.S. officials that he was exasperated with the Greek situation. The British, Macmillan said, were constantly obliged to step in and see that the Greek government upheld its side of the Varkiza Agreement. Macmillan believed the rightists in the government were out for revenge and that Prime Minister Plastiras was unable to control them. Plastiras therefore "would not do" and would have to leave in a month's time.[14] Ironically, although their reasons

[10]DSR 868.00/3-1045.
[11]DSR 868.00/3-1645; DSR 868.00/3-1045.
[12]Woodhouse, *Struggle for Greece,* p. 144–45.
[13]DSR 868.00/3-1645.
[14]DSR 868.00/3-2245.

differed, the KKE's desire to replace Plastiras coincided with the British perception that the Greek prime minister was ineffective.

As for the demands for an inter-Allied commission and the establishment of a representative government, these found more concrete expression during the proceedings of the Eleventh Plenum of the Central Committee of the KKE, held April 5–10, 1945. In addition to extended discussion and analysis of the party's past mistakes, the plenum also considered the KKE's program for the coming year. If the decisions reached at Varkiza and Yalta were to be realized in Greece, the KKE maintained, it was essential to form a representative government under the auspices of an inter-Allied commission.[15] In addition, the KKE argued that EAM had now to be reorganized to meet the new conditions in Greece. Of EAM's two goals, the liberation of the country and the assurance of the sovereignty of the people, the first had been achieved, so all EAM's forces had now to be oriented toward the fulfillment of the second. To this end, EAM was now to become a purely political coalition of parties.[16]

Examination of this program reveals that the underlying purpose was to undertake a political strategy to diminish and ultimately remove British influence from Greece. The statement that it was necessary to achieve the people's sovereignty, made while the British continued to retain forces in Greece, clearly implied that the future political campaign would be directed at the British. An inter-Allied commission was most likely desired as a means of checking British influence by the introduction of Soviet influence. The reorganization of EAM for a purely political struggle indicated that, for the moment, the KKE was pursuing the conciliatory policy suggested to it in December. Finally, the campaign for a representative government sought to shift the government toward the left, with the possible inclusion of the Communists, and more particularly, the elimination of Plastiras. Including the Communists held obvious advantages; removing Plastiras was necessary because of his hostile attitude toward ELAS. He himself wanted to engage in a punitive expedition against ELAS,[17] and with his government under the pressure of virulent anti-Communists he was unable to control, any modus vivendi with the KKE was unlikely.

In retrospect, the first several months of 1945 were a period in which

[15]*Rizospastis*, April 24, 1945.
[16]Ibid.; also DSR 868.00/5-145.
[17]Woodhouse, *Struggle for Greece*, pp. 133, 146. Plastiras was also titular head of EDES, which had been dispersed by the ELAS forces in the initial stages of the December revolt.

KKE policy was still in its formulative stage. Political initiatives like the fall of Plastiras had more to do with British motives and anti-Communist pressure than any overt Communist policy. Only when the British became a direct object of criticism and the KKE possessed a coherent and realizable plan of action could the KKE begin to affect developments in Greece. The plenum was just a start toward a policy based on political infiltration and parliamentary maneuvers. Given these conditions, it is no surprise that the KKE had little contact with the Soviet Union during this period. With no real program and a weak party organization, the KKE could offer the Soviets little help in extending their influence. Stalin would seem to have simply awaited further developments that would allow him to use the Greek Communists for his purposes.

If the KKE was little use to the Soviets at this time, the same could not be said of diplomatic contacts with the Greek government. Back at the height of the December uprising, Stalin had announced the appointment of Mikhail Sergeiev as Soviet ambassador to Greece. But Sergeiev never reached Athens, and his appointment was soon recalled. An analysis of the various explanations provided for this rather strange turn of events tends to support the hypothesis that the Soviets were attempting to use their diplomatic contacts to register their disapproval of the Greek government and quite possibly force a change in leadership.

According to the Soviets, the appointment of an ambassador was withheld because they did not want to complicate the British position in Greece. Instead of Sergeiev, Admiral Konstantin Rodionov was to be sent as ambassador to Greece, but he was temporarily delayed because he was attending the founding meetings of the United Nations at San Francisco. It is interesting that the Soviet explanation was passed to Greek foreign minister Iannis Sofianopoulos (whose close affiliation with the Soviet Union was to be crucial in months to come) through the Greek naval attaché in Turkey.[18]

The British and Greek governments received a second version. When Sofianopoulos met with British ambassador Reginald Leeper in early March, he informed Leeper that his Greek counterpart in Moscow had reported increasing criticism of the Plastiras government. More important, the Greek foreign minister added that the Soviets did not intend to appoint an ambassador until the Greek Communists entered the government.[19] The British Foreign Office concluded from this version that it was very

[18]FO 371-48294 R7276, April 13, 1945.
[19]FO 371-48294 R4504, March 6, 1945.

unlikely the Soviets would do anything to imply support for the Plastiras government.[20]

Finally, there was a third version from the KKE. The secretary for EAM in Macedonia, Nikos Dilaveris, claimed that the reason Russia had no diplomatic representatives in Greece was because it did not recognize the present government. In addition, Bakirtzis reported that Chernichev had told him shortly before leaving Greece in early March that all Russian missions were being withdrawn from Greece because of Russian disapproval of the Greek government. This information, apparently gained from direct contact with Soviet officers,[21] is misleading: subsequent investigation revealed that a "mission" of sorts remained in Greece. While there was a hiatus in the formal diplomatic presence, Soviet officials of some sort were in Greece continuously from summer 1944 until November 1945, when full diplomatic relations were restored.

The conclusion from these explanations is that, Soviet excuses notwithstanding, Stalin was attempting to use the limited means then at his disposal to assist the KKE in bringing about a change of government in Greece. Also worth noting is the nature of the proposed new Soviet ambassador to Greece. Rodionov was an admiral and had served before his trip to San Francisco as the Soviet naval attaché in Turkey.[22] His appointment may well have reflected Soviet interest in using Greece as a pressure point against Turkey.

The fate of other diplomatic and official contacts between Greece and the Soviet Union also supports the hypothesis that the Soviets were doing what they could to deny to the Plastiras government a much-needed sense of legitimacy. Colonel Popov, nominal head of the Russian Military Mission, disappeared some days after the signing of the Varkiza Agreement, and his place was subsequently taken by N. Velichonskii, the Soviets' Tass correspondent in Athens.[23] Besides clandestine contacts, the only Soviet presence that remained was a "repatriation" mission officially attached to the Allied powers; the Soviet Union now had no official contact with the Plastiras government.

[20]FO 371-48294 R4873, March 17, 1945.

[21]OSS L55474, April 6, 1945. Chernichev evidently never left Greece. He entered Greek territory as a member of the Russian Military Mission to ELAS forces in July 1944; remained as a member of the Soviet "repatriation" mission; and then, when the Soviet Union appointed an ambassador to the Sofoulis government in November 1945, became a member of the Soviet diplomatic representation in Greece, becoming first secretary of the Soviet Embassy on March 19, 1946.

[22]FO 371-48294 R7276, April 13, 1945.

[23]DSR 868.00/6-145, no. 1114.

The Soviets also used contacts within the Greek government in their attempts to pursue their interests, the most interesting example being Foreign Minister Sofianopoulos. Although not a Communist, Sofianopoulos had a history of sympathizing with Greek Communist policies. In 1936, as leader of the Peasant party, he sided with the KKE in the Communist-led "popular Front" that played a crucial role in the developments of that year. During the period of the National Resistance, Sofianopoulos represented his party at the Lebanon Conference and again sided with the KKE politicians when they refused to accept the results of the conference. When the Plastiras government was initially formed, Sofianopoulos was given the Foreign Affairs portfolio primarily because of his friendly relations with EAM, thereby giving the Communist cause a powerful voice within the government.[24]

The new Greek foreign minister also distinguished himself for his views on the Soviet Union. According to Sofianopoulos, the Soviet Union was gradually moving away from "world revolution and simon-pure communism."[25] This optimistic conception of the Soviet Union as ultimately benign suited Sofianopoulos' belief that Greece's future lay in close and cordial relations with the Soviets as well as the British, and it provided a convenient rationale for his own political ambitions. As the young and ambitious leader of a small, agrarian party, Sofianopoulos could not hope to accede to the premiership solely on the strength of his popular following. Any perceptive Greek politician, however, was able to see that to maintain power in Greece, it was necessary to accommodate the Great Powers as well. But while some politicians threw their lot in with the British and others with the Soviets (as did the KKE), Sofianopoulos sought to distinguish himself with a policy that purported to advocate the harmonious presence of both Britain and Russia in Greece. Sofianopoulos thus had staked out his political career in such a way as to make him extremely susceptible to Soviet pressure. The evolution of events demonstrates that this fact was not lost on the Soviets, who successfully manipulated the foreign minister in pursuit of their objectives. Indeed, even MacVeagh ultimately concluded that Sofianopoulos was a fellow traveller and an example of the KKE's penetration into the Greek cabinet.[26]

The behavior of Sofianopoulos at the Varkiza talks illustrates his support of Soviet policy. It was he who suggested a partial amnesty that

[24]D. George Kousoulas, *Revolution and Defeat: The Story of the Greek Communist Party, 1918–1949* (London: Oxford University Press, 1965), pp. 108 ff., 216.
[25]Laird Archer, *Balkan Tragedy* (Manhattan, Kan.: MA-AH, 1983), p. 279.
[26]DSR 868.00B/1-2847, no. 3579.

included only high-ranking Communist officials, leaving the rank and file unprotected.[27] This limited amnesty served Soviet policy by restoring the KKE political leadership while minimizing the possibility of military action without effective political control. As the year progressed, Sofianopoulos proved his value to the Soviets in other, more important, ways.

After several months of relatively passive articles, Soviet propaganda and press reports began to increase their criticism of the Plastiras government. On January 11, 1945, *Izvestiia* accused Plastiras of agreeing to talks to end the fighting while simultaneously seeking the unconditional capitulation of EAM/ELAS. Stalin obviously knew of the Greek prime minister's desire to destroy the Communists in a punitive expedition, and the Soviet leader was most likely seeking to avert the complete annihilation of the KKE. A Tass dispatch published in Moscow papers on March 3 constituted the sharpest expression of dissatisfaction with the trend of events in Greece. The dispatch alleged that while EAM observed the Varkiza Agreement, the extreme Right wished to use it to destroy all leftist elements.[28] Two days later, *Pravda* continued this line of attack by implying that the current Greek government was sabotaging the Varkiza Agreement, restoring the Metaxist police system, and failing to deal with relief problems.

In mid-March the Moscow press began to reflect more closely the demands of the KKE and EAM. A Tass dispatch on March 9 recounted the various EAM protests on February 26 about violations of the Varkiza Agreement. Also included in the dispatch was a report of the EAM delegation's visit to the regent to demand the formation of a representative government.[29] A later Tass dispatch quoted the Greek newspaper *Eleftheria* in arguing that the Greek government had no desire to stop the terror enveloping Greece.[30] Even after the fall of the Plastiras government, Moscow showed disapproval of the new premier, Admiral Petros Voulgaris, by quoting a Siantos statement in which the new government was described as an instrument of "monarchofascist dictatorship" that had excluded all democratic elements.[31]

This emergence of a close correspondence between KKE demands and Soviet press statements coincided with the arrival of the Tass representa-

---

[27]Kousoulas, p. 216.
[28]A summary of the dispatch is in DSR 868.00/3-445.
[29]DSR 868.00/3-1245.
[30]Ibid.
[31]DSR 868.00/4-2445.

tive in Athens in March. According to one observer, Velichonskii's job consisted of presenting himself regularly at EAM headquarters, collecting the latest party handout, and cabling it verbatim to Moscow.[32] By the end of March, therefore, the Soviet government had begun faithfully to reflect most KKE demands: an end to the terror, the replacement of Plastiras, and the installation of a representative government. The Soviet press did *not*, however, repeat the KKE's demand for the intervention of an inter-Allied commission.

May–August 1945: The Shaping of Political Gradualism

The months after the fall of the Plastiras government coincided with a series of significant events both within Greece and in the international system. In May the war in Europe was finally brought to a close, thereby fulfilling one of Stalin's principal objectives. In Greece, the return of Zachariadis into the Communist ranks held out the promise of a new KKE policy under a leadership untainted by the errors of the past. The period through August 1945 was therefore a critical one; now the KKE had to formulate an assertive policy that would convince Stalin that Greece could prove useful to his plans.

The Soviet pressure on Turkey intensified during this period. On June 7, Molotov met with Turkish ambassador Selim Sarper and presented the argument that Turkey should cede to the USSR the two provinces of Kars and Ardahan. In further exchanges Molotov also made known the Soviet desire to acquire bases in the Straits, which the Turkish ambassador naturally rejected. Molotov finally proposed an agreement between Turkey and the Soviet Union on changes in the Montreux Convention. Since the other signatories to the convention had to be considered, the discussion ended with no concrete results. The Turkish ambassador did, however, derive the impression "that if Turkey would break away from its alliance with Britain, the USSR would not feel it necessary to insist" on its demands. This surprise move, accompanied by reports of Soviet troop movements along the Bulgarian frontier, was designed to pressure the Turks into accepting Molotov's demands.[33]

---

[32]Kenneth Matthews, *Memories of a Mountain War: Greece, 1944–1949* (London: Longmans Green, 1972), p. 167.

[33]Xydis, p. 84, 83–85; see also DSR 868.00/6-145. In July 1945 the British Military Mission in Sofia relayed to the Foreign Office a message that reflected the intensity of the

The Soviet pressure on Turkey was not restricted to direct approaches alone: given its strategic significance, Greece was to serve as a Soviet pressure point. During the San Francisco conference for the creation of the United Nations, the Soviet delegation had warned Sofianopoulos that any Greek "effort to unite with Turkey against Moscow's efforts to 'keep the Straits open'" would be looked upon with great disfavor.[34] Elements within the KKE were apparently also convinced that Greece was being used to influence Turkey. After a conversation with Zachariadis on July 10, 1945, Bakirtzis told OSS agents in Athens, "Russia will take positive action to obtain [a] stronger hold over Turkey regardless of what Britain does." The OSS agents concluded that the agitation on the Greek frontier might be a smokescreen to conceal preparations for an attack on Turkey.[35]

Other indications of a Soviet interest in consolidating their position in the Balkans and exploiting the chaotic situation in Greece were accompanied by a concern to prevent the instability from spreading across Greek frontiers and jeopardizing other Soviet objectives. Soviet sensitivity on this point quickly became evident whenever the subject of territorial demands was discussed. In Albania, Stalin could not rely on Soviet military power; consequently, the Soviets countered Greek demands for Northern Epirus by arguing that Albania's existence exerted a stabilizing effect on the Balkans. In Bulgaria, the strength of the Red Army allowed for a forceful Soviet response to Greek territorial demands. In May 1945, for example, General Sergei Biriuzov made it clear that Russia would support Bulgaria in resisting what he alleged were British-backed Greek territorial claims on Bulgaria.[36]

Soviet anxiety also showed in a series of border incidents on the already-tense Bulgarian frontier. The assistant military attaché to the U.S. Embassy compiled a list of border violations in northern Greece during the months of May and June which led Ambassador MacVeagh to conclude that although most of the incidents were insignificant in themselves, in

---

Soviet desire to pressure Turkey. The mission had just received the information that Marshal Rodion Malinovskii's and Fedor Tolbukhin's armies would not remain long in Bulgaria and Romania. Apparently, "[t]hey were being concentrated for the purpose of browbeating the Turks into accepting Russian proposals for the Straits. [The p]rocess of frightening the Turks into submission was not expected to take many weeks." The report concluded by stating that the "information did not come actually from Stalin but is (?considered) as sure": FO 371-48774 R11408, July 5, 1945.

[34]Archer, p. 279. See also DSR 868.00/7-2845, no. 1252, for Soviet hostility to the formation of a Greek-Turkish bloc.

[35]DSR 868.00/7-1445, no. 708.

[36]DSR 868.00/6-145, no. 1114; DSR 868.00/6-2045, no. 1210.

total they were "undeniably impressive" and must be considered "as having at least a psychological importance in connection with the present international situation in the Balkans."[37]

Closer examination of some of the incidents supports the contention that the Soviets were trying to take advantage of the unsettled situation to discover the scope of British and Greek activities in the region. Especially interesting is the arrest and detention of a British-Greek patrol that accidentally crossed the Bulgarian frontier on May 29. The group was surrounded by a Bulgarian force and eventually taken to Petrich. On the next day a Russian colonel arrived from Sofia and proceeded to interrogate the members of the patrol on "British and Greek troop distribution and strength, unit identifications, morale, equipment, whether or not the British troops were going to the Far East, economic conditions in Greece, the strength of ELAS, etc."[38] An OSS source also supported this view of Soviet activities. It stated that in May 1945, several Greeks of Russian origin were in contact with a Russian army captain, who was alleged to be engaged in intelligence activities in Greece and who traveled frequently between Greece and Bulgaria.[39]

Soviet information collection was aided by the apparently lax attitude of British patrols in the area. On April 24, a party of Russians appeared at a border post and were refused entry by the Greek National Guard. Returning the next day, the party met a British patrol; the leader, Major-General Zukov [Zhukov?], explained to the patrol that he was on sick leave and wished to visit Thessaloniki. The British let the Soviets through and chaperoned them on a one-day excursion to the Greek port city. News of the visit angered British authorities, especially because the Soviets had repeatedly refused them access to Bulgarian territory. Concerned that a flat refusal to admit Russians onto Greek soil might offend the sensibilities of an ally, they tried to resolve the problem by stipulating that further crossings would be permitted only with the written permission of the British representative to the Allied Control Commission (ACC) in Sofia.[40]

[37]DSR 868.00/7-445, no. 1282.
[38]Ibid.
[39]OSS XL29925, November 16, 1945.
[40]FO 371-48294 R7505, April 27, 1945; R7753, May 2, 1945. The other members of the Russian party besides Zukov [Zhukov?] were listed as Captain Melnik (no first names available), two drivers, and one guard. While in Thessaloniki, the party was graciously put up in the Mediterranean Hotel, from which they were escorted to the border the following day. The Soviets, while quite willing to take advantage of British and Greek hospitality, apparently did not invite their hosts to reciprocate; the "suggestion of a return visit to Sofia did not meet with any encouragement": FO 371-48294 R7505, April 27, 1945.

The Soviets were not, however, deterred from placing their people inside Greek territory. Less than two months later, on June 23, British military authorities informed the British Embassy of a much more serious incident. According to the British diplomatic representative in Thessaloniki, "Five Russian officers arrived at Koula [on the Bulgarian frontier north of Siderokastro] . . . saying they wished to travel to Kavalla [Kavala] and presented [a] pass purporting to emanate from ACC Sofia. As no identification had been received from Sofia reference was made to [the] ACC who replied that no such pass had been issued. Meanwhile, orders had been given to hold the officers at Siderocastron [Siderokastro] pending a reply, but owing to a misunderstanding they were allowed to proceed and are now, it is believed, on their way to Athens."[41] Worse, the Soviet officers were not located and escorted to the Greek border until June 30. These and similar incidents indicate the Soviets successfully gathered information in Greece using their own operatives long after the British had found it all but impossible to enter Bulgaria. British troop dispositions were evidently a major Soviet concern, but the Soviets no doubt took the opportunity to gather a great deal of information on the political situation in northern Greece.[42]

This manifestation of Soviet interests had the misfortune of increasing British mistrust. The turning point in the British attitude toward the Russians apparently came after the episode involving the capture and detention of the British patrol on May 29. Another cause of the growing suspicion was an active campaign by the Communist party in the north of Greece aimed to intensify the mistrust.[43] Ironically, the increasing tension on the northern border would soon become a liability for Stalin's plans as it militated against the general Soviet and KKE goal of not antagonizing the Western Allies so as to ease the British gradually off the Balkan Peninsula without their being supplanted by the United States.

Singling out the British for responsibility for the present state of Greek affairs was a Communist tactic that went hand in hand with distinguishing

---

[41]FO 371-48294 R10861, June 26, 1945; R11238, July 2, 1945. One of the officers in the Soviet party, Captain Brylov (also referred to as Briulev), remained in Greece because he was a member of the "repatriation" mission: ibid. The Soviets appear to have gotten away with more than just crossing the border; once they were located, the consul in Thessaloniki stated that they would be conducted to the frontier, adding that the British authorities would retain the Soviets' jeep "in exchange for the British one taken to Sofia by [the] Russians some weeks ago": FO 371-48294 R11238, July 2, 1945.

[42]The Soviet "repatriation" mission undoubtedly performed similar intelligence functions.

[43]DSR 868.00/7-445, no. 1282.

between American and British policies. In the first place, Britain was quite obviously the power responsible for maintaining and changing the successive Greek governments. Second, it was British forces that were the sole stabilizing influence in Greece. Even so, the British remained a negative rather than a positive force: they could prevent any one side from taking power, but they could not, or would not, exercise the influence necessary to allow Greek government policies to produce positive results; for that would have required a degree of intervention in Greek affairs the British were unwilling to undertake. Given this posture, it was inevitable that the conditions in Greece would deteriorate, thereby further burdening the British commitment.

The American posture was one of unwillingness to become involved in Greek affairs. Throughout 1945 the U.S. government evinced no interest in actively intervening to help the Greeks. In July, in response to a series of incidents on the Greek-Yugoslav frontier, the United States offered to join in sending an international mission of investigation but did not pursue the proposal against opposition.[44] American policymakers viewed the U.S. agreement to participate in the observation of the Greek elections as merely a short-term involvement. Even as late as January 1946, when ambassadors MacVeagh and Leeper recommended a much more extensive American involvement in Greek affairs, the U.S. government replied, "The measure of financial assistance apparently advocated by Mr. Mac-Veagh and the degree of responsibility for internal Greek affairs which he [MacVeagh] seems to contemplate are greater than the Departments of State and Treasury, and the President, are willing to assume."[45]

It was in navigating between the deteriorating British position and the American reluctance to dirty their hands that the future success of Soviet policy lay. A strategy of pressure against Turkey could not succeed if it were not also accompanied by an effort to exploit this potential division between the two Western Allies in adjacent regions such as Greece and Iran. It was, therefore, no accident that Stalin's attitude toward Greece began to change soon after the conclusion of the war in Europe: Soviet policy was a direct reflection of the new strategic configuration of the postwar era. It became eminently sensible to pursue a policy of political gradualism and infiltration, to capitalize on the deterioration of British influence without simultaneously activating an American response. Formulating a policy based on this discrepancy between British and American

---

[44]Woodhouse, *Struggle for Greece,* p. 157.
[45]DSR 868.00/1-1546, Harry C. Hawkins to Secretary Bevin, January 15, 1946.

attitudes proved somewhat difficult in the opening months of 1945, but once Greek Communist attacks began to focus on the continued presence of British troops as the real evil, their criticisms formed the basis for increasingly strong support from the Soviet press as the year progressed.

In addition to this tacit Soviet endorsement, KKE morale received a boost from two key events in the middle of 1945: the return of former KKE general secretary Zachariadis and the Labour party's victory in the British general elections. The role Zachariadis played after his return to Greece has been the subject of heated debate, debate that unfortunately has most often been extemely polemical and usually based on conflicting accounts of what transpired. Zachariadis' role is construed here in a way that is both straightforward and crucial: as a rational actor attempting to achieve certain objectives in the presence of constraints. Zachariadis returned to Greece to pursue a policy that served Soviet strategic interests, although he was apparently handicapped by an incomplete knowledge of Stalin's objectives. His policy encountered serious problems because many within the KKE Central Committee expressed serious doubts about the feasibility of his plans. But Zachariadis was aware, probably more than anyone else in the KKE at the time, that any political force in Greece would meet with failure unless it secured the support of at least one of the Great Powers. Greek political realities thus compelled the KKE leader to find ways to obtain Soviet sympathy and support.

The manner of Zachariadis' return to Greece suggests he had the opportunity to make contact with Soviet forces. He had spent the war years in the Dachau concentration camp, completely out of touch with events in Greece. Upon his release, however, he immediately reported (as another Communist source alleges) to the Soviet Command and requested to be sent as soon as possible to Athens.[46] The Soviets no doubt used this opportunity to brief him on the broad outlines of their objectives in Greece. Once back, Zachariadis almost immediately became active in party work. His authority benefited from the fact that he was untainted by the December 1944 defeat of ELAS but suffered from his lack of contact with Greece for so many years. Several of his statements so clearly reflected external influence that they cost the KKE much domestic support.

Zachariadis' arrival in Athens coincided with the appearance of a new element in KKE policy: the use of territorial claims. But in advancing territorial claims favorable to Soviet interests, Zachariadis placed the

---

[46]Enver Hoxha, *With Stalin: Memoirs* (Tirana: "8" Nentori, 1979), p. 199.

KKE in an unpopular domestic position. Of all of the demands raised by the Greek government, the one with the greatest popular support was that of Northern Epirus. All political parties supported this claim, and with what they considered good reason: the large Greek population in Northern Epirus. The difficulty from the Soviet point of view was that the demand constituted a serious threat to the integrity of Albania; indeed, if Greece received its claim, there would be little to prevent Yugoslavia from absorbing the remainder. Thus it was in Stalin's interest, as well as Hoxha's, to see the Greek claim to Northern Epirus somehow blunted. Here Zachariadis apparently served Soviet purposes. On May 25, right before his return to Athens from Paris, the former KKE general secretary reportedly stated that the Greek claim to Northern Epirus constituted a danger to the peace and cooperation of the Balkan nations.[47] Popular and press reaction was swift and violent, and the KKE soon found itself having to backtrack to save face.

The KKE was also opening up a claim farther east. On June 3, 1945, *Eleftheri Ellada,* the EAM organ, initiated what was to become a campaign for the inclusion of Eastern Thrace among Greek territorial claims. Needless to say, this new claim to part of Turkish territory coincided with the return of Zachariadis and the increase of Soviet pressure on Turkey. During the summer of 1945, the claim to Eastern Thrace was reiterated several times and once even augmented to include the islands of Imbros and Tenedos.[48] In the meantime, the Communists continued their back-pedaling on Northern Epirus. In a June 7 interview with MacVeagh, Zachariadis claimed that his position had been misrepresented in the press. He did not deny that Greece had a claim on Northern Epirus; rather, the KKE leader claimed he objected only to the proposal that it should be occupied at once by force of arms.[49]

Under the leadership of Zachariadis, the KKE now defended a set of territorial claims tailor made for Soviet interests. In another policy devel-

[47]DSR 868.00/6-145, no. 1114; FO 371-48343 R9216, May 28, 1945. That Zachariadis' statements regarding Northern Epirus had a negative impact on KKE rank and file is reflected in an OSS report of the KKE's Epirus Regional Committee meeting. In a brief summary, the report concluded: "With regard to the question of Northern Epirus, most of the senior members of the Committee disagreed with Zachariades's views; and the ordinary KKE members who inhabit both sides of the present frontier are also said to favor the annexation of Northern Epirus to Greece, although they avoid expressing this opinion for fear of Enver Hodja": OSS XL21027, August 31, 1945. Zachariadis' views on the Epirus question surely did not come from anywhere inside of Greece.

[48]DSR 868.00/6-2045, no. 1210; DSR 868.00/7-245, no. 1233; DSR 868.00/7-2845, no. 1252. Imbros and Tenedos are Turkish islands at the mouth of the Dardanelles.

[49]DSR 868.00/6-2245, no. 1211.

opment not unrelated to the issues of territoriality and pressure on Turkey, the Twelfth Plenum of the Central Committee of the KKE (June 25–27, 1945) declared that while it was opposed to Slav encroachment, it denounced the efforts of the Greek government to observe solidarity with Turkey on the question of the Straits.[50] Once again, Soviet interests appeared to motivate KKE actions.

In the period between the eleventh and twelfth plenums, (April–June 1945), Zachariadis (now back in his position as general secretary) increased the offensive against the British. On June 5 he attacked the British presence in Greece, linking the current situation in the country to the actions of the British. In a further development designed to pressure the Voulgaris government, the KKE Politburo warned on June 16 that if the prerequisites for free expression of the people's will were not assured, the Communist party would consider abstaining from the elections.[51] The necessary prerequisites were of course none other than the demands the KKE had previously voiced; but in their new form, they picked up support from centrist groups also alarmed at the prospect of rightist terror affecting the elections. There were also increasing indications of a more violent Communist policy. Zachariadis spoke of the possibility of a "new armed struggle" at his first press conference in Athens, on June 1.[52] Statements such as this had a dissonant ring when compared with overall KKE policy, but the chaotic situation in the north of Greece made such belligerent outbursts appear to be more than political rhetoric.

Besides reemphasizing and clarifying previous policy objectives, two more developments at the Twelfth Plenum of the Central Committee of the KKE indicated the evolution of a more complex and refined strategy. On internal policy, Zachariadis publicly called for a "mass self-defense,"[53] already in existence since early 1945. The ostensible aim of this self-defense (*aftoamina*) was to protect the party organization from extermination by the Right; with its emphasis on defensive militancy and the use of weapons, the *aftoamina* could, however, serve other purposes as well. Alekos Papapanagiotou has pointed out (as have former ELAS commanders such as Giorgis Blanas) that the *aftoamina* units were

[50]DSR 868.00/7-1745, no. 1332.
[51]Ibid.
[52]Woodhouse, *Struggle for Greece*, p. 151. The date given by Woodhouse for the press conference was May 29, but this is difficult to accept, since Zachariadis only just appeared in Athens on that day. I have chosen to use the date suggested to me by Ole Smith.
[53]Ibid. The memoirs of Giorgis Vontitsos-Gousias, Giorgis Blanas, Vasilis Bartziotas, and Dimos Votsikas, as well as statements by Zachariadis, also confirm that the *aftoamina* was officially created at the Twelfth Plenum (specific references follow).

intended to serve as basic units in a policy designed to develop gradually into civil war.[54] For the moment, however, the stated purpose was strictly defensive.

The other development concerned foreign policy. The Twelfth Plenum was the occasion for Zachariadis to launch what has now become known as the "theory of the two poles." In analyzing the wartime policy of the KKE, Zachariadis maintained that the Greek Communists neglected to consider the preponderant British power in the eastern Mediterranean. Hence, "during the conditions of the Second World War . . . a realistic foreign policy on the part of EAM and PEEA would have been to move between the two major poles: the European-Balkan with its center in Soviet Russia . . . and the Mediterranean with its center in England. A correct foreign policy would have been that which constituted a Greek axis, which would join these two poles."[55]

Scholars have interpreted this analysis in a number of ways, usually critical of the KKE general secretary for an anti-Soviet, anti-Greek, or pro-British policy. A more recent analysis plausibly argues that Zachariadis was actually referring to the wartime period, not to postwar Greece.[56] But when one considers that, later in 1946, Zachariadis attempted to secure Soviet consent for the neutralization of Greece, it would seem that the two-pole theory represents the beginnings of a delicate balancing act by which Zachariadis tried to weave KKE policy between the reality of a deteriorating British presence and the Soviet desire for a gradual and careful penetration into Greece. The final resolution of the Twelfth Plenum did not refer to Zachariadis' analysis but instead stressed the "need of establishing equally friendly relations with Great Britain and Soviet Russia and a close collaboration with the United States of America and France."[57] Such a statement was more in line with earlier demands for an inter-Allied commission to reduce the dependence on Britain.

Thus Zachariadis' theory, while primarily directed toward the wartime situation, also fit conveniently into the persistent KKE political demand

[54]Foivos Oikonomidis interview with Alekos Papapanagiotou, *Anti*, May 22, 1981, p. 40.

[55]*Deka Chronia Agones, 1935–1945* (Athens: Poreia, 1977), p. 273.

[56]Ole L. Smith, "On Zachariades' Theory of the Two Poles," *Scandinavian Studies in Modern Greek*, no. 5 (1981), 29–35.

[57]DSR 868.00/7-1745, no. 1332. Zachariadis' attempts to achieve a neutralization of Greece under Great Power auspices, including the Soviet Union, are revealed more fully in the documentary excerpts from the KKE archives (chap. 4). Zachariadis continued to maintain as late as 1963 that his conception of the two poles applied to the postwar era and implied the neutrality of Greece; see Nikos Zachariadis, *Provlimata tis Krisis tou KKE* (N.p.: Laikis Exousias, n.d.), pp. 22–24.

for a reduction of the British presence. It was therefore an elegant rationale that connected legal appearance with political reality. The reality of the situation in Soviet eyes was that Britain, though in decline as a military power, would continue to retain diplomatic and political influence for some time. Hence, while supplanting the British was only a matter of time, Stalin had to move carefully lest the British skillfully utilize their remaining resources to engage American commitment. The KKE leadership apparently shared this view: In the new Europe being shaped at the Potsdam Conference, Britain would count for little; Soviet–American differences would be confined to the Far East. Russia, therefore, must eventually come to dominate the Balkan scene.[58] The KKE demands for the intervention of an inter-Allied commission in Greece were, therefore, an elaborate fiction that provided the juridical context for Soviet intervention in Greek affairs. With all the Great Powers in Greece, the passage of time would lead to the erosion of the British position and the ultimate ascendance of the Soviets.

Unfortunately for the Greek Communists, the Soviets would not budge until two conditions had been met: politically, it was necessary to avoid creating the impression of a Soviet intervention in Greece, thereby setting a precedent for the intervention of Western states in Eastern Europe; militarily, the British forces currently stationed in Greece had to be removed. Once this was accomplished, the Soviets would be free to move aggressively on the political level. It was precisely for these reasons that Stalin refused to take part in the observance of the Greek elections. Once the elections in the Eastern European countries were a fait accompli and the British forces had left Greece, the question of a Soviet political presence could be contemplated more seriously.

The importance of the notion of Greece as a balancing factor thus lay in that it provided the KKE with the basis for a reasonable political strategy. The Soviet Union could enter Greece by means of an inter-Allied commission, and as the perceived political realities developed, its presence would ultimately become the dominant one. The KKE, for its part, had the task of forcing the British to leave—always, of course, without antagonizing the Western Allies or allowing them to become convinced that the Communists sought power.

The weeks after the Twelfth Plenum were marked by an increase in the violence of attacks against the British presence. In northern Greece, *Laiki*

[58]DSR 868.00/7-2845, no. 1252.

Foni developed the habit of referring to the British as "Occupation Forces."[59] EAM's announcement of its Program for Popular Democracy on July 31 also continued the foreign policy trend set at the Twelfth Plenum. According to the EAM program, "Greece, being a Balkan as well as a Mediterranean country, must be a factor of balance between the Great Allies. . . . This necessitates equal understanding and collaboration with Great Britain and the Soviet Union, and friendship with all the major Allies."[60] This statement was proof that Zachariadis was not merely restricting himself to an analysis of wartime conditions but was attempting to extract from this analysis an effective policy by which the KKE could neutralize the British position of primus inter pares in order to allow Soviet political intervention on favorable terms.

The British Labour party's victory at the polls in July was also an event that significantly affected the course of Greek politics in several respects. In the first place, it stunned the rightists and emboldened the Left. Second, it marked an intensification of British attempts to base the Greek government on a weak or nonexistent Center.[61] This was an ideal situation for the Soviet-oriented aspects of KKE policy because it reinforced the Communists' own desire to have a weak (possibly left-leaning) government, which in turn would provide the opportunity for continued instability and the possibility of KKE representation.[62] That state of affairs could then be utilized to tax Britain's commitment to the breaking point.

In the wake of the British elections, the Greek Communists became even more aggressive in their political demands. The KKE Politburo had apparently met on July 28 and 30 and reached a number of decisions that, according to MacVeagh, "heralded a disturbing changeover from the defensive policy so carefully pursued by [the] KKE since the Varkiza agreement." The new policy, as reflected in the resolutions of the EAM Executive Committee on July 30, was to be "based on the enforcement by all means in its [KKE] power of demands for the recognition of the

[59]Ibid.; *Laiki Foni* is a KKE organ.
[60]DSR 868.00/8-2145, no. 1426; see also, Zachariadis, *Provlimata tis Krisis tou KKE*, pp. 23–24.
[61]Lawrence S. Wittner, *American Intervention in Greece, 1943–49* (New York: Columbia University Press, 1982), p. 30–31.
[62]Some U.S. officials anticipated such a turn of events after the government of Themistoklis Sofoulis came to power in November 1945. Some months after that, MacVeagh became convinced that "the idea of using the aged liberal leader Sophoulis as a cover for . . . a 'constitutional' attempt to seize power has been much in the thoughts of the communist leaders": DSR 868.00B/1-2847, no. 3579.

Resistance movement as it has been recognized in other countries. This, of course, involves the participation in the Govt of leaders of the Resistance and of KKE and by public meetings, protests to the Govt and to foreign Embassies, backed if necessary by the threat to call a general strike[. I]t is hoped to create serious trouble necessitating eventual Allied intervention."[63]

Four days after the EAM resolution, Archbishop Damaskinos, the regent of Greece, reported to the British chargé that he was under the strongest pressure to create a new "political" government and that Voulgaris was unhappy and wished to resign.[64] Sensing that a possible turning point was near, the KKE continued its offensive. Several days later, Siantos reiterated the demand for a representative government (by now a euphemism for the participation of the Communists), and when informed that other parties were unlikely to agree to a government that included EAM, he responded that EAM was ready to undertake the formation of a new government.[65] Simultaneously, the KKE, EAM, and ELAS planned to have a mass meeting of their supporters on August 6. The assembly was subsequently banned by the government, and the Communists responded by issuing a press release declaring that unless a "representative political government" was formed, they would abstain from the "fake" elections being prepared.[66]

Despite the intense KKE pressure, the British did not budge, and the new British foreign secretary, Ernest Bevin, in a speech on August 20, reaffirmed the basic line of British policy in Greece. Zachariadis, however, increased the militancy of his campaign.[67] In a speech in Thessaloniki on August 24, he attacked the British presence and denounced the

[63]DSR 868.00/8-845, no. 817.
[64]DSR 868.00/8-345, no. 796.
[65]DSR 868.00/8-845, no. 817. The KKE's aggressive turn is reflected in the results of an August 1 Politburo meeting at which it was decided that there should be an all-out attack on the regent and the Voulgaris government, accompanied by demands they leave office. It was also resolved to propose to the EAM Central Committee that it take the initiative in forming a representative government with whatever assistance from the "democratic Left and resistance movement." This was the first time since the second round that the Greek Communists considered it wise to come out in open opposition to the regent and the Republican and Populist parties: FO 371-48276 R13056, August 3, 1945.
[66]DSR 868.00/8-845, no. 817.
[67]DSR 868.00/9-345, no. 1289. According to this document, it was Bevin's speech that crystallized KKE policy: the KKE was "to strengthen Russia's prestige by all possible means and to prove that Russia alone—not Britain—can ultimately reverse the state of helpless confusion prevailing in Greece."

elections being prepared. According to the KKE leader, British prime minister Clement Attlee and Bevin would be held responsible if the Greek people's limit of self-restraint was exceeded by dishonor and they arose to the cry of "onward ELAS for Greece."[68] In a speech several days later at Naousa, Zachariadis stated that opposition to the Voulgaris government was a national necessity and added that it was essential for the British to leave Greece and for a representative government to be created.[69]

By the end of the month it was clear that the Communist policy was having effects. The campaign for the inclusion of the KKE in the government was obviously affecting the Voulgaris government, which was also plagued by a series of resignations in key ministries. The direct attack on the British presence was making progress as it threw British inability to deal with the situation in Greece into the international limelight. There were negative consequences as well. On the all-important question of British policy, the new Labour government stood firm, and Zachariadis' speeches had the disadvantage of worrying the Greek government so much that it felt uneasy about any diminution of British support. Mac-Veagh noted in late August how agitated the Greek foreign minister became when the American ambassador inquired whether the British had given any indications of an early withdrawal from Greece.[70] The Greek Communists were finally having a major impact on Greek politics, but they had still not succeeded in the two primary aims of a change of government and the withdrawal of the British.

Another aspect of KKE policy was designed to ensure that internal economic conditions in Greece remained chaotic, thereby preventing any pro-British government from carrying out a successful (and popular) program of reconstruction. The return to Greece of Kyriakos Varvaresos in late May thus posed a threat to the Greek Communists. The British had invested a great deal of their confidence and prestige in Varvaresos,[71] and he was consequently given the posts of vice-premier and minister of supply in the Voulgaris government. The hope was that under the guidance of Varvaresos, the Greek economy would recover and provide the British with a much-needed success in their Greek policy. The new vice premier felt confident that by taxing profits and instituting rigid control of prices and supplies, he could save the situation. He admitted, however,

[68]*Rizospastis,* August 25, 1945.
[69]DSR 868.00/8-3145, no. 949.
[70]DSR 868.002/8-2945, no. 935.
[71]DSR 868.00/9-1145, no. 1295.

that his program was likely to meet with opposition from the wealthier and more conservative sections of society.[72]

What was unexpected was that the Left would be hostile to the Varvaresos initiatives. The British speculated that this was because the Left assumed that any solution Varvaresos might be able to offer would preserve the interests of capital.[73] This was only a partial explanation for the Communists' position, however, so when KKE hostility to the Varvaresos program intensified in July, the British were at a loss to explain the situation: "It is difficult to see what justification there is for the attacks which have been launched from the Left, who ignore the heavier taxation of the wealthier groups, concentrate their fury on the taxes on the small shopkeepers . . . and then use the argument that the fall in prices is illusory anyway since the same shopkeepers whose profits must not be taxed are making further illegal profits by the hoarding of goods and the skillful use of the back door for favored clients."[74]

The real explanation of the Communist stand is that Varvaresos' program, if successful, would have fulfilled the KKE's demands without allowing it into the govermment. The Greek Communists had always used to good effect the argument that Greece was becoming a dependency of the British, effectively losing its independence. This claim was not without justification and appealed to certain sections of the population. Varvaresos, unlike most right and center Greek politicians, took a similar view. According to MacVeagh, Varvaresos was "disturbed at the apparent attitude of many Government officials that their problems are so difficult that only foreign aid can solve them and what they can do is so small that it is not worth doing." Furthermore, the vice-premier was especially critical of plans to use external assistance to enlarge the Greek armed forces.[75] If Varvaresos succeeded in improving conditions in Greece, he would therefore not only provide a victory for British policy but rob the KKE of one of its most effective criticisms of the Greek government.

[72]DSR 868.oo/6-145, no. 114. A more extensive treatment of Varvaresos' economic programs and the resistance they encountered from the Right can be found in Christos Hadziiossif, "Economic Stabilization and Political Unrest: Greece 1944–1947," in *Studies in the History of the Greek Civil War, 1945–1949*, ed. Lars Baerentzen, John O. Iatrides, and Ole L. Smith (Copenhagen: Museum Tusculanum Press, 1987), pp. 25–40.

[73]DSR 868.oo/6-1345, no. 1204.

[74]DSR 868.oo/7-2045, no. 1243.

[75]Lincoln MacVeagh, *Ambassador MacVeagh Reports: Greece, 1933–1947*, ed. John O. Iatrides (Princeton, N.J.: Princeton University Press, 1980), p. 684.

The Greek Communists thus had to compromise the Varvaresos program. Their efforts were aided by a parallel effort by the wealthy, conservative stratum of Greek society. The British intelligence analysis of Varvaresos' resignation on September 1 accurately depicted the vice-premier's downfall as the result of a coalescence of hostile factors. In the first instance, the attack on Varvaresos was part of a concerted plan by the organizations of major industrialists. The National Bank of Greece also wanted to "break" Varvaresos and replace him with "a man of straw of their own." A third group attacking Varvaresos was a clique of government and press officials, among the most important of whom were Dimitris Lambrakis and his associate, Konstantinos Doxiadis, who, upon his return from the United Nations Conference on International Organization in San Francisco, encouraged a campaign against Varvaresos with the story that the U.S. State Department had officially expressed disapproval of the vice-premier's economic system.[76]

Independent of these actions, the Communists supported the shopkeepers and employees who felt the plan would unfairly burden them. But the KKE went much farther than mere passive support. The Communists gave orders to their members who worked in the taxation department to take every opportunity to lay the heaviest taxes on people of the small-shopkeeper and employee class in order to drive them into an alliance with the proletariat. More specific instructions show the extent to which KKE strategy was tailored to damage specific aspects of Varvaresos' program:

Caracalla also adds the following information regarding instructions issued by the Central Executive Committee of the KKE on August 23 and the City Committee of KOA on August 25 to KOA organizations on the Government's financial policy: a) 11th Achtida [leading cadres] (tradesmen, industrial workers, members of Liberal professions, etc.) are to exert all their activities against the Government's financial laws. b) Protests and strikes are to be organized with the slogan, "None shall pay the Varvaressos tax this month." c) 1st, 2nd, 11th, and 12th Achtides (all those organized on the basis of occupation and not locality) are to organize a "Strike Treasury" under [KKE union chief Kostas] Theos and [Vasilis] Nefeloudis, to support strikes against taxation, which are to be in every way encouraged. Compulsory levies of 200–300 drachmae are taken from workers' weekly wages by KKE financial committee; the money goes to the election campaign and the purchase of votes.[77]

[76]OSS XL21021, September 14, 1945.
[77]Ibid.

The implication of these orders is clear: the KKE had a hand in the downfall of Varvaresos and even encouraged making the workers' condition worse in order to achieve their aim. Ultimately, Varvaresos resigned and no one competent in economic affairs succeeded him. The mention of strikes brings up the last aspect of KKE policy: the use of the labor movement to disrupt the economy. The second round and its aftermath had a severe impact on Communist strength in the trade union movement. During the Papandreou government of national unity, Porfyrogenis, an EAM member and minister of labor, had succeeded in placing enough members of the Communist-affiliated Workers' National Liberation Front (EEAM) on the executive committee of the General Confederation of Greek Workers (GSEE) to constitute a majority.[78] Had this move proved successful, the KKE would have had complete control over the governing body of the labor movement. Unfortunately, the events of December 1944 cost the Communists dearly and allowed non-EEAM unionists to take the initiative. The labor minister under Plastiras promptly announced that the previous GSEE executive was invalid and appointed his own, made up exclusively of non-Communists. This was of course contested by the old GSEE executive, and the stage was set for a legal and political battle that lasted on into 1946.

The KKE thus had first to regain control of the labor movement before it could use labor influence as a policy instrument. The first step was to reform the EEAM, which was accomplished in March 1945, when the Communist Workers' Antifascist League (ERGAS) was created. The league promptly launched into a campaign to gain control of the labor movement through an electoral victory. An appraisal of this effort in early June concluded that the KKE was still not all-powerful in the labor movement but added the warning "The nationalist unions [(as opposed to the Communist ones) had] been thoroughly penetrated by crypto-Communists with the object of lulling the Government and Right-wing circles into a false sense of security." The report concluded that much of the vitality behind the trades union movement was supplied by the KKE.[79] As in the case of Varvaresos, penetration of the rank and file of other organizations was to prove an essential part of Communist strategy.

By mid-June 1945, leftist strength in the union movement had become more apparent. In light of the growing KKE strength, Victor Feather,

[78]For this and a more detailed discussion of the Greek labor movement, see Christos Jecchinis, *Trade Unionism in Greece: A Study in Political Paternalism* (Chicago: Roosevelt University, Labor Education Division, 1965), pp. 62 ff.

[79]DSR 868.00/6-145, no. 1114.

British Trade Union Council representative, decided to permit a modification of the GSEE General Executive. Even with the modification, however, the pro-government faction retained the majority of votes.[80] It was evident, however, that the KKE was rebuilding its strength and might soon be in a position to challenge the government majority. Meanwhile, failure to control the governing body of the labor movement did not prevent the KKE from using Communist-controlled unions in a series of strikes aimed at crippling the economy. Short, disruptive strikes were preferred over a general strike, presumably because the latter was less popular. Strike activity increased during May, corresponding to the launching of the KKE's policy of infiltration, and continued increasing in frequency and intensity as the year progressed.

In diplomatic relations, the Soviet Union continued to keep the Voulgaris government in a state of uncertainty through its failure to appoint any diplomatic representative. In fact, in May 1945 the only recognition Stalin bestowed upon the Greeks went to EAM. In a telegram that coincided roughly with the beginning of the KKE's gradualist policy and the conclusion of the war in Europe, Stalin sent his congratulations to the general secretary of EAM and to "the freedom loving Greek people who suffered great sacrifices in the struggle against fascism and its assistants." MacVeagh interpreted this as a rebuff to the Greek government and Stalin's official benediction to EAM[81] or, more precisely, EAM's *policy,* coming soon after the start of the KKE's new campaign. The U.S. ambassador also noted the ambiguous reference to the "assistants" of fascism. While this gesture in itself was not overwhelming, it did indicate the low regard Stalin had for the new Greek government, especially since the Greeks had sided with the Soviets on the question of admitting Argentina to the United Nations. Furthermore, there was little more Stalin could do at the official level lest he arouse British suspicions.

The Soviets were also wary of participating in any Allied commission to observe elections, despite the repeated KKE/EAM calls for Allied intervention in Greek affairs. On July 13 the U.S. and British ambassadors in Greece indicated to the Greek prime minister their governments' willingness to approach the governments of the Soviet Union and France with the proposal for Four Power supervision of the upcoming Greek elections. The U.S. State Department also noted that it might be possible to overcome a potential Soviet objection that this constituted a violation of

[80]DSR 868.00/7-1745, no. 1332.
[81]DSR 868.00/6-145, no. 1114.

Greek sovereignty by pointing out that EAM and the KKE were especially insistent on "Allied supervision."[82] Evidently, the KKE felt its domestic political position would be strengthened by the participation of its Communist patrons, but the Soviets viewed matters in a different light and refused such involvement. The necessary preconditions for Soviet diplomatic involvement in Greece simply did not yet obtain. British forces were still in Greece; Stalin had yet to consolidate his grip on that part of Europe which the Red Army already controlled. The Soviet dictator could countenance the further expansion of his influence in the Balkans only when to do so would not damage gains already made; the refusal to participate in the supervision of elections reflected the Soviet judgment that conditions in Greece were not yet ripe for a more assertive role.

The Potsdam Conference, held in the latter part of July, revealed another, perhaps more important, reason for the Soviet refusal: unless such action were given an exceptional status, it could be construed as a precedent allowing for Western demands to participate in elections in Eastern Europe. To establish a safe basis for a greater Soviet political role in Greece, Stalin attempted to use the conference to disengage the Greek case from the rest of Europe. The best way to accomplish this was to argue that the Varkiza Agreement, *not* the Yalta declaration, constituted the legal basis for Allied intervention in Greek affairs; for whereas Yalta applied to the countries of liberated Europe generally, Varkiza pertained solely to Greece. Under the Soviet proposal, criticism of Soviet policy in Eastern Europe would have no juridical basis because of the "exceptional" character of the Varkiza Agreement. One of the two obstacles that prevented the Soviets from playing a more positive role in Greece would thus be eliminated.

The proceedings of the conference reveal that the Soviets approached the subject of Greece in two ways. First, they used it as a defensive shield to deflect American and British criticism of the Soviet failure to implement the Yalta declaration in Romania and Bulgaria. Molotov painted a picture of Greece in the throes of anarchy and terror, for good measure, depicting the Greek government as possessed by insatiable territorial demands that threatened the peace of the Balkans.[83] Second, they attempted to manipulate the internal affairs of Greece in a more direct fashion. On July 20, Molotov circulated a document that directly attacked the Greek government for failing to control terrorism against "the democratic ele-

[82]DSR 868.00/7-1445, no. 452, Secretary of State to U.S. Embassy, Athens.
[83]*FRUS: The Conference of Berlin (The Potsdam Conference), 1945*, vol. 2 (Washington: USGPO, 1960), pp. 150–55.

ments." The Soviets then proposed, in opposition to the Western proposal for Allied supervision, that the Great Powers recommend to the regent immediate measures for creating a "government in the spirit of the agreement reached at Varkiza . . . between representatives of the then existing government of Greece and the representatives of Greek democracy."[84] Some days later, the Soviets circulated another proposal, slightly different from that of July 20, asserting that because order had not been created in Greece and the Varkiza Agreement was not being implemented, the British government should urge the regent to change the composition of the Greek government to conform to the spirit of Varkiza.[85] These actions clearly support the argument that the Soviets were attempting to create what they considered to be the necessary preconditions for a policy that gradually would broaden their involvement in Greek affairs without affecting their unchallenged position in Eastern Europe.

Worth noting is that the second Soviet proposal mentioned only Great Britain and not the Great Powers, perhaps, as Xydis has argued, because of the Soviet desire to prevent American interference in Greek affairs.[86] Finally, much of the Soviet argument was couched in language very similar to that employed by the KKE. While some of the similarity could arguably be a mere reflection of KKE propaganda, terms such as "democratic elements" must have been used with the knowledge that those "elements" encompassed organizations faithful to Soviet interests.

After the British Labour victory, the Soviets, like the KKE, appeared to become more aggressive in their policies, as information from politically sensitive Turkey seemed to suggest. In early August, Rafail Rafail, the Greek ambassador in Ankara, had an exchange with his Soviet counterpart, Sergei Vinogradov, in which the Soviet ambassador was strongly critical of the Greek government. According to Rafail,

> Vinogradov . . . launched into a vigorous enunciation of "the scandalous internal situation and Rightist terror in Greece." The Ambassador said that in all parts of Europe occupied by Soviet troops there was peace and unity and only in Greece was there a backward government and tyranny. This state of affairs could not and would not be continued after the change in the British Government. The labor success would be extended also to Greece where Churchill's personal policy had previously prevailed. Churchill had lost because the British people could not understand why British troops

[84]Ibid., p. 1044.
[85]Ibid., pp. 1592, 525.
[86]Xydis, p. 114.

should be used to kill the best Greek patriots. The British Army must evacuate Greece as the USSR was evacuating its troops from the other European countries.[87]

Vinogradov's outburst is interesting because it coincided with a more vigorous Greek Communist policy and repeated many of the KKE's demands. Most important, however, was the impression in Vinogradov's accusations that a decisive stage had been reached with the British Labour victory. Stalin's gradualist and cautious policy derived from his perception of the primacy of international factors, and he must have taken Churchill's defeat as a sign that Soviet policy toward Greece could become more aggressive. The Conservatives' loss probably led the Soviets to believe that all wartime agreements (such as the percentages agreement of October 1944) were now void, leaving the field in Greece open once again for Soviet penetration.

The actions of Sofianopoulos during this period also indicate that the Soviets' sympathetic ally was doing what he could to further Soviet policy by weakening the government from within. He caused great consternation in Western circles by voting with the Soviet Union against the admission of Argentina to the San Francisco Conference on International Organization. This was an independent initiative on the part of the Greek foreign minister, which took the British completely by surprise.[88] It was a clever maneuver and demonstrated the extent to which he depended on Soviet support to maintain his cabinet position; for when some officials considered recalling Sofianopoulos, Leeper argued that was impossible because such an action would be interpreted by Russia as an unfriendly act.[89] Besides demonstrating his source of support, Sofianopoulos' action came near to provoking a governmental crisis, which was averted in part be-

[87]DSR 868.00/8-1445, State Department, memorandum of conversation. Participants: Greek ambassador, F. D. Kohler, L. H. Henderson.

[88]OSS L56891, May 24, 1945.

[89]OSS L56331, May 24, 1945. Sofianopoulos was clearly an opportunist, but there is no evidence from Western sources to link him directly to the Soviets. Greek Communist sources, however, suggest much closer relations between the KKE and the former foreign minister. In a September 1, 1947, letter to Andrei Zhdanov in Moscow, Zachariadis transmits the opinions of Sofianopoulos "who is now in Paris and who is collaborating with us," to the effect that the Soviets should publicly express their sympathy with the Greek people and their unwillingness to tolerate Greece as a base for the American military. Zachariadis concurs with Sofianopoulos' advice and closes this section of the letter by adding that "Sofianopoulos expresses the wish to go to Moscow": *Avgi*, December 30, 1979.

cause the Right restricted its attack solely to the foreign minister, realizing that he had acted independently of instructions.[90]

The talks Sofianopoulos had with the Soviet delegation to San Francisco (including separate talks with Molotov and Ukranian delegate Dimitrii Manuil'skii), in which the Soviets apparently expressed their willingness to recognize the Greek government only if it included the Communists, support the hypothesis that the Soviets may have implied their support for Sofianopoulos if he could form another government. Later developments also support this contention. On July 23, one day after returning to Athens from San Francisco, Sofianopoulos tendered his resignation. In a remarkable coincidence with Communist demands, the Greek foreign minister stated to MacVeagh that he was convinced after talking with Molotov that the only hope of achieving the desired relations with the USSR lay in establishing a political government representative of all the parties. When the former foreign minister called on the American ambassador the next day, MacVeagh related that Sofianopoulos "appeared very cocky and on my remarking that one of the royalist leaders had just told me a political govt is 'impossible,' replied 'that depends on who would be its chief,' apparently meaning himself."[91] This Soviet-inspired resignation, coming as it did on the eve of the British elections, in the middle of the Potsdam discussions, and in the midst of an aggressive turn in the KKE's gradualist strategy, suggests that the Soviets were attempting to coordinate available internal and external sources of influence to destabilize an already shaky Greek government.

The conclusion to be drawn from all this diplomatic activity is that the Soviets disapproved of the Voulgaris government and were attempting to affect the internal affairs of Greece. The combination of the resignation of Sofianopoulos, the British Labour victory, and the resignation of Varvaresos seriously weakened an already frail government. Furthermore, the way these events and Soviet claims coincided with KKE demands and policies was more than merely fortuitous.

Soviet press and propaganda during the summer of 1945 closely mirrored EAM demands and reflected the growing hostility of the Communists toward British policy. The most popular topic was the supposed

[90]DSR 868.00/5-1645, AGIS Weekly Report, no. 29.
[91]DSR 868.00/7-2445, no. 746. Sofianopoulos did not receive the premiership, but the possibility surfaced again several months later: when it appeared the Sofoulis government might fall in late December 1945, Sofianopoulos was considered the logical choice to succeed him: OSS XL32200, December 20, 1945.

crescendo of terror being unleashed on EAM and the Communists. Events in Greece began to appear with increasing frequency in Soviet papers. An article in *New Times,* which appeared on June 15, painted the darkest picture yet of internal conditions, laying most of the blame on British policy. A Tass dispatch published in the Moscow press on June 17 reiterated the "monarchist" terror and also cited the opinion of Republican leaders that free elections were impossible under existing conditions.[92] On June 25, *Pravda,* citing the *New Statesman* and *Nation,* again hit upon the wave of terror in Greece. On July 6, the Moscow press quoted *Rizospastis* on the alleged preparations for a monarchist coup, adding for good measure that the British authorities knew of these preparations and could put an end to them if they wished.[93] On August 22, *Izvestiia* carried an article providing the Soviet rationale for not participating in the observation of elections. Such activity, *Izvestiia* maintained, was not consistent with the principle of state independence and sovereignty; an odd argument for the Soviets to make, since at Potsdam they were not averse to using Great Power pressure to force a change in the Greek government.

In general, Soviet press reports served two important functions: First, they allowed the KKE to have its demands heard by an international audience, thereby keeping the British and Greek governments constantly occupied with justifying their position. The KKE could quote themselves once their story had been amplified through the Soviet press to reach a world audience. Thus, *Eleftheri Ellada* reproduced a stern broadcast by Radio Moscow on the state of internal security in Greece. The Soviet broadcast, however, originated from a Tass report, which was based primarily on citations from the Greek left-wing press.[94] Second, the Soviet press reports served as a kind of alarm that would be set off, should the Communists' position appear seriously threatened, as in the case of the preparations for a right-wing coup.[95]

Soviet internal press also began to reflect a strong anti-British character. On August 14, a Soviet Balkan specialist by the name of Belenkov

[92]DSR 868.00/6-2045, no. 2176.
[93]DSR 868.00/7-845, no. 2477; *Pravda* for July 6, 1945, also ridiculed the Greek claim to Northern Epirus.
[94]DSR 868.00/7-245, no. 1233.
[95]DSR 868.00/7-1745, no. 1333, reveals that the British were concerned about a possible right-wing coup in midsummer. DSR 868.00/7-845, no. 2477, indicates that the Soviets were aware of this possibility and attempted to give it full press. Later in 1945, the KKE, apparently concerned over the possibility of a right-wing coup, prepared for a countercoup in March 1946; see Ole L. Smith, "Self-Defense and Communist Policy 1945–1947," in *Studies in the History of the Greek Civil War, 1945–1949,* ed. Lars Baerentzen, John O. Iatrides, and Ole L. Smith (Copenhagen: Museum Tusculanum Press, 1987), pp. 159–78.

delivered a public lecture marked by sharp antipathy to British policy, bitter hostility to the present Greek government, criticism of the anti-Communist elements among the democratic parties, and an emphasis on the positive role of the Communists.[96]

September 1945–March 1946: From Political Activity toward Civil War

The months remaining until the Greek elections in March 1946 were marked by continued Soviet pressure in the two areas the Soviet Union considered most important: Turkey and Albania. In Turkey, Stalin remained content to keep the question of the Straits unresolved. The Turks still had not received from the Soviets a satisfactory guarantee of the territorial integrity of Turkish frontiers. The Soviet demand for a base in the Straits, discussed at the Potsdam Conference, was renewed in a different form. In late February, Soviet ambassador Rodionov approached the Greek prime minister with the suggestion that the Soviet Union supply Greece with food, coal, and other items in exchange for a Soviet repair base for its vessels on a small island in the Dodecanese.[97] In Albania, where the Soviets were trying to make the best of the access to Adriatic ports, the protective attitude persisted. As a foil to the Greek government's demands for Northern Epirus and as a rationale for the independent existence of Albania, Soviet press began to present that country as a "factor of stabilization" in the Balkans.[98]

The attempt to exacerbate the chaotic situation in Greece continued, with the goals of establishing a more pliable government and detaching the British presence appearing more possible as the weeks passed. To this end, the Soviets took an active and direct interest in Greek affairs in early 1946 by bringing before the United Nations the question of the British military presence in Greece and by giving specific advice to the Greek Communists as to what the Soviets desired the KKE to do during the elections.

In addition to consolidating gains and attempting to prevent a stabilization of the British presence in Greece, the Soviets continued to exploit Anglo-American differences over Greece. Soviet and Greek Communist propaganda tried to portray the British as the central evil, while they

[96]DSR 868.00/8-1845, no. 2957.
[97]DSR 868.00/3-646, State Department, memorandum of conversation.
[98]*Krasnaia Zvezda*, September 17, 1945.

avoided severe criticism of the United States. There was still some cause for hope on this score; for although the Americans were becoming increasingly skeptical about Soviet intentions, they still advanced no concrete policy on the Balkans. President Truman had become convinced by early January that the Soviet Union had to be faced with "an iron fist and strong language." He thereupon began a gradual slowdown in the demobilization of American forces in Europe and resolved to inform the American public of the serious situation the USSR was causing in the international arena.[99] Despite his resolve, a firm American response was not forthcoming for another fourteen months, and then only when the British announced that they could no longer maintain their commitment to Greece. The only evidence of a new U.S. attitude was the visit to Greece of the cruiser *Providence* and the granting to Greece of $25 million in credit.[100] In the crucial area of cooperating with the British, the Americans persisted in their reticence. On January 15, when Ambassador Mac-Veagh proposed initiating a much more extensive aid program to Greece, the U.S. government refused.[101] The hardening of the U.S. attitude toward Stalin was not yet accompanied by any substantive or coordinated measures.

Meanwhile, the Soviets and the KKE hammered away at the British. Waves of bitter and highly critical propaganda pounded the British from KKE papers, while the Americans were treated comparatively well. Even as the elections approached, the Soviets echoed the same theme. In commenting on a speech by Secretary of State James F. Byrnes, which attempted to clarify the American position on the international observers then being sent to Greece to oversee the elections, Moscow Radio centered on Byrnes's remark that the United States would not fight for reactionaries and interpreted it to mean that the United States thought genuinely fair elections should be held in Greece. The Russian commentator then argued that "real, honest elections" could not be held as scheduled in Greece and that the only people who wished to have elections immediately were monarchofascists.[102] Later, in March, Byrnes explicitly rejected this Soviet view by strengthening his statements in support of the British position that the election date should remain unchanged.

This effort to center on the British presence and postpone the Greek elections fit conveniently into overall Soviet objectives. The basic thrust

[99]Xydis, pp. 155–56.
[100]The original Greek request, however, had been for $250 million, ibid., p. 145.
[101]DSR 868.00/1-1546, Harry C. Hawkins to Secretary Bevin, January 15, 1946.
[102]DSR 868.00/3-546, no. 361.

of the policy was simultaneously to pressure the British and to present them with the choice between making a long-term commitment to Greece or leaving that area of the world to be "organized" by a power more competent for the task. Since the British were in no position to undertake such a commitment, the question would then become whether the United States would act decisively to supplant British interests. If U.S. ambivalence prevented a commitment to the extended support of the Greek government, the field would be left to the actors in the domestic context. The success of Soviet policy would then hinge upon the ability of the KKE, the principal means by which the Soviets could exert influence, to remain loyal to Soviet interests. It was along these lines that Soviet policy proceeded in early 1946; it was to fail precisely because domestic and international developments did not unfold as anticipated.

Expressions of Greek Communist policy were increasingly belligerent and violent. On September 8 the KKE Politburo issued its most strident attack in a public manifesto, with choicest criticism reserved for the Voulgaris government (now seriously weakened by the departure of several key ministers) and the regent. Both leaders were portrayed as supporting a program of liquidation of Greek democrats. The British received their share of criticism and the bulk of the blame for creating and supporting the entirely unjust conditions. The recommendations were similar to earlier ones, although there were some additions: not only was it necessary for Voulgaris to leave, but the "collaborationist" regent had to leave as well. The British "occupation forces" also had to leave the country, "so that the fascist reactionaries will be deprived of the open support which they [the British] are giving it [sic]."[103]

As a further counter to the alleged terrorism of monarchofascism, the manifesto urged the expansion of the popular self-defense (*aftoamina*). Keeping in mind the long-range objectives of the *aftoamina* mentioned earlier, this meant that the Communists were seriously contemplating a future military option. In the manifesto, however, the KKE put itself officially on record as depicting the *aftoamina* purely defensively, to meet government-sponsored force with force. According to the manifesto, the "people's struggle . . . is a political struggle." To continue and resolve this struggle, the KKE also demanded the formation of a representative government based on EAM. Finally, the KKE reiterated the demand for a general amnesty, characterizing it as an "immediate, basic and popular demand." Although the tone was violent, the manifesto stopped short of

[103]DSR 868.00/9-1445, no. 1511.

advocating any active nonpolitical measures to overthrow the government. The closest the manifesto came was an ominous statement that the British must eventually come to terms with EAM in Greece because otherwise "a wound will be opened which will finally be closed as the people wishes . . . let it cost what it may in blood and even if it lasts for years."[104]

Zachariadis' activities in September confirmed that the KKE political offensive was under way. The Greek Communist leader took the occasion of a visit to Patras to again press for genuine elections and a government founded on EAM.[105] Several days later, at a mass rally for the fourth anniversary of the founding of EAM, Zachariadis definitely committed the KKE to abstention from the elections if held in 1945 under the conditions then in existence.[106] The abstention threat now became a persistent theme in Greek Communist demands; the KKE apparently hoped to postpone the elections until a later date, allowing more time for the rehabilitation of their forces while simulatneously increasing the pressure on the British, already burdened by the weight of their commitment of forces to Greece.

While the Seventh Congress of the KKE occupied internal Communist affairs for the first week of October, the antigovernment and anti-British attacks did not stop. In fact, a group from the EAM Central Committee, which included Siantos, visited the American ambassador on October 4 and presented the now-familiar demands.[107] Then, on October 8, three days after it attempted to fix the election date at January 20, the Voulgaris government resigned. Weakened as it was by defections and a failure to deal with the internal condition of the country, the attempt to fix an election date in the face of vigorous Communist opposition and strong Republican reservations sealed the fate of the third Greek prime minister in ten months. The next six weeks (October 8–November 21) brought the Greek political system to the brink of collapse. With the exception of a brief tenure by Panagiotis Kanellopoulos as premier, the government drifted in a virtually leaderless state as the result of persistent pressure of internal actors to realize their own interests at the expense of others, combined with the repeated British efforts to establish a government on a nonexistent Center.

The impossibility of compromise and the British insistence on a middle-of-the-road solution gradually began to have an impact on British officials in Greece. The aggressive KKE campaign most likely tipped the balance

104Ibid.
105DSR 868.00/10-345, no. 1635.
106DSR 868.00/10-945, no. 1332.
107DSR 868.00/10-1345, no. 1699.

in their favor; for the British began to think the success of their policy hinged on a government still farther to the left. On October 15, amid efforts to find a workable coalition, Leeper informed his American colleague that a left-of-center government was still the best solution in the long run but that it was only possible to form such a government if the regent was assured that the British would back him against Royalist intransigence.[108] Finally, after the fall of the Kanellopoulos government, the British took the initiative and sent Undersecretary of Foreign Affairs Hector McNeil to Athens. The result was the formation of a new government under the leadership of Themistoklis Sofoulis on November 21, 1945. This government, containing prominent members of the Republican parties in Greece, was the farthest left of any yet appointed—and Sofianopoulos reappeared in the position of foreign minister.

American officials chose not to involve themselves in the British initiative. MacVeagh believed that such a drastic measure adopted at foreign instigation was only too likely to stir up national resentment. The U.S. ambassador concluded: "Existing British involvement Grk pol situation may justify risking such reaction but unless we willing to become equally involved believe US participation unwise." MacVeagh also added that the details of the British plan appeared to indicate that they contemplated controlling Greek economic life to an extent even greater than the Germans.[109]

These developments furthered the objectives of the KKE's policy of political gradualism, so there was an immediate shift in attitude in the Communist press. The Greek Communists now officially announced their support of all government measures that tended to restore political equality and tranquility, so that free and honest elections might be held as soon as possible. This marked change in tenor was accompanied by a noticeable absence of the specific Communist demands for amnesty, recognition of the resistance movement, and a representative government.[110] That the KKE considered this change of government significant is apparent from the writings of Partsalidis. According to the KKE Politburo member and EAM general secretary, the Communist-led EAM was willing to give the new government a chance to prove itself. Thus, "EAM did not hesitate to express itself openly, on November 24, 1945, against the printers' strike, emphasizing that while it considered the demand for a wage increase justified, it maintained that the moment chosen for the announcement of

[108]DSR 868.00/10-1645, no. 1169; see also DSR 868.00/10-3045, no. 1220.
[109]DSR 868.00/11-1645, no. 1304.
[110]DSR 868.00/11-2345, no. 1342.

the strike was the most unsuitable—there had just been formed, despite the reaction of the Right, a government of the democratic Center and the strike, which was incited by agents of the Right, aimed at the creation of an abnormal situation."[111]

This benevolent attitude, however, soon began to dissipate and was rapidly replaced by the intransigence of previous KKE policy. In a December 1 editorial in *Rizospastis,* Zachariadis again demanded the government be broadened to include EAM. Three days later, EAM returned to the demands it had omitted less than two weeks earlier: a general amnesty, purge of government agencies, revision of electoral registers, and direct measures to relieve economic suffering.[112] These demands were repeated in a statement handed to the minister of justice and reaffirmed at a public meeting on December 7, which included the threat to "reconsider" the Left's support of the present government.[113]

Still other developments indicated that the initial changes in KKE policy were purely ephemeral. By late November the KKE had decided to reorganize the "self-defence groups" (*omades aftoaminas*) created at the Twelfth Plenum into a larger and stronger organization to be known as "popular self-defence" (*laiki aftoamina*). This reorganization, still in the preliminary stages, aimed at the mobilization of the entire population to come out into the streets as required.[114] The KKE was also actively engaged in the penetration of the Greek Armed Forces. The existence of the Communist Organization of the Army and Security Forces (KOSSA) was known to British and American intelligence and has been openly acknowledged by former high-ranking members of the KKE.[115] The strength of KOSSA had been the subject of some discussion at the KKE Seventh Congress in October,[116] but the organization apparently began to assume a more important role in KKE eyes later in 1945. The existence of such organizations as KOSSA combined with a restructuring of the *afto-*

[111]Dimitris [Mitsos] Partsalidis, *Dipli Apokatastasi tis Ethnikis Antistasis* (Athens: Themelio, 1978), p. 184.
[112]DSR 868.00/12-445, no. 1407.
[113]DSR 868.00/12-1045, no. 1435.
[114]DSR 868.00/12-445, no. 1952.
[115]OSS XL46486, February 1946; and see, for example, Giorgis Blanas, *Emfilios Polemos, 1946–1949: Opos ta Ezisa* (Athens: n.p., 1976), pp. 56–64; Vasilis Bartziotas, *O Agonas tou Dimokratikou Stratou Elladas,* 2d ed. (Athens: Sygchroni Epochi, 1982), pp. 27–39 passim; Dimos K. Votsikas, *I Ipeiros Xanazonetai T'Armata* (Athens: n.p., 1983), pp. 83–86; Giorgis Vontitsos-Gousias, *Oi Aities gia tis Ittes, ti Diaspasi tou KKE kai tis Ellinikis Aristeras* (Athens: Na Iperetoume to Lao, 1977), vol. 1, pp. 128–36.
[116]OSS XL46486, February 1946.

amina indicated that, although no aggressive plans had as yet been made,[117] the KKE had the means of aggression at its disposal.

The creation of the Sofoulis government was therefore a critical point in the evolution of Communist strategy. The emergence of a weak, center-left government brought the KKE to a choice between, on the one hand, at least temporary support of that government and a purely parliamentary policy or, on the other hand, continued underground activity against the government and open opposition at the first sign of a "reactionary" policy. Partsalidis, from what has already been mentioned and from later developments, appears to have presented himself as an advocate of the former, while Zachariadis endorsed the more aggressive line. The rationale for a more militant policy was evident: The KKE realized (as did the rightists) that the Center in Greece was too weak to stand on its own because it lacked the support of the population and large industrialists. To leave matters as they stood was thus tantamount to inviting the Right to penetrate the Sofoulis government. To preempt rightist penetration, the KKE would itself have to penetrate or bring down the Sofoulis government. In retrospect, this rationale, despite the risk of escalating conflict that it entailed, was more realistic than a *purely* parliamentary approach. Nor was the aggressive approach long in coming: after a government proposal in mid-December to relieve prison congestion, EAM announced the withdrawal of its support and accused the government of making no real change. Simultaneously, Zachariadis drew increasing public attention to the mass popular self-defense created six months earlier.[118]

Meanwhile, the gradualist political strategy continued operating. An EAM delegation had been sent abroad in October 1945 (almost one year after Dimitrov's advice to that effect) to gain an international forum for KKE demands. On January 4, 1946, *Humanité* in Paris carried an interview with the EAM delegates in which they argued against international observation of the Greek elections in terms similar to the rationale provided by the Soviets in August 1945.

With the new year came a final KKE push to secure postponement of the elections (tentatively set for March 31, 1946) and a strong verbal attack on the British presence, designed to serve as a prelude to a January Soviet complaint to the same effect in the United Nations. In a New Year's speech in Thessaloniki, Zachariadis sharply criticized the Macedo-

[117]Blanas, among others, complained bitterly of the KKE's lack of clear and consistent planning: pp. 42–75 passim.

[118]DSR 868.00/12-1245, no. 1444.

nian autonomist movement, charging it was promoted by the British to create trouble in the Balkans. The KKE general secretary again repeated his demand for an end to the foreign intervention and the participation of EAM in the government.[119] Coinciding with the KKE leader's speeches was a wave of strikes that intensified as the month progressed, the most serious ones occurring in the north of Greece.

In fact, the situation in northern Greece was deteriorating rapidly, and the assistant military attaché of the U.S. Embassy reported that the leftists in northern Greece were more self-confident and eager for some kind of military move than their counterparts in the south, probably largely because the northern detachments were not involved in the unsuccessful fighting in December 1944. American officials concluded that very little provocation could cause a revolutionary outbreak under Communist leadership but that British troops, while they remained, were likely to cause the Communists to exercise caution.[120] Once again, a troubling contradiction had reappeared in KKE policy: while it was acknowledged by all parties that the British were the sole restraining influence in Greece and the last support of the Sofoulis government, more extreme KKE activities were convincing the Western powers of their need to remain to control the situation.

The arrival of the EAM delegation in Moscow on January 15 provided an opportunity to determine the Soviet attitude toward events in Greece. When Partsalidis presented his case to members of the International Department of the CPSU on January 17, the EAM general secretary emphasized the growing terror against leftists in Greece and expressed his opinion that it would be extremely difficult to avoid an armed conflict. The implication was that the KKE was considering carrying out its threat of abstaining from the elections. In response, Petrov, Balkan specialist for the CPSU International Department, informed Partsalidis that the advice of the CPSU leadership was to take part in the elections; after that, the KKE was to "wait and see." The CPSU leadership also instructed the EAM delegates to continue strengthening the paramilitary "popular self-defense."[121] There were indications of tension between the EAM delegation

[119]DSR 868.00/1-646, no. 25.
[120]DSR 868.00/1-2346, no. 121.
[121]Partsalidis, *Dipli Apokatastasi tis Ethnikis Antistasis*, p. 199. On the advice to strengthen the *aftoamina*, see Partsalidis' interview in *Tachydromos*, no. 25, 1977 (as cited in Ole L. Smith, "The Boycott of the Elections 1946: A Decisive Mistake?" *Scandinavian Studies in Modern Greek*, no. 6 (1982), 87 n), and the interview with Papapanagiotou in *Anti*, May 22, 1981, p. 40. In a later interview (*To Vima*, January 6, 1980), Partsalidis recalls that while in Moscow in January 1946, he met with Deputy Minister of Foreign Affairs Anatolii I. Lavrent'iev to discuss the situation in Greece. After this, he received a

and their Soviet hosts. On January 23, EAM gave a news conference in Moscow, but Soviet censors omitted the specific territorial claims to Cyprus, Eastern Thrace, and Northern Epirus. Two days later, British ambassador Archibald Clark Kerr informed the Foreign Office that EAM representatives had expressed to the Greek ambassador their dissatisfaction with their treatment at Soviet hands. In particular, they objected to the way the news conference was conducted and the twisting of their remarks to suit Soviet propaganda.[122]

About the time of these events, Soviet policy toward Greece took an aggressive turn. On January 21, Vyshinskii, Soviet delegate to the United Nations, used the international organization as a forum for an attack against the British presence in Greece.[123] Simultaneously, the KKE in Athens published a manifesto that detailed charges against the British "occupation forces" and stated that the British, more than any other group or organization, were responsible for the desperate condition of the country.[124] During the discussions that followed (including the debate in the Security Council on February 1–6), the Soviets stressed the themes KKE propaganda had emphasized for some time. In presenting his case, Vyshinskii made reference to copious communications sent by EAM to the Soviet government and the meetings of the Great Powers. After detailing the familiar arguments, the Soviet delegate went on to argue that the British had stationed troops in Greece to protect the communication lines of their forces in defeated countries, a purpose for which they were no longer needed. Now the British troop presence was actually being used to influence the internal affairs of Greece. Bevin responded that British soldiers were in Greece at the request of the Greek government, adding that once his country had fulfilled the obligations it had undertaken in Greece, military forces would be withdrawn.

While the Soviets used the United Nations forum to keep Britain on the diplomatic defensive, the Greek Communists intensified their campaign. The British were becoming alarmed; for increasingly reports indicated the KKE was leaning more and more on subversive activities and possible military activity. Zachariadis continued the political campaign nonethe-

---

directive from the KKE to meet with Petrov in the International Department, where the order to participate in the elections was given. The only questionable point in this account is whether Partsalidis actually met with Lavrent'iev. See note 129 for the source of the confusion.

[122]FO 371-58735 R1298, January 26, 1946.

[123]Xydis, pp. 163–67.

[124]Evangelos Averoff-Tossizza, *By Fire and Axe: The Communist Party and the Civil War in Greece, 1944–1949* (New Rochelle, N.Y.: Caratzas Brothers, 1978), p. 158.

less; in early March, with the Sofoulis government weakened by resignations and dissatisfaction within its ranks, the KKE general secretary proposed an electoral coalition of the Left and Center with a fifty-fifty
division of seats won.[125]

But with the prospect of abstention appearing greater and greater, the
KKE's policy of political gradualism was approaching its limits, as the
crucial decisions reached at the Second Plenum of the Central Committee
of the KKE (February 12–15, 1946) showed. It was at this meeting that
the KKE leadership, at the urging of Zachariadis, resolved gradually to
develop an armed insurgency.[126] The Greek Communists would begin
implementing a more militant approach in concert with the parliamentary
aspects of their policy. The question was thus not whether there would be
a resort to arms but when and how.

Indeed, the belligerence of KKE/EAM statements increased signifi-
cantly as the election date drew near. During the U.N. debate on the
British presence, Theos, the Communist labor leader, told officials at the
U.S. Embassy, "If this situation [the British occupation] continue[d], the
Greek people [were] ready to declare a new war of liberation against the
British." On March 14, the *Herald Tribune* reported EAM had declared
that if the elections were held as scheduled, civil war would follow.
Apparently, the KKE, despite Soviet advice, was seriously considering

[125]*Rizospastis,* March 7, 1946.

[126]The most explicit on this point is Bartziotas, *Agonas tou Dimokratikou Stratou
Elladas,* pp. 27–30. The decision appears to have caused much confusion through different
interpretations. There is no evidence Stalin's election speech of February 9 had any impact
on the decision although it could have been taken as justification. Perhaps more significant,
when the question of influence came up in discussions with former partisans, the general
reaction was bewilderment; those who did comment apparently genuinely believed Stalin's
speech had no bearing on KKE policy. There *are* competing interpretations of the proceedings of the Second Plenum. Heinz Richter, for example, argues that nothing was decided
about military policy, and as a consequence, the KKE drifted into civil war without a
coherent strategy; see Richter, *British Intervention in Greece: From Varkiza to Civil War*
(London: Merlin, 1985), pp. 482–95. Lefteris P. Eleftheriou, in his recollections of discussions with Zachariadis in 1956, believes that in February 1946 Zachariadis still had not
opted decisively for civil war; see Eleftheriou, *Synomilies me ton Niko Zachariadi* (Athens:
Kentavros, 1986), pp. 32, 33–35. For an interpretation similar to the one found here, see
Ole L. Smith, "The Problems of the Second Plenum of the Central Committee of the KKE,
1946," *Journal of the Hellenic Diaspora* 12 (Summer 1985). The manner by which the
KKE numbered the Central Committee's plenary sessions can be confusing. Plena were
numbered consecutively until the convocation of a party congress, after which the sequence
would begin again with the first plenum. Therefore, the sequence of Central Committee
plena for 1945–1946 is as follows: Eleventh Plenum (April 5–10, 1945), Twelfth Plenum
(June 25–27, 1945), Seventh Congress of the KKE (October 1–6, 1945), First Plenum
(October 7, 1945), Second Plenum (February 12–15, 1946).

making good on its threat to abstain. This was, in fact, what transpired. When Partsalidis returned from Moscow and informed the KKE Politburo of the Soviet stand, Zachariadis violently attacked him, declared that the Comintern no longer existed, and threatened to use Siantos in EAM to enforce his views.[127]

This was a surprising stand for Zachariadis to take, especially in view of the argument presented here that the general secretary's policy was inspired by Stalin. It is possible that Zachariadis received separate information from Moscow that contradicted Partsalidis' instructions, but no evidence for this has surfaced. Vasilis Bartziotas, a member of the KKE Central Committee (and later the Politburo) and ally of the KKE leader, has argued that because the decision to take up arms (albeit gradually) had been taken at the Second Plenum in February, the issue of the elections was of secondary importance. Abstention from the elections could therefore be only a tactical error and not one of decisive importance.[128] Closer examination of the considerations weighing on Zachariadis tend to support Bartziotas' analysis. In early 1946, KKE policy was driven by the need to conform to broader Soviet interests while simultaneously responding to the deterioration in Greece and increasing dissension within the party. As these considerations began to pull KKE policy in different directions, Zachariadis was forced to find a course that avoided explicitly violating any of them.

This was particularly difficult when it came to determining the nature of Soviet objectives in Greece and the Balkans, because precise information was hard to obtain. The KKE could only point to the *advice* (there is no evidence that it took the form of an explicit order) in January to participate in the elections while developing defensive military forces in reserve. But even this information was helpful, for it revealed that although Stalin preferred at the time to see a parliamentary policy in Greece, he was not opposed to the expansion of Communist military forces. After all, the Soviets must have been aware that through their encouragement of the expansion of the *aftoamina*, they were advising the Greek Communists to

[127]DSR 868.00/1-2546, no. 136; Partsalidis, *Dipli Apokatastasi tis Ethnikis Antistasis*, p. 196. While Markos Vafeiadis supports Partsalidis in this instance—see Dimitris Gousidis, *Markos Vafeiadis: Martyries* (Thessaloniki: Epikairotita, 1983), p. 28—Zachariadis had his own interpretation. In a piece written some years later, Zachariadis denies there ever existed advice from any outside party and blames the failure to register in the elections on Partsalidis and Siantos; see Zachariadis, *Provlimata tis Krisis tou KKE*, pp. 20–21. His interpretation must be viewed with some skepticism, as by the time he wrote it, Zachariadis was having to defend his position against attack by the majority of the KKE.
[128]Bartziotas, *Agonas tou Dimokratikou Stratou Elladas*, p. 38.

move toward an eventual reliance on force. Soviet attitudes toward Greece appeared to function at two levels: in the near term, the KKE was to participate in legal political activity; in the longer term, however, Stalin was still undecided (if he had definite plans, he evidently kept them to himself) and encouraged the Communists to develop all resources at their disposal. This helps explain why the Soviets refrained from explicitly ordering KKE participation; they viewed participation as a preferred *tactic* under existing conditions rather than as a commitment to parliamentary democracy. In a January 1950 meeting with KKE leaders, Molotov explicitly supported this view, arguing that participation in the elections "would have permitted the KKE to evaluate the situation continuously [*kathe fora*] and, depending upon developments, to throw its weight sometimes into legal forms of mass struggle, and other times into armed struggle."[129] Participation was therefore desirable but by no means indispensable. For the Soviets, the goal was to preserve the opportunistic qualities of KKE policy, a goal best exemplified by Stalin's later endorsement of the gradual development of an armed struggle.

Inside Greece, Zachariadis confronted an entirely different set of problems. In particular, it was becoming increasingly difficult to defend KKE members from the excesses of the Right and parastate organizations. As time passed, too, the authorities were uncovering more arms caches, reducing the store of weapons the Communists were to rely on in a resort to arms. Zachariadis had to respond to increasing pressure within the KKE for a more militant policy, as more and more of the Communists felt their best chances were slipping away from them. Pursuit of a purely parliamentary policy risked not merely party cohesion but the KKE's control over the growth of resurgent military forces throughout the country. Furthermore, if the tenor and content of Zachariadis' speeches is to be believed, he evidently expected military force to form at least a part of any future policy on dealing with the Greek government. Thus logic and local conditions made him favor abstaining from the elections despite Soviet advice (and apparently the views of other parties in the EAM coalition).[130]

[129]Interview with Mitsos Partsalidis in *Avgi,* March 2, 1976. Later in the interview, Partsalidis makes a crucial mistake in discussing the Soviet officials that the EAM delegation met with in Moscow in January 1946. The former EAM general secretary stated that the delegation was received by "Lavrent'iev, who later represented the Soviet government on the Balkan Commission" of the United Nations. In fact, Anatolii I. Lavrent'iev was the Soviet ambassador to Belgrade; A. A. Lavrishchev served on the Balkan Commission of Inquiry in 1947. It is impossible to tell which of these two Partsalidis met with.

[130]For the effect of the activities of other leftist parties on the KKE, see Hagen Fleischer, "The 'Third Factor.' The Struggle for an Independent Socialist Policy during the Greek Civil War," in *Studies in the History of the Greek Civil War, 1945–1949,* ed. Lars

This interpretation of the relations between the CPSU and the KKE makes it possible to provide a plausible explanation for why Zachariadis felt abstention was the better alternative at the time. First, he knew that in doing so, he would not be committing a fatal error in the eyes of Stalin, because he still oriented KKE policy toward preservation of opportunities and resources he knew would be useful in the future. Second, he would be able to direct his efforts toward reasserting KKE control over the rapid growth of military bands throughout Greece. Third, he could thus mollify other parties in EAM and on the left that also had opted for abstention. Finally, and perhaps most intriguing of all, he could use the abstention as a means of extracting from Stalin some clarification of his longer-term intentions in Greece.

The KKE had decided more than six weeks before the elections to pursue the gradual development of armed struggle; yet this decision had been reached without concrete information from the Soviets.[131] Hence Zachariadis could have taken the abstention as an opportunity to present Stalin with a fait accompli when the Soviet leader met with him in early April after the elections.[132] With the KKE out of the parliamentary pro-

---

Baerentzen, John O. Iatrides, and Ole L. Smith (Copenhagen: Museum Tusculanum Press, 1987), pp. 189–212; and idem, "EAM 1941–1947: An Approach for Reconsideration" (Paper presented at the Lehrman Institute Conference on the "Third Round" of the Greek Civil War, 1945–1949, Copenhagen, June 1987).

[131]Gerasimos Maltezos, a former high-ranking officer in the Communist Democratic Army of Greece, is the only source that explicitly states the decision for armed struggle made at the Second Plenum was due in part to "the promise of the Soviet Union and the Socialist countries that they would assist our struggle"; see Maltezos, *DSE: Dimokratikos Stratos Elladas* (Athens: n.p., 1984), p. 28. Somewhat later (p. 81), Maltezos argues that the "gradual movement toward armed struggle" was specifically a creation of Stalin and Dimitrov, and he justifies this strategy by arguing that gradualism was "a general line which pertained to form and did not bind our revolutionary movement to a fixed degree of mobilization of our armed forces, or to a time period." Unfortunately, he provides no supporting evidence, and his reasoning sounds more lucid and concrete than circumstances reflected. Against this is the testimony of Zachariadis at the Seventh Plenum of the Central Committee of the KKE (February 1957), where he maintained that Dimitrov first approved the strategy of gradual movement toward armed struggle at the congress of the Czechoslovak Communist party in March 1946, more than one month *after* the Second Plenum; see Panos Dimitriou, ed., *I Diaspasi tou KKE* (Athens: Themelio, 1978), vol. 1, p. 94.

[132]Evidence supporting the existence of this meeting is scant. Filippos Iliou, making use of Greek Communist archival material, mentions Zachariadis' meeting with Stalin in Crimea in April 1946: *Avgi,* December 12, 1979. Eleftheriou (pp. 34–35) maintains that there were *two* meetings, one with Stalin, Molotov, and Zhdanov in Moscow, and a second, secret meeting a week later in Crimea with only Stalin present for the Soviet side; at this second meeting, Stalin supposedly approved the gradual movement toward armed struggle. The dates correlate well with Zachariadis' travels in Europe after the Second Plenum; in March he traveled to Belgrade and then Prague for the congress of the Czechoslovak Communist party, where he certainly had the opportunity to meet with the Soviets.

cess, Zachariadis could argue that his hands were effectively tied, leaving him no option but to expand the military component of KKE policy. Since the Soviets evidently did not preclude the expansion of military forces, this was not an entirely inconsistent position; moreover, it had the virtue of finally forcing Stalin to be more specific about his intentions in Greece. Zachariadis was thus able to achieve a variety of goals at the cost of an error having only tactical significance.[133] Further indirect evidence that Zachariadis' decision did not seriously displease Stalin is that even after the complete defeat of KKE forces, Stalin retained him as KKE general secretary.

Even though he had committed the KKE to abstention from the elections, Zachariadis, for reasons still unclear, changed his mind some time later. Without endorsing complete participation, he maintained that there should be a "symbolic" candidate in each electoral district to represent the parties of the united Left.[134] By that time, however, the deadline for the submission of candidates had passed, leaving the KKE out.

The infiltration of the labor movement had also run into difficulty. The KKE and its front in the labor movement, ERGAS, had made significant gains in restoring their popularity among the rank and file, enabling them to mount a serious challenge to the government-sponsored GSEE provisional executive. In addition, Communist-inspired strikes were becoming more frequent as the year progressed, further impairing government reconstruction efforts. British intelligence had learned in September 1945 that the strikes had as their object the creation of anarchic conditions that would serve the regent as proof that the elections and plebiscite had to be postponed.[135] By the time the Eighth Pan-Hellenic Labor Congress opened in early March 1946, the KKE appeared to be in the saddle. Three delegates from the World Federation of Trade Unions, one of whom was a Soviet, spoke at the congress. Coinciding with the labor congress, a new strike movement was underway, affecting utilities, telephone workers, and U.N. Relief and Rehabilitation Administration (UNRRA) drivers.

But the KKE rebound in the unions was marred by a significant setback. The new minister of labor had contested the legitimacy of the old, pro-KKE general executive of the GSEE and established a new provisional executive, leaving the ERGAS faction in the minority. In early 1946 the

---

[133]This raises the interesting possibility that Zachariadis abstained from the elections intentionally in an effort to gain Soviet consent for the decisions of the Second Plenum. No evidence supporting this possibility has come to light.

[134]Zachariadis, *Provlimata tis Krisis tou KKE,* pp. 20–21.

[135]OSS XL21000, September 13, 1945.

matter had gone to the courts, and a long legal battle ensued, lasting into the summer of 1946.[136] Ultimately, the KKE lost the battle and failed to gain control of the executive offices of the labor movement.

A conflict between Soviet policy and the reality of local Greek conditions was beginning to emerge. By the time of the elections on March 31, 1946, the political component of the KKE's policy had encountered serious difficulties. Instead of any significant achievements, the KKE was now decisively out of the government, struggling in its attempt to control the labor movement, and slowly being weeded out of the armed forces. For most Greek Communists, who were for the most part nationalistic and relatively unconcerned about Soviet objectives, all signs pointed to the urgency of preparing for a military confrontation.

In contrast, Greek-Soviet diplomatic relations through January 1946 indicate the Soviets remained generally unmoved at the serious setbacks KKE interests were suffering yet content with the manner in which events in Greece were creating problems for the British. Their inability to create a stable Greek government and the failure to ameliorate postwar conditions increased the pressure on the British. The Sofoulis government was undoubtedly the kind of weak government that the Soviets wished to see in the region. Since it rested solely on British support, the Soviets would have excellent possibilities of establishing their influence once the British left.

In view of this potential pliability and evident weakness, the Soviet attitude toward the Sofoulis government improved dramatically. The Soviet ambassador to Turkey, Vinogradov, had earlier spoken disparagingly of the Greek government. Less than one week after the creation of the Sofoulis government, the Greek ambassador found that Vinogradov's attitude had changed completely. In a conversation with his Soviet counterpart on November 28, 1945, Ambassador Rafail noted that Vinogradov was friendly and remarked that he was glad to see Greece "was beginning to see the light." Rafail interpreted this as Soviet relief to find an opportunity to change their attitude toward the Greek government and appoint an ambassador there. One day later, the Soviet government announced the long-delayed appointment of Ambassador Rodionov.[137] All sectors of the Greek press responded favorably to this sudden improvement in Greek-Soviet relations. The improvement continued gradually during the month of December. The Greeks contributed to it by recognizing the Republican

---

[136]Jecchinis, pp. 96–105.
[137]DSR 868.00/11-2945, no. 1501; DSR 868.00/11-3045, no. 1380.

regime of Tito in Yugoslavia. Such efforts were encouraged by the receipt of messages from Stalin and Manuil'skii to the "Gr[ee]k gov[ernmen]t and people," and the arrival of Rodionov on December 30, 1945.[138] Several days later, the regent, Sofoulis, and Foreign Minister Sofianopoulos received New Year's messages from Stalin, Molotov, and Mikhail Kalinin.[139]

Sofianopoulos, the former foreign minister whose activities had helped undermine the Voulgaris government, continued to play an influential role in Greek politics. In an article he wrote for the *News Chronicle* of September 11, 1945, he revealed more clearly his affinity for KKE policy and the importance of a Soviet presence in Greece for his personal career. Sofianopoulos praised Varvaresos' attempt to reconstruct the Greek economy and blamed a "clamorous campaign on the part of capital" and the "treacherous opposition" of Varvaresos' fellow ministers (of which he was one) for the fall of the former vice-premier. He made absolutely no reference to the hostility the KKE showed toward the Varvaresos initiatives nor to the program it instituted to sabotage the reconstruction efforts. Sofianopoulos then went on to reiterate the demand for a representative government. In defending the viability of such a government, the former foreign minister dwelt upon his close connections with the Communists: "If today the Regent claims that the formation of such a government is not possible on account of the refusal of the old Republican parties to work together with the Communists, *I am in a position to inform him that the Communists would agree to being represented in the Government by two or three persons* who . . . would not meet hostility from Conservative Rightists" (emphasis added).

The frank affinity of Sofianopoulos for the Communists again became important when the Sofoulis government came to power, restoring Sofianopoulos to his former post as foreign minister. His tenure in this position turned out to be brief, however, as British and Soviet interests came into open conflict in the United Nations in late January 1946. This was precisely the kind of situation the foreign minister had to avoid, as it was fatal to his personal political position. In the U.N. debate that ensued, Sofianopoulos refused to support the British position entirely; instead, he tried to avoid a conflict between Britain and the Soviet Union and proposed that the Greek delegation quietly support Vyshinskii's proposal and defer consideration by the Security Council until April.[140] For his refusal

138DSR 868.00/12-3045, no. 1492.
139DSR 868.00/1-1346, no. 69.
140DSR 868.00/1-2746, no. 144. Note the suggested April date was to be postelection, assuming elections were held as scheduled.

to obey orders, Sofianopoulos was dismissed, causing another shake-up in the Greek government at a critical moment. The significant point is that, despite his dismissal, Sofianopoulos remained as loyal to the Soviet position as possible under the circumstances. The former foreign minister surfaced again some weeks later, when he declared his support for a postponement of the elections. But by then his utility as some one capable of disrupting the Greek government at crucial moments no longer existed.

These diplomatic developments stand in marked contrast to the deteriorating position of the KKE's political strategy, an indication that the Soviets focused on the strategic objective of removing the British presence, while the KKE had the control of Greece as its fundamental objective. This reasoning is further supported by the fact that Vyshinskii's complaint in the United Nations against Great Britain increased the unpopularity of EAM in all classes because of the anti-Slav feeling prevalent in Greece.[141] In addition, Greek nationalist feelings could not but be offended by the keen interest the Soviet Union was showing in the Greek islands near the mouth of the Straits (in addition to Mytilini and Chios). A short time after his appointment, Ambassador Rodionov even suggested establishing a Soviet repair base in the Dodecanese.[142]

The course of events through March 1946 reveal the changes that took place in Soviet policy. In late 1944, Stalin made no attempts to act in Greece, choosing instead to consolidate his control of Romania. In the early months of 1945 the Soviets still refrained from any activity or encouragement of the KKE, preferring to wait and see if local Communists forces could successfully reestablish themselves. By the summer of 1945, events in Greece combined with clear evidence of British inability to control the situation to convince Stalin that a cautious attempt to implement a gradualist policy was worth the risk; the Soviets began to support Zachariadis in his attempt to get the KKE to pursue a policy of political gradualism that entailed the infiltration of governmental, social, and political institutions, combined with gradual preparations for armed conflict. This policy conformed with the overriding Soviet objective of removing British influence from the eastern Mediterranean without alarming the Western Allies.

This characterization of Soviet policy helps explain the apparently indecisive and unresolved Soviet attitude toward using KKE military forces. Stalin must have been aware that, even if domestic conditions in Greece

---

[141]DSR 868.00/2-1146, no. 1702.
[142]DSR 868.00/2-2646, State Department, memorandum of conversation.

were stabilized, a gradual increase in Communist military forces still risked alarming the British and Americans. Yet if the Soviet leader was interested in the postwar expansion of his sphere of influence, these substantial political and military assets in Greece were too tempting to squander or sacrifice. The major strategic impediment to the immediate implementation of the KKE assets was the emerging global confrontation between the United States and the Soviet Union: in Germany, Eastern Europe, Turkey, and Iran, Soviet efforts to consolidate and extend political control contributed to an escalation of tensions and the crystallization of American resolve.

In the context of confrontation over these major Soviet objectives, Greece assumed secondary importance. The logical alternative was to place KKE forces in reserve until other, more pressing, Soviet objectives were achieved; then the Soviets could initiate more aggressive action in Greece. (Perhaps it was this thinking that occupied Stalin when in 1945 he told Milovan Djilas, "The war shall soon be over. We shall recover in fifteen or twenty years, and then we'll have another go at it.")[143] Since political activity in Greece *was* acceptable, Stalin endorsed it, while remaining uncommunicative on military activity (at least with the KKE). The Greek Communists, after all, operated in an environment in which Stalin had only limited control; to counsel a rapid build-up of forces might serve to escalate developments beyond the Soviets' ability to impose restraint.

Hence what appeared to KKE leaders throughout 1945–46 as indecision and a lack of information was actually a prudent and opportunistic Soviet response to the need to devote attention and limited resources to more pressing postwar objectives. But for Stalin's prudently expansionist policy to have even a minimal chance of success required a degree of short-term domestic stability sufficient to prevent a renewed Western commitment to the region. As long as it was possible to maintain this minimal internal stability, Soviet and KKE political gradualism could achieve results, as in the appointment of the Sofoulis government, which marked the high point for the strategy, as it left Greece with a fragile, unpopular government whose sole basis of support was an already over-burdened British presence.

Further success in Soviet policy would prove elusive, however, as domestic conditions deteriorated and other postwar crises continued to

---

[143]Milovan Djilas, *Conversations with Stalin,* trans. Michael Petrovich (New York: Harcourt, Brace & World, 1962), pp. 114–15.

occupy Soviet attention. Stalin would continue to view a gradualist strategy as a means of preserving assets for a future occasion, but nationally minded Greek Communists, who viewed an immediate and vigorous policy as essential for their survival, came to see in Soviet strategy a program for military action. Once the KKE had abstained from the elections, the pressure for a military option only increased. The stage was set for the most serious complication; for as Stalin continued to try to orient the KKE toward conserving its forces, the urgency of action impelled Greek Communists to move rapidly toward insurgency. Therefore, the spring of 1946 marks a critical juncture: whereas the Soviets had previously been able to pursue a policy that matched developments, now the pace of events began to outdistance strategy. The tension between Soviet requirements and Greek realities was to affect the KKE profoundly, creating division within this basic instrument of Soviet policy and rendering it ineffective for the attainment of Soviet aims. Similarly, the resulting hesitancy induced in KKE leaders would prove fatal to their efforts to pursue a coherent policy. The role of Soviet interests in the failure of KKE policy bears closer examination.

Zachariadis' "Dual" Strategy: The Impact of Soviet Interests on KKE Policy

One way of assessing the impact of the conflict between Soviet strategic imperatives and Greek Communist realities is to examine Zachariadis' efforts to implement his policy in the presence of sharp conflict within the KKE. That the Greek Communist party leaders were divided on questions of strategy has come to be accepted by most scholars studying this period.[144] What is lacking in almost all accounts, however, is an explanation of Zachariadis' behavior after his return to Greece. The KKE general secretary is more often than not depicted as a traitor, as a man ignorant of the context in which he was working, or as a leader who committed the most egregious of errors. When his policy is considered marred by a fatal hesitancy or inability to act, the reasons remain unexamined; analysis is restricted to the unhelpful conclusion that he was wrong.[145] How could he

---

[144]For example, see Woodhouse, *Struggle for Greece*; Kousoulas; Dominique Eudes, *The Kapetanios: Partisans and Civil War in Greece, 1943–1949* (New York: Monthly Review Press, 1972).

[145]This is especially true of the charges former and present KKE members hurl at each other. Blanas, p. 62, condemns Zachariadis as fatally unsure of strategy and sometimes

have succeeded in remaining KKE general secretary for three decades had he been incompetent or anti-Communist? Furthermore, despite the complete defeat of Greek Communist forces in 1949, he was retained as general secretary under the watchful eye of Stalin. Had he committed some terrible blunder in the eyes of the Soviets, they could easily have seen to his removal at that time.

The basis for explaining Zachariadis' behavior can be established by elaborating the model of the KKE general secretary as a rational actor pursuing a specific policy under constraints that undermined coherent and effective action. In this instance Zachariadis attempted to pursue a policy that accommodated Soviet interests, but factional division within the KKE forced him to respond in ways that had damaging consequences for Soviet and Greek Communist aims. While Zachariadis continued to push the Soviet-inspired strategy of gradualism and penetration, the means he used caused conditions within Greece to deteriorate, which adversely affected Soviet strategic objectives. A parallel problem was that the division within the KKE leadership delayed opting decisively for civil war, thereby fatally damaging KKE prospects.

The leadership conflict revolved around several key areas of Communist activity, one of which was nationality issues. Zachariadis' statements on Northern Epirus were not well received by local party committees. In fact, most ordinary members of the Regional Committee of Epirus favored annexation.[146] Ethnic differences were also important in the difficult relations between the KKE and the Communist Party of Macedonia.[147] More fundamental, however, were issues of overall strategy, where differences were compounded by Zachariadis' initial unfamiliarity with conditions in Greece after his nearly ten years of imprisonment. His relative ignorance of Greek affairs served to highlight the difference of opinion among KKE leaders. Zachariadis tended to analyze events from the international per-

---

even argues that he was a traitor. Bartziotas takes a different line, arguing that the years in prison in Korfu and Dachau somehow altered Zachariadis' capacity for innovative and active thought; see Bartziotas, *Agonas tou Dimokratikou Stratou Elladas*, p. 35. He also adds that the KKE leader, having been away from the historic developments taking place within Greece during the period of the resistance, was acting in ignorance of the historical conditions. Woodhouse follows neither of these interpretations but concludes that the return of Zachariadis resulted in more confusion than conscious policy—that the KKE was still reacting to events rather than acting decisively; see Woodhouse, *Struggle for Greece*, p. 144. While some of these views may have validity, none eliminate the possibility that Zachariadis had a conscious policy difficult to follow given conditions in Greece and KKE disorganization.

[146]OSS XL21027, August 31, 1945.
[147]OSS XL38975, January 14, 1946.

spective, while other Politburo members and ELAS officers emphasized the importance of internal factors.[148] More important, divisions emerged within the party organizational structure, creating the potential for dissident groups, or groups that simply misunderstood party directives, to gain a dangerous degree of autonomy. This was especially true of military and paramilitary organizations, given that policy differences centered on how these organizations should be used.

Zachariadis' position, already elaborated in the previous section, may be summarized briefly. At the Twelfth Plenum of the Central Committee of the KKE in late June 1945, Zachariadis presided over his first party gathering since the beginning of World War II. During the course of the discussions, he elaborated on the two-pole theory and pressed for a policy that involved the use of mass organizations and parliamentary activities combined with covert penetration of state bureaucracies. In addition, the mass popular *aftoamina* was officially inaugurated as an element of KKE policy. Its ostensible function was protection from rightist terror but it was paramilitary and could serve as a military foundation in the development of armed insurgency.

The Seventh Congress of the KKE in October reemphasized the dual policy advocated by Zachariadis. The importance of the *aftoamina* was again pointed out, but in sharper fashion. Outwardly, the congress left the

---

[148]Some days after the Varkiza Agreement, MacVeagh reported that the unsurrendered arms would pass into the hands of the KKE. He added, "There seems to be no reason to quarrel with this, or with the expression of the possibility that there will be trouble between political and military authorities of ELAS on this matter": DSR 868.00/2-2745. Thus, even before Zachariadis returned, the question of military power was seen from a different perspective by military leaders. Blanas, pp. 66–69, and Bartziotas (*Agonas tou Dimokratikou Stratou Elladas*, pp. 17–26) argue exclusively from the internal situation and are opposed to Zachariadis' interpretation of issues such as the two-pole theory and territorial matters. Their argument rests primarily on the assumption that a revolution in Greece had to be carried out without substantial external support and therefore rapidly. Vontitsos-Gousias (*Aities gia tis Ittes, ti Diaspasi* 1:129), on the other hand, praises Zachariadis for his clear analysis of the international situation at the Twelfth Plenum. He agreed with Zachariadis' argument that it was important to realize the Soviet Union could not afford a rupture with the Western Allies (p. 128). Some months later, after the Second Plenum, Gousias mistakenly believed that Zachariadis' entire line had changed and that the Soviets no longer supported the position that Greece should occupy a neutral position (p. 133–34). The problem with Gousias' argument is that the Soviets, according to available evidence, never desired to see Greece neutralized. Rather, they believed that given existing international conditions, a policy of gradualism was best suited to Greece. The neutrality argument was put forward by Zachariadis as a tactic because he realized that a gradual evolution of civil war would ultimately require the involvement of the Soviets; thus it was expedient to involve them in some officially sanctioned capacity in Greece, thereby strengthening any future stand the KKE might take.

impression of little change in policy, but its creation of the Panhellenic Military Committee was a portent. In fact, Bartziotas maintains that the orientation toward armed struggle emerged at the Seventh Congress.[149] Consequently, as conditions in Greece continued to deteriorate, Zachariadis responded by progressively moving from a purely parliamentary policy to a dual strategy involving the simultaneous intensification of political action *and* preparations for armed action. As KKE policy shifted from political gradualism to this new orientation of dualism, it clearly risked deviating from Stalin's desire, manifest in January 1946, to hold KKE forces in reserve.

There is sufficient evidence to conclude that at the Second Plenum of the Central Committee (February 12–15, 1946), Zachariadis successfully argued for the dual policy he had initiated. Here, however, the policy received an important alteration, as the general secretary maintained it was necessary to *develop* (in contrast to *prepare for*) the armed struggle, "in such a way as to avoid the direct, armed military intervention of the English forces that were in Greece." Zachariadis made the curious argument, however, that an immediate military plan was unnecessary because an open insurgency was not yet the objective of the strategy. According to Bartziotas, Zachariadis envisioned the gradual (as opposed to immediate) development of armed struggle as constituting "an additional, forceful means of pressure on the adversary for . . . peaceful, smooth development."[150] The gradual evolution of military activity was meant to complement the KKE's political activity; it was initially designed to ensure that the opposition not be tempted to resolve matters through the use of force.

This is precisely what the general secretary maintained was determined at the Second Plenum. In Zachariadis' view, the plenum had decided on a "progressive development of the movement, with the strengthening of the groups of the persecuted, for the gradual passing into partisan struggle, into armed resistance." In addition, the movement of the masses was to be strengthened, including the policy of reconciliation and unity. Simultaneously, there would be a further unfolding of the "popular struggles and of popular resistance with the creation of mass popular *aftoamina* in the cities and with the pushing forward of . . . groups in the mountains."

---

[149]Bartziotas, *Agonas tou Dimokratikou Stratou Elladas*, p. 22.

[150]*Voithima gia tin Istoria tou KKE* (KKE, 1952), p. 260, in Ole L. Smith, "On the Beginning of the Greek Civil War," *Scandinavian Studies in Modern Greek*, no. 1 (1977), 25. Smith also discusses the dual strategy, although from a somewhat different perspective. Bartziotas, *Agonas tou Dimokratikou Stratou Elladas*, pp. 28–30. See n. 126 above for explanation of the KKE's system of numbering plena of the Central Committee.

The objectives of this policy were to give the appearance that the KKE was acting in defense and to isolate the British. Given this line of reasoning, Zachariadis understandably felt he was correct when he concluded that no military plan existed because only a political decision had been taken: armed action was only an adjunct to a policy still within a parliamentary framework.[151]

Zachariadis was apparently alone in suggesting this strategy of legal activity combined with the "gradual" passing into partisan activity. The Central Committee was divided into two groups, but neither initially supported the general secretary. Bartziotas relates that the majority of the Central Committee was in favor of the "*immediate* formation of armed struggle," with all preparations complete in 1946.[152] In this way, KKE forces would be in a position to deliver the decisive blow against the Greek government in late 1946 or early 1947 at the latest. The minority held that the armed struggle should be put off while the partisan forces regained their strength, and in the interim the party would be occupied with the mass struggle. Zachariadis was thus squarely in the middle, arguing that the simultaneous but gradual development of both aspects of KKE policy would produce the best results.

The reasons Zachariadis provided in support of his position reflect an effort to harmonize KKE policy with Soviet interests. It was of crucial importance, the KKE general secretary argued, that British intervention be avoided because of the KKE military weakness after Varkiza, but this goal also meshed conveniently with the Soviet interest in getting the British out of Greek affairs. His second reason was that it was necessary for the kind of struggle the KKE was waging to pressure progressively and as far as possible the wavering elements of the Center and Right.[153] Here again, the justification reflected a Soviet preference for avoiding civil war for the time being.

The majority of the Central Committee was not satisfied with Zachariadis' views, yet he prevailed. The possible reasons why provide an interesting insight into the real sources of persuasiveness in Communist debates. Zachariadis undoubtedly benefited from his absence during the failed December revolt; he returned to Greece untainted by the disastrous second round. More important, the KKE membership held him in such high esteem that his view prevailed in many instances solely because it was *his*

---

[151]Dimitriou, *I Diaspasi tou KKE,* 1:92–94.
[152]Bartziotas, *Agonas tou Dimokratikou Stratou Elladas,* pp. 27–28; emphasis added.
[153]Ibid., p. 30 (see also Zachariadis' speeches already cited in n. 150).

opinion. The party at that time suffered from a "cult of personality" (*prosopolatria*) that placed Zachariadis on a plane beyond question. Bartziotas is quite frank about this, admitting that despite strong reservations about the strategy of gradual development of partisan warfare, the Central Committee unanimously consented to the plan.[154]

There was an added psychological lever that Zachariadis and Ioannidis (who at that time was faithfully serving the general secretary[155]) employed: the implication that the dual strategy should be pursued because other Communist parties, especially the Soviet, concurred with the opinion of the KKE chief. Thus, when the Panhellenic Military Committee convened shortly after the Seventh Congress to discuss military matters, Blanas, chief of Command Headquarters for the Democratic Army of Greece (DSE) in Thessaly, inquired as to what was to be done given the likelihood of a renewed military intervention by the British. Ioannidis' reply was that "there [were] other old men [to take care of us] now." This was apparently in reference to the Soviets because Blanas goes on to comment somewhat bitterly that when external aid appeared, it was "deficient."[156] In light of later developments, the Yugoslavs and Albanians could not be faulted for providing deficient aid. A second instance of this tactic was mentioned by Bartziotas in reference to the discussions at the Second Plenum: "The hint by [Zachariadis] that his view was in concert with certain of our friends outside of Greece also played a part [in convincing the Central Committee to accept the resolution of the Second Plenum]."[157] Whether or not this expectation of Soviet bloc aid was true or merely a tactic is still unknown. At least one scholar argues that Zachariadis "knew something" that others did not about Soviet intentions in Greece.[158]

The view opposed to Zachariadis was shared by most members of the KKE Central Committee as well as many of the ex-ELAS officers. Their opinions were more nationalistic, as reflected by their dismay over the party policy on Northern Epirus.[159] There was also severe criticism of the two-pole theory, the majority of dissenters considering this stand to be an

[154]Bartziotas, *Agonas tou Dimokratikou Stratou Elladas*, p. 30.

[155]Blanas, chap. 1 passim.

[156]Ibid., p. 71.

[157]Bartziotas, *Agonas tou Dimokratikou Stratou Elladas*, p. 30.

[158]According to Alekos Papapanagiotou, "Zachariadis knew something, which no one else knew, and because of this until the end of his life insisted that the abstention from the elections was a tactical mistake and not of a strategic nature"; Foivos Oikonomidis' interview with Alekos Papapanagiotou, *Anti*, May 22, 1981, p. 40. Unfortunately, Papapanagiotou does not reveal what it is that Zachariadis knew, leaving this interesting piece of information to await further elaboration.

[159]Bartziotas, *Agonas tou Dimokratikou Stratou Elladas*, p. 36.

error in the party's thinking about the position of the British. Internal factors in general weighed much more heavily than international ones. This way of viewing the problem makes it understandable why Blanas would ask: "Why is it indispensable to support equally the friendship of Britain and the Soviet Union?"[160] Using Greece as a balancing factor between the two powers only made sense if the Soviet argument was accepted: that it was of primary importance not to trigger a renewed British intervention.

Zachariadis and the proponents of a more militant line also differed on whether KKE forces could succeed in neutralizing the British military presence. Here it would appear that Zachariadis' opponents were both more optimistic and more realistic in their assessments of the outcome. Blanas and Bartziotas both argued that if events resulted in an armed confrontation with the British, the KKE would do well if it had made adequate preparations. Blanas states that if immediate preparations had begun for an armed confrontation after the Seventh Congress or the Second Plenum "at the latest," the Communists would have been "in the middle of things."[161] The correlation of forces, argued the former DSE chief of Thessaly, was favorable to ELAS forces even after the signing of the Varkiza Agreement. He maintained ELAS did not lose even one-tenth of its fighting strength in its confrontation with the British.[162] Bartziotas was also confident about any future clash with the British military forces. As a supporter of immediate and total mobilization for civil war, he accepted that the British would have to be expelled militarily. Thus, he maintained that if all preparations were made in 1946, the basic blow could be rendered to the Greek government forces, and then the Communists could turn and confront the "English occupation forces."[163] The former political commissar of the DSE General Staff was also confident about the outcome of this confrontation: "It was necessary . . . to take the decision to begin the armed struggle immediately . . . so that we could deliver the decisive blows to the enemy by the end of 1946-early 1947. . . . The problems of food supply, clothing, and military materiel . . . could have been solved correctly then."[164]

There was also extreme pessimism about the probability of achieving any lasting success from the parliamentary route. Blanas, Bartziotas, Partsalidis, and others depicted the peaceful activities of the KKE as being

[160]Blanas, p. 69.
[161]Ibid., p. 61.
[162]Ibid., pp. 26–28.
[163]Bartziotas, *Agonas tou Dimokratikou Stratou Elladas,* p. 28.
[164]Ibid., pp. 33–34.

obliterated under the pressure of rightist and government terror. The analysis of Blanas in particular stressed that the only real options were military: "According to the correlation of forces we had either to maintain, without exposing these groups [the *aftoamina* and groups within the government armed forces], until the moment when, upon our command, they would pass to the side of revolution; or, opportunely disperse, diverting the soldiers to the *andartes* [guerrillas]." Similarly, Bartziotas believed, "Essentially there existed no other route except that of taking up arms."[165] They saw no room, apparently, for any "third course" such as Zachariadis suggested. The militant forces in the KKE thought the choice was between taking up arms now or taking them up later. A parliamentary policy was simply not decisive when it came to a final reckoning with the British.

In this respect, the militant wing of the KKE was more realistic in its appraisal of alternative policies. Looked at from an internal perspective, the Greek Communists' situation was a classic example of the Leninist dictum *kto-kogo?*—"Who will defeat whom?" Either the British would stay and, over time, resuscitate the feeble Greek government and completely extinguish the KKE's chance for power, or the KKE could mobilize rapidly and attempt to deal a fatal blow to the British forces. It was foolish to think that the British would be gradually edged out of Greece while a partisan uprising was simultaneously being developed. There was, therefore, no possible middle road in Greece.

This was precisely the dilemma of Zachariadis' position, primarily because he was trying to take Soviet interests into account. Furthermore, he believed that the KKE's chances of military success depended heavily upon obtaining external support, which the Soviets were still unwilling to provide. Consequently, despite the fact that anything less than a military strategy was ill-suited to Greek reality, the KKE leader was forced to create his dual approach in the hope that it could eventually lead to securing Stalin's consent for more aggressive policies. Whereas the majority of the KKE Central Committee stressed the need for immediate military action, the crucial requirements for Zachariadis' policy were time and a disciplined party apparatus. Unfortunately, he had neither: disorganization was still rampant in the party, and the British (as well as the Americans) were gradually becoming aware of KKE intentions. Zachariadis' persistence in his policy despite the degenerating situation in Greece implies that the KKE general secretary was leaning heavily on international considerations, especially the influence of the Soviet Union. This is in fact what occurred; subsequent developments reveal that Zachariadis

[165]Blanas, p. 57; Bartziotas, *Agonas tou Dimokratikou Stratou Elladas*, p. 22.

succeeded in eliciting Stalin's support for his dual strategy, though the degree of approval was not as strong as he might have wished.

While the evidence available reveals the key decision at the Second Plenum in favor of the dual strategy, there is almost no evidence on the role of Soviet influence. The scant information that does exist, however, combined with the knowledge that the KKE was aware of the broad outline of Soviet interests, suggests that at a minimum, the dual strategy at least fell within the limits of acceptability marked out by Stalin's opportunistic policy. Once the decision was made, Zachariadis had to concern himself with gaining support for his policy from other Communist parties and with extracting from Stalin a more concrete commitment to the use of force.

In the weeks after the plenum, Zachariadis traveled abroad seeking pledges of assistance and support from "fraternal" parties. His first stop was Belgrade, where Tito apparently expressed complete agreement with the concept of the dual strategy. Zachariadis then went on to Prague to attend the congress of the Czech Communist party (February 28–March 3, 1946). There Zachariadis requested, and evidently received, Czech Communist support for the armed struggle; in particular, the Czechs promised to provide heavy weapons and other general assistance.[166] The next stop was Moscow (via Belgrade), for meetings with the Soviet leadership in early April. Evidently, there were two meetings: one with Stalin, Molotov, and Andrei Zhdanov in attendance; then a private meeting in Crimea between Stalin and Zachariadis. It was at the second meeting that Stalin apparently consented to the dual strategy, arguing that the KKE should "proceed gradually from the villages to the cities, in order to avoid an untimely British intervention, and, with the objective of finding a compromise."[167]

[166]Eleftheriou, p. 34.
[167]Ibid., p. 35. Ole L. Smith has reservations about the reliability of Eleftheriou's account of these meetings. In his opinion, however, the scarce evidence does support the conclusion that Zachariadis met with representatives of the CPSU at the party congress of the Czech Communists and felt confident that the Soviets had accepted the policy adopted at the Second Plenum; Smith, "The Problems of the Second Plenum of the Central Committee of the KKE, 1946," pp. 57–59. In his analysis of the civil war, Filippos Iliou is more optimistic about the existence of a meeting between Zachariadis and Stalin in 1946, alluding to it on at least three occasions but without providing supporting documentation; Iliou, *Avgi*, December 2, 12, and 30, 1979. Despite this disagreement, both interpretations support the basic contention that the KKE Second Plenum produced a policy without the benefit of Soviet instruction, after which Zachariadis traveled abroad in an effort to secure Soviet consent to the new line. Zachariadis' own account of his contacts can be found in his discussions with Gousias and in his speech at the Seventh Plenum of the KKE Central Committee (February 1957); see Vontitsos-Gousias, 2:250, and Dimitriou, *I Diaspasi tou KKE* 1:94.

The timing of these meetings correlates almost precisely with the KKE's abstention from the Greek elections, corroborating the argument that Zachariadis decided to abstain in part to present Stalin with a situation in which a resort to military force was the only logical alternative. If the information on this timing is accurate, it implies that Stalin was placed in a position in which there was little he could do: the KKE had abstained from the elections, effectively closing the parliamentary route; other Communist parties had enthusiastically endorsed the Greek Communist strategy; and party organs in Greece were under increasing attack. Under the circumstances, Stalin's response to Zachariadis was the farthest the Soviet leader could go in sanctioning military force while still trying to keep Greek Communist forces in reserve. Zachariadis was disappointed in the response, apparently hoping for a firmer commitment to military action. Years later, he argued that it was the unwillingness of Stalin to detail a precise strategy that contributed to the hesitation and incoherence in KKE policy, which was poignantly expressed in the party's simultaneous, yet contradictory, demands for a political "reconciliation" on one hand and the strengthening of the armed struggle on the other.[168] Stalin's prudence in dealing with Greece would profoundly affect the evolution of KKE policy and, by implication, Communist prospects for success.

If Zachariadis was concerned with gaining Soviet consent for his policy, the militant wing of the KKE rejected any considerations but those that pertained to the internal situation. They inclined toward a strategy of what might be called "dual power": in opposition to the Greek government, a competing power had to be established which could then carry out the struggle against, rather than within, the state. This position had powerful and simple appeal. It correctly maintained that compromise was impossible with opposition forces. Once a rightist government came into power, as was foreseeable even in late 1945, the Communists would be quickly shut out of the state bureaucracies. A second point was even more

---

[168]This was certainly Zachariadis' opinion in his conversations with Lefteris Eleftheriou in 1956: Eleftheriou, p. 35. Unfortunately, it is difficult to determine whether Zachariadis was making use of *post festum* arguments in support of his analysis. At least one other KKE leader makes an argument similar to that of Zachariadis, however; Partsalidis maintains that the CPSU was skeptical of a Greek Communist insurgency, despite the fact that the KKE considered it inevitable. This pessimism notwithstanding, Partsalidis points out that the Soviets did not advise the KKE to abandon the course of civil war. Instead, the KKE attempted for some time to "utilize the armed struggle as a means of achieving reconciliation and compromise"; see Partsalidis, *Dipli Apokatastasi tis Ethnikis Antistasis,* pp. 199–200. Here again, Soviet vacillation and desire to achieve a negotiated solution short of force emerge as key to KKE military policy.

persuasive: the longer the delay in action, the greater the likelihood that the British would uncover the arms hidden by ELAS. In addition, the Greek government would regain some strength and, under rightist direction, begin purging the armed forces of Communist sympathizers. These groups in the armed forces would play a key role in any bid for power, so their elimination would seriously damage KKE chances. In fact, very soon after the elections, the purging of the armed forces did begin. Blanas and Dimos Votsikas, former political commissar in the DSE and attaché to Zachariadis, have related how many of their subversive groups were purged.[169]

Finally, the longer the delay in mobilization, the greater the chances that the Greek government would act to deprive the KKE of its most vital resource: manpower. In particular, many KKE members were concerned that the dual strategy would create confusion, especially since Zachariadis did not as yet see the necessity for a detailed plan (nor is there any evidence to suggest that he succeeded in eliciting Stalin's consent to such). Furthermore, a gradual mobilization was deemed dangerous because it would forewarn the Greek government of Communist intentions, leaving the recruits that had not yet been mobilized in an exposed position. Blanas remarked that the Central Committee's lack of a clear mobilization plan left many KKE fighters in the cities, only to be arrested and sent to prison by the government.[170] Sometimes, Zachariadis' policy created such absurd results that it furnished the opposing faction with evidence of its uselessness. In Naousa, for example, when the word was disseminated that the Second Plenum had opted for military action, over two thousand volunteers appeared in the city and requested to be sent to the mountains. The response of the local KKE leadership was to inform the volunteers to disperse and return to their villages, where they should continue the popular struggle.[171] This incident also underscores the difficulty of making KKE rank and file comprehend the concept and necessity of a gradual mobilization. All these reasons contributed to the powerful appeal of the argument for immediate and total mobilization. The militant faction maintained that the potential for a successful strike against the Greek government and the British existed, but time was slowly eroding this advantage.

Differing conceptions of how the armed struggle was to develop also significantly affected the conception of how organizations were to be

[169]Blanas, p. 62; Votsikas, p. 84.
[170]Blanas, p. 59.
[171]Related to the author in an interview with a former partisan, Athens, May 1984.

used. The most important organization was the *aftoamina*, which could be quickly converted from defensive to offensive activities. Zachariadis clearly believed that the *aftoamina* was one instrument among the many he could employ simultaneously with other aspects of the policy of gradual partisan revolt. To him, using the *aftoamina*, therefore, did not imply that anything else was necessarily to follow; it was an instrument that acquired its meaning and purpose from the use to which the party leadership put it.

This view of the *aftoamina* was not shared by the military members in the KKE, nor by members of the Politburo. For this group, the creation and implementation of *aftoamina* meant that a sequence of events had been set in motion which inevitably led to partisan struggle. In elaborating the duties of the *aftoamina*, Blanas states that it "must be considered as a step in the development of the revolt against the fascist state or parastate mechanism." Somewhat further into his explanation, Blanas gets to the heart of the matter: "The progress from *aftoamina* [to] armed struggle or war is *uninterrupted and continuous.*" Bartziotas also reflects the same logic, stating, "Mass Popular *Aftoamina*, up to a certain point, can be effective and usually develops into armed struggle."[172] Hence, the creation of *aftoamina* intensified the division within the KKE. While Zachariadis tended to see it as a political instrument that took on meaning as the leadership saw fit, the more militant members of the party saw it as the signal for the initiation of a policy that had as its final objective partisan war. This explains their consternation at Zachariadis' stand during the Second Plenum, when they must have viewed the general secretary's arguments as illogical.

The difference in interpretation of the significance of the *aftoamina* was however, more than merely abstract. The formation of this illegal self-defense organization was done separately from other party organizations.[173] Because it was staffed in many cases by ex-ELAS officers who

[172]Blanas, pp. 44–45; 47, emphasis added; Bartziotas, *O Agonas tou Dimokratikou Stratou Elladas*, p. 22. Blanas is also susceptible to some of the same criticisms he levels at Zachariadis as to confusion and incorrect interpretation of strategy. Almost immediately after confidently stating what the aim of the *aftoamina* is, Blanas goes on to say something quite different: "The aim of popular *aftoamina* must be the strategic aim of the party, which each time serves the organization (revolutionary center). It should repulse the enemy terror in order to push forward the mass legal activity, or carry the form of struggle of the party up to revolt, when this is necessary and expedient." Here, he views *aftoamina* like Zachariadis: as an instrument serving party interests, useful in a variety of ways. Usually, however, Blanas does stick to his conception of *aftoamina* as one step in an unbreakable chain of events leading to war.

[173]Blanas, p. 42.

were partial to a more militant policy, any military decision to act alone would result in a dangerous organizational division within the party.

This division within the KKE and its significance can be examined by addressing three key questions: (1) Did the more militant members actually have at their disposal the capacity for carrying out the policy they were supporting? If objective conditions such as a lack of adequate manpower or armaments prohibited implementation of a more aggressive policy, then the support for the militant position would be weak and the argument would be only academic. (2) How did Zachariadis manage this split in the leadership? (3) What were the consequences of Zachariadis' handling of the situation?

Information now available indicates that, despite the ex-ELAS officers' optimistic appraisals of Communist military strength, the KKE still did not have in the beginning of 1945 a detailed plan or sufficient organizational capacity for a swift and disciplined attempt to seize power. The defeat in December 1944 had seriously affected the party's organs, and its ability to control dissident elements was limited. The reconstruction of the party apparatus discussed in previous sections was meant to remedy this situation, but even by June 1945, U.S. intelligence continued to maintain that the KKE was not strong enough to take on the opposition and even wondered if the Communists could defend themselves in the event of attack. ELAS, though it continued its intelligence operations on a more limited scale, was judged to be more of a political than a military organization.[174]

In materiel and manpower, however, the Communists were far more successful. Bartziotas and Blanas both agree that there were ample arms in hidden caches, which could have fielded a sizeable force. American sources estimated there were approximately fifty thousand weapons in good condition available to ELAS at this time.[175] In addition, the hiding of these arms was done efficiently and under the direction of a central command. Before the dissolution of ELAS, Blanas notes that arms caches had

---

[174]DSR 868.00/7-645, no. 1291.

[175]Ibid. KKE estimates of the number of weapons tend to be lower. Blanas, p. 95, notes that twenty thousand weapons were hidden by ELAS after the December 1944 fighting. Iannis Ioannidis provides two conflicting estimates of the number of weapons that were hidden. At one point he states that the weapons the Greek Communists fought with "did not reach the number of 60,000 or 70,000 . . . because if you take away 25–30,000 useless [ones] you can see how many are left." This seems to imply the number of hidden weapons was anywhere between thirty and forty-five thousand, but in the next breath Ioannidis emphasized that ELAS forces hid enough arms for an army of thirty thousand; see Ioannidis, *Anamniseis: Provlimata tis Politikis tou KKE stin Ethniki Antistasi, 1940–1945* (Athens: Themelio, 1979), pp. 292–93.

been distributed throughout Greece, with specific allocations of weapons to designated groups.[176] Support was also expected from other Communist parties,[177] who were obviously in a position to take advantage of the unsettled situation in the north to prevent the government from securing its own borders.

KOSSA, the secret Communist organization within the armed forces, possessed considerable power at this time, according to Communist estimates. American intelligence sources provided a somewhat more conservative, though still troubling, estimate: Communist control of the armed forces and security organs was at 17 percent of the air force, 15 percent of the army and National Guard, 5 percent of the navy, and 2 percent of the police force. Communist strength in the Attica Command was listed at 10 percent.[178] "Attack groups" (synergia krousseos) were also mentioned, but with no elaboration of their functions.

Another organization that deserves mention is the League of National Resistance Fighters (Syndesmos Agoniston Ethnikis Antistaseos), which served as the reserve of KOSSA. This organization was reported to have an estimated strength of 8,000 men in the Attica area and considerable equipment reserves in Macedonia.[179] In addition, ELAS members were reported to have joined a "Pan-Hellenic Union of Fighters" that, while outwardly serving as a veterans' association, performed a valuable service as a recruiting agency for any future military force. (The British estimated the contribution of this organization to be between 3,000 and 4,000 men.) When one adds to this the estimated 25,000 men that could be taken from the countryside,[180] the total size of a potential fighting force rises to approximately 33,000 men. This, combined with the facilities to train and

---

[176]Blanas, pp. 35–36.
[177]Bartziotas, *Agonas tou Dimokratikou Stratou Elladas*, p. 26. KKE leaders differed considerably on the possibility of outside aid and the extent to which it was wise to depend upon it. Blanas was most skeptical and consequently stressed the KKE capacity to proceed alone; Bartziotas noted that the prospect of aid from abroad helped support the militant faction's argument. Partsalidis (*Dipli Apokatastasi tis Ethnikis Antistasis*, p. 199), also skeptical, stated that the Soviets advised participation in the elections; the Communist parties of Italy and France were of the opinion that armed struggle would not produce results; and the Yugoslavs, in a meeting with Zachariadis on his return from Prague in March 1946, promised support for the Communists. With so little concrete information about Soviet intentions to provide arms, the prospect of outside help was generally used as necessary to support various positions.
[178]DSR 868.00/9-1845, no. 1538; OSS XL46486, February 1946.
[179]OSS XL46486, February, 1946.
[180]DSR 868.00/9-1845 no. 1538.

retain another 20,000 men, which Zachariadis claimed the Yugoslavs later granted him,[181] added up to a sizeable force.

When these figures are combined with the fact that the Greek government was steadily weakening, the temptation to try and employ these forces as soon as possible seems reasonable. But the organizational control was still lacking, and the party failed to develop a plan. Stalin's desire to hold Greek Communist forces in reserve, translated by Zachariadis into a dual strategy, had the effect of developing existing forces but with no comprehensive and detailed plan for their implementation. The prospect that the entire effort might degenerate into incoherence was therefore high, and the resulting need to supervise the reconstruction of military forces occupied much of Zachariadis', as well as the Soviets', time.

The return of the KKE chief in May 1945 was followed by a number of developments that indicated the party was beginning to try to reestablish its control throughout Greece. Since the military leaders were largely out of touch with the Central Committee,[182] it was only reasonable that Zachariadis would attempt to restore some unity of action among the KKE military. In mid-June, Zachariadis met with senior ex-ELAS officers and discussed the reorganization of ELAS, and a little over a month later, the orders for the formation of the veterans' associations just mentioned were reportedly given out.[183] These moves, combined with the initiation of the *aftoamina* organization, clearly implied that Zachariadis was undertaking the reconstruction of the KKE's military potential under some semblance of party control.

During the months that followed, Zachariadis continued to meet with members of the Communist military, using his cross-country tours as a convenient camouflage for these meetings. In late September he passed through Macedonia, and British intelligence reported that the reorganization of ELAS was discussed at this time. On September 17 and 18, British sources reported another secret meeting between Zachariadis and military leaders, on the reconstruction of ELAS.[184] Thus it appears that up to the

---

[181]This was the figure mentioned by Zachariadis in his speech at the Seventh Plenum of the KKE Central Committee (February 1957); the proceedings are published in Dimitriou, *I Diaspasi tou KKE,* 1:95. For further discussion of this point, see Ole L. Smith, "A Turning Point in the Greek Civil War 1945–1949," *Scandinavian Studies in Modern Greek,* no. 3 (1979), 40–42.

[182]This situation lasted through the crucial Second Plenum; see Smith, "Beginning of the Greek Civil War," p. 24.

[183]DSR 868.00/9-1845, no. 1538.

[184]DSR 868.00/10-1745, no. 1714.

Seventh Congress, Zachariadis was engaged in serious discussions on the reemergence of a new Communist military force and, in the process, was trying to extend his own influence and establish some unity of views. Although Stalin was unable to control events in Greece, the sensitive task of reconstructing KKE military forces made some form of Soviet oversight essential to assure the orderly development of policy. The Soviets tried to accomplish this by using diplomatic and military personnel to monitor conditions and transmit information back to Moscow. The evidence currently available indicates the Soviets maintained clandestine and public contacts and representatives in Greece throughout 1945, supposedly a time when they professed to have no interest in this region of the Mediterranean.

On a formal diplomatic level, the departure of Novikov from Cairo in July 1944 left the Soviets without a representative to the Greek government. The hiatus in Greek-Soviet relations was ended finally in November 1945, when Ambassador Rodionov was appointed as Soviet diplomatic representative to the Sofoulis government. The intervening sixteen months created something of a dilemma for Stalin: while it was advantageous to pressure successive Greek governments by threatening to withhold Soviet recognition, such action risked depriving them of the opportunity to place representatives in Greece who could then make contact with Greek Communist forces. The Soviets solved this dilemma when, in October 1944, Vyshinskii asked the British for facilities for a "repatriation" mission in Greece.[185] The British acceded to the request, and a Soviet mission was established in Greece under the formal jurisdiction of British military authorities. Stalin was thus able to maintain official representation in Greece without having to recognize the postwar Greek government.

Establishing a Soviet right of access to Greece was perhaps the most obvious benefit deriving from the repatriation mission. Red Army officers could argue that they had a legitimate purpose in entering and remaining in Greece, as did the group who crossed into Greece without British permission in June 1945, were intercepted, and then allowed to proceed unmolested to Athens.[186] In November 1945, Soviet officers stationed in Belgrade applied to go to Athens to inspect the work of the mission, but British authorities, by then eager to see the mission's departure, denied the request.[187] In addition to bringing in new Soviet representatives, the

185FO 371-48294 R11064, June 29, 1945.
186FO 371-48294 R11238, July 2, 1945.
187The only Red Army officer positively identified in Belgrade was a Colonel Kutuzov: FO 371-48294 R18803, November 6, 1945.

mission made it possible to retain the balance of the Russian Military Mission that had been dropped into the Greek mountains in July 1944. While the Russian Mission's titular head, Popov, apparently left for Moscow, this was not the case with Chernichev. The latter, who functioned as de facto chief of the earlier mission, remained in Greece through 1945 and later became first secretary of the Soviet Embassy in Athens.

The repatriation mission's mandate made it an invaluable Soviet asset for gathering intelligence information: the Russians had virtual carte blanche to travel throughout Greece in search of Soviet nationals allegedly eager to return to their homeland; and whenever it appeared that all Soviet citizens had been accounted for, the Soviets would assert that some new pocket of previously unaccounted for nationals had turned up, requiring them to extend their stay. This was certainly the basis of Soviet demands to visit Crete in October 1945.[188] Later in 1946, when the mission's personnel had been incorporated into the new embassy, the Soviets persisted in this tactic. The petition of several thousand Armenians in 1946 for repatriation to the Soviet Union gave Vladimir D. Karamanov, second secretary of the Soviet Embassy, the opportunity to visit Thessaloniki several times, ostensibly in connection with consular affairs. Karamanov's search for Armenians took him deep into remote parts of Greece— on one occasion as far as Mount Athos to visit the Russian, Serbian, and Bulgarian monasteries![189]

The British both suspected and disliked the activities of the repatriation

[188]FO 371-48294 R17971, October 23, 1945. This document also reveals that the Soviets were trying to exert other forms of diplomatic pressure on the British. In a meeting with Sir Alexander Cadogan, Konstantin Kukin brought up the case of a former Soviet prisoner of war (last name given as Gurskii), who was allegedly murdered in Thessaloniki. The Soviet counsellor complained that the murderers, whom he believed to be Greek rightists, were not yet apprehended and that the Soviet ex-POW's funeral was attended by only two of his comrades. Several days later, the British consul in Thessaloniki reported that the Soviets were "completely misinformed" about the incident; Gurskii was actually murdered by three other Russian ex-prisoners of war with whom he had been drinking heavily: FO 371-48294 R18341, October 28, 1945.

[189]FO 371-58735 R11578, August 6, 1946. Karamanov also had contact with American officials while in Thessaloniki in July 1945. Army Major Spencer, who was in Macedonia on an informational tour for U.S. Headquarters in Cairo, reported that he ran into Karamanov "in a Salonica restaurant a few days ago. The following afternoon Karamano[v] . . . burst in on [Spencer's] siesta to inform him, in very bald terms, that the Macedonian autonomist movement was a 'reactionary' affair and received no official sponsoring from the Yugoslav and Bulgarian governments nor had it the approval of the Soviet" government: FO 371-58749 R11945, August 7, 1946. Because it was impossible for the Soviets not to be aware of Yugoslav enthusiasm on the question of Macedonia, Karamanov's action suggests the Soviets were concerned to impress the Americans with their disinterest in Macedonian affairs.

mission,[190] but their desire to avoid affronting an ally combined with Soviet diplomatic dexterity to defeat the lackluster British efforts to remove the mission. In late spring 1945, the British expressed to the Soviets their opinion that the work of the mission in Greece was finished, to which the Soviets responded that the mission could be dissolved only by Allied military authorities, since it was originally created under the headquarters of General Scobie. When the supreme Allied commander declared on July 7 that the work of the repatriation mission was completed, the Soviets temporized and continued to insist on the presence of significant numbers of Soviet nationals in Greece. The British continued through the summer to request the Soviets to leave, but compliance was not forthcoming. By autumn, the British had stopped providing facilities to the mission, but the Soviets appeared unperturbed. In fact, Ambassador Leeper concluded that cutting off facilities to the Soviets would accomplish little, as they were no doubt counting on Greek Communist support.[191]

Once the Soviets extended recognition to the Sofoulis government in November, it became impossible to remove the mission. In response to a direct request by the British government to remove the Soviet "repatriation" mission Konstantin A. Kukin, the Soviet counsellor at the embassy in London, replied that the Soviet government did not recognize such a request because Greece was a sovereign state and any requests should come directly from them. Kukin added for good measure that to accede to the British request would constitute interference in the internal affairs of Greece. Ultimately, the Soviets removed any possibility of further British protest by incorporating the mission's members into the embassy staff.[192] Thus the Soviet Union succeeded in retaining an official presence in Greece during 1945, which provided them with the means and opportunity of supervising KKE activities.

Other evidence indicates the Soviets were active in clandestine operations designed to oversee Zachariadis' efforts at reconstructing Greek

---

[190]In June 1945 the British Embassy in Athens argued that the Soviet repatriation mission had completed its task and concluded there was no reason it should remain in Greece. The British added: "Indeed, we should be glad to see the last of it": FO 371-48294 R11064, June 29, 1945.

[191]FO 371-48294 R18803, November 6, 1945.

[192]FO 371-58375 R1092, January 22, 1946; FO 371-59375 R2798, February 22, 1946. As of spring 1946, the diplomatic officers at the Soviet Embassy in Athens were Konstantin Rodionov, ambassador; Nikolai P. Chernichev, first secretary; Vladimir D. Karamanov, second secretary; Ivan Bourtsev, second secretary; Vasilii Rassuzhdaev, commercial representative; Avraam K. Muradov, attaché; Ivan G. Orlov, attaché; Petr F. Sokolov, attaché; and Mikhail I. Turalin, attaché.

Communist military forces. The relevant portions of an OSS document on this matter indicate the Soviets' method of operating:

> 2. A third and independent sub-source has informed source that fourteen Russians have been living in Salonika at the houses of . . . three Greeks for some weeks previous to 18th September. On this date four of these Russians left for Kilkis, two left for Kalamaria and four more went to Ekaterini [Katerini].
>
> 3. These Russians accompanied certain KKE officials who about 20th September were visiting various KKE offices in Macedonia. *The object of these visits was to check up on the activities of these offices since the visit of Zachariadis to Macedonia.* Each official had to present a progress report on the work done by the particular office he visited. This inspection tour, according to sub-source, was camouflaged as a visit of EAM political enlighteners to various towns on the pretext of arranging celebrations for the 4th anniversary of EAM.[193]

The Soviets evidently wanted to watch carefully the activities of Zachariadis and the impact of his policies on the local KKE elements. The timing of the Soviet "visits" also strongly suggests that the Russians were aware beforehand of KKE policy. Further evidence of covert Soviet activity in Greece came from the British Military Mission in Sofia, which reported that Russians in civilian clothing were operating with the Communists in northern Greece.[194] This information on Soviet operatives in Greece and their activities suggests that during the period from the Seventh KKE Congress in October 1945 and into the following year, there were emerging, in the presence of Soviet agents, both an attempt to reunify the political and military branches of the KKE *and* a set of organizations capable of undertaking subversive, paramilitary, and military operations.

Given this state of affairs, and taking account of the perception of a strong military base for action, the KKE proponents of immediate military action had a powerful and realistic argument in their favor. Furthermore, the creation of organizations such as the *aftoamina* led military leaders and certain Central Committee members to believe, unlike Zachariadis, that the party was now irrevocably committed to a military seizure of power. This helps explain why the Central Committee's consternation and frustration was so great when Zachariadis lobbied for a policy that appeared to correspond so little with the perceived objective strength and

[193]OSS XL29925, November 16, 1945; emphasis added. This apparently originated from British intelligence.
[194]FO 371-48718 R18233, December 19, 1946.

potential of the KKE and its organs. Perplexity at Zachariadis' position vanishes, however, when one considers that having as yet no decisive commitment from Stalin in favor of civil war (this was before his trip to Moscow in April 1946), he was compelled to urge restraint on his KKE comrades. This meant that the dual strategy was to continue, despite a strong domestic push for military action.

There simply were too few Soviets in Greece to provide more than information and oversight, meaning that the burden of restraining recalcitrant KKE members rested primarily on Zachariadis. This brings up the second question: how was the KKE general secretary able to enforce his own decisions in the presence of this powerful argument in opposition to the strategy of gradual evolution of the partisan struggle? The existence of a personality cult has already been mentioned, and Zachariadis' dominant personality was indeed important. The general secretary was also a skillful party politician, however, and he apparently used several ingenious methods of dissipating the force of the militant faction.

Most prominent was his technique of splitting the military and political aspects of strategy, a partition not restricted to argument alone. Most decisions at the Seventh Congress were political, military matters were taken up at a separate meeting of the Panhellenic Military Committee after the congress. This meeting was chaired by Zachariadis and Ioannidis, which allowed them to control the agenda. Similarly, the Second Plenum was divided into two meetings, the major one restricted to political matters, the later meeting on military planning. Here again, Zachariadis had to face the more militant members of the Central Committee. According to Bartziotas, the KKE general secretary argued that the time had indeed come for the historic decision to take up arms, although he declined to go into details at that time, declaring that he preferred to hear the opinion of all the members of the Central Committee first. After the close of the plenum, Zachariadis pledged, there would follow a military meeting that would put together the military plan of the armed struggle.[195]

This technique allowed Zachariadis to push through his own policy at the official meeting and then allow the military meeting to languish.

---

[195]Bartziotas, *Agonas tou Dimokratikou Stratou Elladas*, pp. 27–28. The meeting did take place, and it was interpreted differently by different persons. Bartziotas was disappointed, as was Blanas, whereas Gousias took the meeting to be the beginning of decisive planning for armed confrontation; see Vontitsos-Gousias, *Aities gia tis Ittes, ti Diaspasi* 1:133–34. Gousias is a bit confused, as he earlier stated the decision was for maneuvering with active defense to avoid provoking British armed intervention (p. 133), which follows Zachariadis' interpretation. Yet when Gousias returned to the Epirus Regional Office, plans were begun for a coup to take place on the eve of the elections.

Although the Panhellenic Military Committee had been created by the Seventh Congress specifically for detailing armed activity, this body met only twice, and no general plan of "development, organization, and leadership of armed struggle was discussed, or even existed."[196] The military meeting after the Second Plenum, chaired by Zachariadis, was similarly disappointing: it lasted barely one hour and did not even begin to elaborate a plan for action.[197] Zachariadis was thus able to avoid a serious confrontation within the Central Committee and continue pursuing his own policy, and the militant faction was left without a forum in which to air its views.

The general secretary was also aided by circumstances in part the result of the December uprising: the Party organs were dispersed throughout the country, and Zachariadis was only beginning to attempt a reimposition of central direction. To a certain extent, this state of affairs worked in his favor, because weak and decentralized organizations cannot easily implement a policy that requires extreme discipline. Blanas' comments on the structure of the Military Committee are instructive on this point. The ex-ELAS officer criticized the Military Committee because it was scattered throughout the country and its entire leadership revolved around Zachariadis.[198] If any party resolution for immediate armed action should have succeeded, it is difficult to see how it could have been implemented by party organs.

By using such favorable conditions in conjunction with his own tactics, Zachariadis hoped to achieve a compromise whereby his policies would continue to be adopted and the military activities could be put off for some time. The characterization of Zachariadis' decision at the Second Plenum as a compromise between military preparations and political action is therefore correct.[199] The explanation of why this occurred can be found by turning once again to the central hypothesis of the chapter. Stalin's desire for a policy of gradual political infiltration created serious divisions within the KKE because Soviet interests affected actors in an area where

[196]Blanas, pp. 74–75.
[197]Bartziotas, *Agonas tou Dimokratikou Stratou Elladas*, p. 31. See also Dimitris Vlantas in Woodhouse, *Struggle for Greece*, p. 178. When Bartziotas privately expressed to Zachariadis his belief that the policy of gradual development of the armed struggle was a mistake, Zachariadis replied vaguely that he would take Bartziotas' opinion into account and told him to "wait and see," the same advice that Partsalidis was supposedly given in Moscow: Bartziotas, p. 31.
[198]Blanas, p. 62.
[199]Woodhouse, *Struggle for Greece*, pp. 170ff. The phrase used in the text is taken from Smith, "Beginning of the Greek Civil War," p. 16.

Soviet control was lacking. The presence of Soviet representatives may have ensured a degree of oversight in Greece, but it was no substitute for the controlling influence the Red Army exerted in Eastern Europe. This absence of control meant that any conflict between policies or objectives could not be authoritatively resolved by Stalin. The result was less a policy than a bewildering succession of ambiguous decisions and actions that reflected an attempt to keep all possible options open. Hence, Zachariadis returned to Greece and attempted to pursue a policy heavily influenced by Soviet interests. When a divergence developed between Soviet and Greek Communist interests, the KKE general secretary was forced into delicate political maneuvering, as internal conditions were hostile to his policy.

The consequences of Zachariadis' handling of this potentially destructive division within the KKE were grave problems. In the first place, there was much confusion within the party about what KKE policy actually was during this time. Most military leaders in the KKE saw Zachariadis' efforts to develop the partisan struggle gradually as a product of doubts and wavering within the party leadership. This perception was reinforced by the fact that time was at a premium if there was to be an armed struggle. Second, the brief military meeting gave many in the Central Committee the correct impression that the KKE leadership was not seriously studying the question of military action.[200]

These impressions were reinforced by two other considerations. Zachariadis, despite his efforts, had still not succeeded in reestablishing central control. Party members, especially military leaders, remained out of touch with the Central Committee. They referred not to a central command but to their local situations for policy guidance. Party resolutions were therefore poorly defined and subject to a great deal of interpretation by local officials. In addition, the KKE leader had to deal with the Greek situation as well as the one within his party, and here too he was not complete master. Some of his directives, rather than addressing KKE exigencies, had to respond to the very real threat from the Greek Right. Several times there were clear indications that the rightists would attempt a coup.[201] Churchill's defeat helped to dampen the rightists' desire for a coup temporarily, but by winter the KKE had apparently received new information that a coup was once again being prepared, with the aim of reinstalling Admiral Voulgaris. The KKE had to order that a plan be drawn up as a counterweight. Blanas relates that a special meeting took place (he does not mention the date), in which the work of the KKE cells

[200]Blanas, p. 59.
[201]DSR 868.00/7-1745, no. 1333.

in the army was detailed and their connections with the *aftoamina* cells were established.[202]

The combination of using strategy as a political maneuver and the real need to defend the Communist organs created a picture of confusion and hesitancy: decisions were made only to be ignored; serious plans were considered at various points only to be dropped when immediate danger appeared to have passed. Zachariadis' political successes were thus marred by the appearance of hesitancy and incompetence in military preparations. Although Zachariadis succeeded in persuading the Central Committee to adopt his policy, KKE military leaders were understandably gaining the impression that the Politburo was squandering precious time in applying a militant line. This perception provided the basis for the most serious problem of all: military leaders, still largely out of touch with the Communist center and faced with ambiguous policy statements that were open to interpretation, began to take the initiative into their own hands.

In this instance, the KKE military, immediately after the Second Plenum in February 1946, began planning for a coup, making use of regular KKE detachments, *aftoamina* units, and cells within the army. In March and April the detachments of *andartes* (guerrillas) *"had already been determined* in the mountains of Thessaly."[203] All other units were in readiness as well, probably a result of planning for the expected coup from the Right. A more specific example of how KKE military leaders chose to interpret the decisions of the Second Plenum in the light of their own arguments and take matters into their own hands is provided by Votsikas:

> Immediately after the convocation of the Second Plenum of the . . . [KKE], there was held a meeting of the *ipefthinoi* [political officers of the KKE charged with overseeing activities within the unit for which they were responsible] of the *aftoamina* for Epirus. Also taking part at the meeting were Michalis Tsantis, secretary of the Epirus Regional Office, and several permanent officers who were serving in the 8th Division of the government army in Epirus. The report was given by Giorgos Vontitsos [later a lieutenant-general and military administrator in the DSE], second secretary of the Epirus Regional Office and secretary of the *aftoamina* in Epirus who said, among other things, that it had been decided at the Second Plenum to make an armed revolt on March 31, 1946 [the date scheduled for the Greek elections].[204]

---

[202]Blanas, pp. 57–58. For a good discussion of the KKE preparations for a coup, and the argument that these were primarily defensive in nature, see Smith, "Self-Defence and Communist Policy 1945–1947," esp. pp. 167–68.

[203]Blanas, p. 51; emphasis added.

[204]Votsikas, p. 83.

Votsikas' record of the meeting is striking in two respects. The meeting's rapporteur, Vontitsos-Gousias, had interpreted the resolution of the Second Plenum to mean that a revolt had been decided upon, which was not the case. The military leaders evidently took the resolution and interpreted it in the light most favorable to them; for there is no mention here of a "gradual" development of the armed struggle. The presence of officers from the government army attests to the fact that the KKE was in earnest when it spoke of cells within the Greek army.

All was in readiness, and the Second Plenum was being viewed as a decision for the seizure of power. Votsikas also leaves little doubt that this seizure was to be in the form of a coup, rather than a civil war: "We had to act with great expertise, so that we could seize power in a few hours." Blanas also indicates that a rapid move was what had been planned: "In the event [our organs in the army] were not able to move first, we could still gain the upper hand. We could, within 2–3 days of publication of the relevant order, use the *aftoamina* in cities and towns."[205]

Plans for the coup included the transformation of the *aftoamina* and the extensive employment of cadres within the government army: "The meeting also organized the *aftoamina* into military groups. . . . Concrete missions were also determined. The military groups which came from the *aftoamina* were given orders to attack the commands, assistant commands, sections, and stations of the Rural Police [*chorofilakis*] on the morning of the revolt. . . . An order was also given to take all measures so that it would not be possible for the officers, on the morning of the 31st of March, to go to their formations." The cadres in the military also had specific instructions, and the officers expressed their confidence to the meeting that "in all of the regiments of the division the leftist forces could prevail already within the first day of the revolt, because in all of the military groups in Epirus there were strong, active party organizations. The overwhelming majority of soldiers were members of the party, EAMites, EPONites."[206]

Preparations for the coup were carried out in extreme secrecy and lasted more than one month. Some days before the elections, a second meeting was held, "which confirmed that the preparations were going well." But these elaborate plans came to nothing, because "on the eve of the elections . . . it was announced that the revolt was postponed indefinitely." Unfortunately, the person responsible for issuing the order postponing the

---

[205]Ibid.; Blanas, p. 58.
[206]Votsikas, pp. 84, 83.

coup was not mentioned, and there is not even enough information available to suggest a possible candidate. Zachariadis had left for Prague after the Second Plenum and was apparently not privy to the secret coup preparations. He was still out of the country (on his way to Moscow) when the orders canceling the coup came through on the night before the Greek elections. The intriguing question of who suppressed the coup must therefore remain unanswered. The decision left the military deeply embittered; for they were confident of the coup's success: it "would have begun simultaneously from one end of Greece to the other."[207] The suppression of the coup preserved, for the time being, the opportunistic orientation of Soviet interests in Greece, but the damage to the future prospects of Greek Communist policy was immense.

The evidence presented so far clearly indicates that Stalin pursued a course of action that sought to minimize the possibilities of strategic conflict, expand the political bases of Soviet influence, and preserve local Communist military forces for a future opportunity. Events such as the attempt to distinguish between British and American policies, Stalin's telegram to EAM in May 1945, and the change in Soviet attitude after the British Labour victory in August 1945, all support the contention that the Soviets were proceeding slowly and gradually, while paying primary attention to the uncertain international context after Hitler's defeat. In addition, the existence of other pressing Soviet interests in the postwar world made sense of Stalin's advice to the Greek Communists to expand political activities while developing military forces only in reserve. The principal weakness in this policy was that to succeed it required a minimal degree of stability and control in the domestic environment. As internal conditions deteriorated, Soviet actions came to be viewed with increasing hostility by the Western Allies, provoking precisely the kind of result Stalin wished to avoid. Had domestic stability been achieved, the strategy of political gradualism would certainly have had greater prospects for success, but the Soviets could do little as their preferences for political activity and cautious military development became increasingly irrelevant in the chaotic Greek context.

This period was also especially important in revealing the variety of instruments Stalin employed in his attempt to achieve policy success. Direct oversight and intelligence gathering were carried out by Red Army officers and agents operating in Greece, as the Soviets sought to maximize

---

[207]Ibid., p. 84.

their room to maneuver. At the same time, the KKE performed a double function by serving as a political vanguard while simultaneously preparing the ground for future military actions. Foreign Minister Sofianopoulos is an excellent example of the use the Soviets made of politicans whose sympathies or political futures rested on increasing Soviet influence in Greece. Finally, the attempt by Stalin and Molotov at the Potsdam Conference to make the Varkiza Agreement the basis for Great Power action in Greece illustrates how the Soviets used diplomatic contacts among major powers to provide the basis for a future role in Greece without threatening their absolute control of the Eastern bloc states.

Soviet policy is of primary concern, but the narrative illuminates as well the impact of Soviet interests on the actions of the Greek Communists. Of critical importance is the conflict created by Soviet attention to strategic factors even though the majority of KKE leaders were impelled by the local situation. Because local KKE leaders were not under the control of Stalin (nor were they ever fully under the control of Zachariadis during this crucial period), they eventually began to opt for solutions that favored their own interests at the expense of Soviet ones. This dilemma for the KKE and its subsequent management, combined with the realization that the Greek Communists required military force to survive in the deteriorating political climate, helps explain the bewildering and ambiguous decisions reached by the KKE at its Second Plenum in early 1946, as well as the inability to act decisively at the optimal moment.

For the second time in as many years, the KKE, by abstaining from the elections, had failed to follow Soviet instructions. More important, however, for the second time in two years, the Greek Communists had adhered to a pro-Soviet line long enough to seriously, if not fatally, damage their own chances for power. The turn toward militancy and civil war had to be dealt with anew, despite the fact that it was taking place in a confused and halting manner. Stalin soon found that he was following events rather than leading them.

4

FROM DUALISM TO DEFEAT, 1946–1949: THE SOVIET IMPACT ON THE THIRD ROUND OF THE CIVIL WAR

In his seminal work on Lenin's contribution to Marxist thought, Alfred Meyer argued that Lenin had grasped the necessity of adapting the general principles of Marxism to local and temporary conditions.[1] Henceforth, the indispensable prerequisite to successful action in a specific context (the sine qua non of a true Marxist-Leninist) was a proper evaluation of the "objective correlation of forces." Ironically, the third major shift of Soviet policy during the Greek Civil War may be viewed as emanating from Stalin's *failure* to employ this cardinal principle correctly. The Soviet dictator continued to pay primary attention to international strategic considerations, even as developments came to be dominated by Greek domestic pressures and Balkan regional interests. Under attack from government and rightist forces, the KKE was increasingly inclined toward the immediate employment of its military resources. This inclination received the strong support of the Yugoslavs, who now became actively involved in the development of the civil war. The growing independence of Tito, however, threatened Soviet interests; for the success of Yugoslav and Greek Communist efforts would mean the eclipse of Soviet influence throughout the Balkans. Consequently, the Soviets first tried to restrain the growing insurgency; that failing, they progressively involved themselves in the civil war, lest Tito take over policymaking in the peninsula.

[1] Alfred G. Meyer, *Leninism* (Cambridge: Harvard University Press, 1957), pp. 12–14.

The enunciation of the Truman Doctrine made this change in Soviet policy easier by removing a key Soviet strategic concern a civil war in the Balkans would have precipitated.

Stalin had to modify the dual strategy of legal activity combined with defensive military preparation as the KKE chose to rely increasingly on its army. The crucial point, however, is that Stalin provided aid not because he intended to allow the KKE to become victorious but to avoid the appearance of following Tito's lead. As the civil war dragged on, the USSR promised the Greek Communists aid but provided it so slowly as to significantly disrupt KKE plans. Greek Communist leaders felt compelled to accept this Soviet parsimony because, although grateful for Yugoslav assistance, they remained suspicious of Yugoslav political and territorial ambitions. By controlling the tempo of events, the Soviets contributed to the defeat of the KKE. While the failure of the insurgency fit in with Stalin's regional efforts to contain Tito, the Soviets continued throughout the war to advance diplomatic initiatives in an apparent effort to achieve a compromise solution that would preserve at least some Communist assets in Greece.[2]

Background: Yugoslavia, Macedonia, and the KKE

The connections between the Balkan states and the Macedonian question have a long and complicated history that defies a quick summary; nevertheless, some background is necessary if subsequent arguments are to be comprehensible. Generally, Macedonia during World War II took on more aspects of an independent entity because there was little effective state control during the German occupation. The "independent" position of Macedonia did not, however, prevent other actors from having interests in this territory in the heart of the Balkans. Yugoslavia stood to gain great territorial advantage if it should succeed in incorporating this area, which stretched to the Aegean Sea. The Greek Communists were equally interested in retaining Aegean Macedonia to maintain support within Greece.

The difficulty was that Yugoslav Communists succeeded in establishing themselves in power, thereby leaving the KKE in a delicate position: Yugoslavia was the logical place for the KKE to turn for material support,

[2]Vasil Kondis also reaches the same conclusion about Soviet objectives in the closing stages of the civil war; see *I Angloamerikaniki Politiki kai to Elliniko Provlima, 1945–1949* (Thessaloniki: Paratiritis, 1984), p. 385.

but to maintain its independent political existence the KKE needed to exercise extreme care on the Macedonia issue. Because the KKE had its most important base of strength in the province of Macedonia, it had to accommodate to local forces. An OSS report documents the complexity of the situation and the resulting tensions as far back as 1943: "Throughout 1943 great confusion reigned in KKE policy in Macedonia. The Communist Party of Macedonia was at loggerheads with the Macedonian political office of the KKE. This meant that, (a) The Slav Macedonians on the Greek side of the border acted more or less independently of Central control and, (b) the Yugoslav Partisans, whose sole means of communication with the Greeks was via Macedonia, held the poorest opinion of the KKE." Also contained in the document were the opinions of "Rennos" (most likely Andreas Tzimas), the KKE representative sent by the Athens office to straighten out relations with the Macedonians. He confided that the KKE completely ignored the rise of Macedonian opinion under Yugoslav auspices. Rennos also commented that the KKE had first founded SNOF (the Slavo-Macedonian National Liberation Front), then disbanded it because it proved impossible to organize along party lines,[3] which irritated Macedonians and further worsened relations between the Yugoslav Partisans and the KKE.

In addition, Svetozar Vukmanović-Tempo, Tito's representative in Macedonia, was initiating actions that would provide more ground for suspicion. In June 1943, Tempo organized a meeting of Yugoslav Partisans, Albanian Communists, and representatives of ELAS at Tsotylio in Macedonia (approximately fifteen miles south of Kastoria), at which he proposed the formation of a joint command for the Balkan resistance movements. As Tempo's aspirations for the incorporation of Aegean Macedonia into Yugoslavia were widely known, the ELAS representatives were suspicious and the plan was not well received. Ultimately, the Greek Communists rejected it on the grounds that ELAS was under command of British General Headquarters in Cairo,[4] although Tempo's outspoken

[3]OSS L53686, February 8, 1945. Also noteworthy in this document is the reference to the existence in Greece of Russians: "A telegram from General Sarafis to Tito, dated 12th April, 1944, states that the Allied Military Mission to Greece has informed him that Great Britain and the U.S.S.R. have concluded an agreement for the transfer to the Middle East of all Russian ex-German P.O.W.[s] now serving with ELAS, and that the British had already transported some. He asks Tito for confirmation that the agreement exists. A letter believed to be from Siantos to Despotopoulos (undated) states that the writer has been informed that the Soviet government have concluded no such agreement. An order must therefore be circulated to inform all Russians still in Greece that they can refuse to go."

[4]Christopher M. Woodhouse, The Struggle for Greece, 1941–1949 (London: Hart-Davis, MacGibbon, 1976), pp. 45–46.

views on the need for an independent Macedonian resistance movement were obviously the real reason.

The creation of SNOF by ELAS also reflected the Greek Communists' discomfort with the attitude of the Yugoslavs. Although a joint Balkan command was not accepted, the Greeks did accede to Tempo's request to form slavophone units within ELAS, and it was these units that became the basis for SNOF. ELAS leaders made sure, however, to fill these units with Bulgarophone recruits.[5] They also attempted to pick a man to lead these units who was reliable, that is, not in favor of autonomy. Much to the dismay of the Greek Communists, the man chosen for the job, Ilias Dimakis (Gotsi), turned out to be a wholehearted autonomist, and ELAS was forced to suppress the SNOF units.[6] Gotsi and some of his forces escaped and fled into Yugoslavia, where they were welcomed. Although Tito appears initially to have been unwilling to sanction any further action on Macedonia's behalf against the Greeks, the legacy of tension remained. Both British and American intelligence sources confirm that the KKE was very sensitive about this question: "ELAS do not want an ind[e]pendent Macedonia and as far as this goes are strongly nationalist. To this end they adopt their usual propaganda met[h]ods . . . . ELAS have Tito's assurance that his ind[e]-pendent Macedonia does not include Greek Macedonia."[7]

During the period of the second round in Athens, it appears that KKE concern over the status of Macedonia flared up once again. In a series of telegrams captured by British intelligence and later forwarded to American officials, it was evident that the formation of the Anti-Fascist Assembly of National Liberation of Macedonia (ASNOM) evoked serious concern about Tito's intentions. Indeed, from the text of the telegrams, the anxiety was apparently warranted; the transformation of ASNOM into a "government" for Macedonia could easily follow:

[5]OSS L53541, February 10, 1945.
[6]Woodhouse, *Struggle for Greece*, pp. 49–50. Further evidence of tensions between SNOF and ELAS is in British ambassador Leeper's report to the Foreign Office on the interrogation of deserters from the Gotsi regiment. According to these men, who had crossed over into Greece from Yugoslavia on April 10, 1945, it was believed that Gotsi had quarreled with ELAS, though none of them knew the precise reason. Significantly, the deserters told their interrogators that they belonged to the Yugoslav Partisan Army: 371-48183 R8242, May 12, 1945. The Slavo-Macedonian version of the question of Aegean Macedonia during the Greek Civil War has recently been presented in Risto Kirjazovski, *Narodnoosloboditelniot Front i drugite organizatsii na makedontsite od ege-jska makedonija, 1945–1949* (Skopje: Kultura, 1985).
[7]OSS XL817, June 24, 1944. Later in 1944, Captain P. H. Evans, the British Liaison Officer stationed in Florina, also reported that the KKE did not have good relations with the Macedonians. Evans commented that the ELAS regiments had Greek officers and Macedonian recruits, a situation that fostered little trust: FO 371-43649 R22039, December 30, 1944.

From Macedonia to KKE Hq. No. 17 for IOANNIDES from LEONIDAS
5.9.44 [September 5, 1944]

. . . In connection with the attitude of the Anti-Fascist Conference on the
Liberation of Yugoslavia . . . held by Marshal TITO and the Anti-Fascist
[Council for the] National Liberation of Macedonia . . . the Supreme Com-
mand of Macedonia has sent a representative to negotiate with the Supreme
Command of Greece and take decisions regarding the Macedonian question
in Greece.

As if this unilateral "invitation" to discuss the future of a part of Greek
territory were not enough, the ensuing telegram (in the order presented by
British intelligence) became even more ominous:

No. 18 From Macedonia (Cont.)

If you fail to send a representative in time the Supreme Command of
Macedonia will take steps to make the position of Marshal TITO's ABNOG
[AVNOJ] and of TSNOM (?) [ASNOM] a "fait accompli." Friendly greet-
ings—Death to Fascism—liberty for the people.[8]

These political developments were followed by even more threatening
military developments one month later. Apparently, Tito's actions had
boosted the morale of the Macedonians in Greece to such asn extent that
the KKE had a difficult time controlling and guiding policy:

From GHQ ELAS. No. 10090 21.10.44. To SIANTOS and MANTAKAS.

Group of Macedonian Divisions reports. Division of Slavo-Macedonians of
the 28th Regiment 900 strong refused to obey order to move to SIATISTIS
area [approximately twelve miles west of Kozani]. This division carried out
compulsory mobilization with "independent Macedonia" as its motto.

In the following weeks, the situation only worsened, as this sample of
telegrams indicates:

From H.Q. Macedonia. To GHEROS [Siantos] from LEONIDAS [Stringos]
10.11.44. [November 10, 1944]

Detachment of 160 autonomists GOTSE [GOTSI] entered KRYSTAL-
OPIGHI [located twelve miles northwest of Kozani on the Albanian fron-
tier] 6 inst. [?] Emblem red star and hammer and sickle. Day before yester-
day another unit was at HALARA. Slavo-Macedonian residents received
them with joy. It is said that a Yugoslav officer accompanies GOTSE.

[8]DSR 868.00/1-2245, no. 427. See the introductory note on transliteration and documentation for information on how the documents have been presented.

From H.W. Macedonia. 75/ a & b for IOANNIDES from LEONIDAS
4.11.44. [November 4, 1944]

Battalion of Slav-speaking GOTSE troops attempted to enter Greek territory coming from HAGIA PARASKEVE, north of FLORINA. They tried to take FLORINA, but after an engagement of two hours withdrew to HAGIA PARASKEVE . . . four political (commissars?) accompany GOTSE. TEMPO made following declaration to our representative: *"I am very much afraid that the KKE together with the British will find themselves up against New Yugoslavia [and] the Soviet Union.* Detachments which arrived will be armed by us and sent south; if ELAS tried to prevent this they will defend themselves. If you attack then we will send assistance." In Serbian Macedonia people shouted at our representatives "Death (to them)—hang them!" They disarmed and denuded Slavo-Macedonians who deserted to us. . . . Situation always critical. Disturbance of our relations with Yugoslavia will damage our cause.[9]

Concern over Macedonian autonomist sentiments obviously had a negative impact on KKE relations with the Yugoslav Partisans. It is even conceivable that ELAS felt compelled to divert forces to that area during the height of the fighting in Athens in December 1944, in order to forestall an uprising by the Macedonians. If true, this forced deployment would be of enormous significance; for ELAS forces stationed in Macedonia could otherwise have considerably strengthened the Communist forces then engaged in the second round in Athens. In any event, the elimination of Gotsi became a necessity for KKE policy.

The situation remained tense after the December fighting, but Tito was not ready to exploit the Macedonian question for the moment, given the resolve that Churchill demonstrated in defeating the Greek Communists. Two points were clarified, however. First, it was obvious that Tito could, when he felt that conditions permitted such a policy, make use of the strongly pro-Yugoslav sentiment in northern Greece in an attempt to realize the goal of a greater Yugoslavia. Such a policy would be especially appealing if the Greek Communists were forced to depend upon the Yugoslavs. Second, it was evident that if the KKE was to preserve its influence in Macedonia, it had to mollify the Slavic element—a fact not lost on Western intelligence sources, which concluded: "EAM's policy towards Slavo-Macedonians [might have been] only local in scope and . . . based merely on expediency, since the Slavo-Macedonians constitute[d] the majority of the population in the Florina area."[10]

[9]Ibid; emphasis in original.
[10]OSS L53758, February 24, 1945.

From the final phases of the war to the period of the Greek elections (March 31, 1946), events moved to confront the KKE with a serious dilemma. The dual strategy could not withstand the increasingly terroristic and unrestrained behavior of rightist political forces, illegal and legal. The KKE's greater dependence on the military aspect of the dual strategy and the Soviets' reluctance to endorse such a course of action during the winter of 1944–45 naturally meant that Yugoslavia was the only place to turn for material assistance. A long border between the two countries also favored this arrangement. As this KKE dependence increased and the situation in the northern regions of Greece continued unsettled, Tito must have seen an opportunity to extend his influence. Hence, during 1945 and into 1946, the level of invective directed at the Greek government by Yugoslavia for alleged persecution of Macedonians continued to rise. Typical was Tito's speech in Belgrade on August 8, 1945, in which he deplored the "fascist terror" reigning in Greek Macedonia and alluded to a number of alleged border incidents caused by the Greek government. Immediately after this speech there was a great increase in western Macedonia in the activity of armed bands, most of which had come across the border from Yugoslavia.[11] Tito had begun to act upon the temptation to capitalize on Greece's disorders in Macedonia, at the expense of the KKE.

The dilemma then faced by the KKE was that the resort to arms meant it relied upon Yugoslav support for its physical existence; yet this very reliance threatened its credibility in Greece as well as its independent political existence. One can thus view the KKE leadership, Zachariadis in particular, in the same manner as previously: as a rational actor under constraints. The KKE general secretary was fully aware that events in Greece necessitated the ready availability of some coercive apparatus should negotiations fail. As he inclined in this direction, however, Zachariadis was constrained by Stalin's unwillingness to allow an immediate resort to force. But Yugoslavia threatened to overshadow the KKE in Greece unless the Greek Communists developed some independent power base. Zachariadis could only depend upon Yugoslavia for immediate physical survival while he simultaneously looked to Moscow for long-range political survival.

The means Zachariadis used in his attempt to solve this dilemma was to continue the dual strategy but at the same time use the Soviet lack of control in Greece to confront Soviet officials with KKE *faits accomplis*. From this standpoint, the differences between Yugoslavia and the Soviet

[11]DSR 868.4016/8-2845, no. 1453.

Union were beneficial for the Greek Communists. As long as Tito was independent and Stalin tolerated him, Stalin would be forced to follow the Yugoslav's much more active lead in Balkan policy. Should the split between Stalin and Tito become unmanageable, however, it would fatally endanger KKE policy. To characterize the differences between Tito and Stalin as *inherently* detrimental to the KKE is therefore incorrect. So long as differences persisted, yet remained within the bounds of "fraternal relations," the KKE could hope to benefit from the situation.[12]

It is not unreasonable in fact to conclude that much that happened in the postwar Balkans can be explained by the triangular Stalin-Tito-Zacharia-dis relationship. While Zachariadis sought to exploit Yugoslav-Soviet differences to his own advantage, Stalin may in turn have made use of the KKE leader's suspicion of Tito's ambitions in Macedonia to restrain Greek Communist policy.[13] But the Soviet leader's ability to manipulate the anxieties and animosities of political elites to his own advantage was compromised by his lack of control over the Balkans. While it might be possible to exploit the sensitive position of the KKE to affect its behavior, not so the Yugoslav Communists, which made Tito the focus of Soviet anxiety.

Relations between Yugoslavia and the Soviet Union carried with them an undercurrent of tension, and the key meetings between the two countries, as recounted by those present, were never marked by cordiality.[14] The independence Tito had achieved by virtue of the success of his Partisans, and the Soviets' inability to penetrate the Yugoslav leadership, must have been particularly vexing for Stalin. But still more serious was the potential influence Tito might wield throughout the Balkans. In Albania, the pro-Yugoslav faction of the leadership under Koçi Xoxe was ascendant until late 1947; plans for a union between Yugoslavia and Albania were not only being considered but in certain instances put into effect.[15] Also in 1947, a delicate rapprochement between Tito and Bulgaria's Dimitrov heightened Stalin's concern. After the Bled Conference

[12]To illustrate the point, had Tito been completely subservient to Stalin, the Soviets, wanting no expansion of aggressive activities, would only have had to order Yugoslavia to shut down the Greek rebellion, and it would have been done.

[13]I am indebted to Ole L. Smith for suggesting this possible hypothesis, which I consider in more detail later.

[14]See, in particular, Milovan Djilas, *Conversations with Stalin,* trans. Michael Petrovich (New York: Harcourt, Brace & World, 1962); Vladimir Dedijer, *Tito* (1953; reprint, New York: Arno, 1972).

[15]William E. Griffith, *Albania and the Sino-Soviet Rift* (Cambridge: MIT Press, 1963), pp. 18–21.

in August 1947, Dimitrov went so far as to say that it was possible for Bulgaria to pass to socialism by its own path, without the dictatorship of the proletariat.[16] Finally, in Greece, the KKE moved progressively toward civil war, thereby increasing its dependence on its Yugoslav patrons. Thus, quite apart from the question of Yugoslav independence, there were serious prospects that Stalin would lose political control throughout the Balkans.

Moreover, Tito's aggressive activities threatened to upset Stalin's strategic plans for the Mediterranean region. Stalin faced a dilemma not unlike that of the KKE; he needed to wrest political control of the Balkans from Tito without destroying the loyalty of Albanian and Greek Communists to the Soviet Union. Stalin succeeded in extricating himself from his dilemma by acting on several fronts. In Bulgaria, the Soviet dictator successfully regained control over Dimitrov and the Bulgarian Communist organization, effectively eliminating the dangerous possibility of any federative arrangements in the Balkans under Yugoslav auspices. In Albania, the logical attraction of the Soviet Union as the protector of Albanian integrity against possible Yugoslav encroachment provided a powerful argument in the Soviets' favor. Soviet success there hinged on the ability to excise carefully the pro-Yugoslav elements. In Greece, the Communists' appeal to Greek national interests was a strong card but not sufficient to meet the Soviet strategic aim of removing and (later) minimizing Western presence in the Mediterranean. Stalin needed a means of providing support to the KKE yet retarding the development of civil war. The most promising means in 1946 appeared to be encouraging Zachariadis to pursue the dual strategy while simultaneously acting to restrain the pace at which its military component evolved.

1946: Soviet Efforts to Preserve KKE Dualism

The KKE abstention from the 1946 elections enabled the Greek Right to shut the Left completely out of the political process. The Right now claimed undisputed political control and proceeded to purge state apparatuses of suspected Communists. The "white terror," which had been unleashed after the December 1944 second round, was seen as vindicated, and parastate groups increased their activities against the Greek Left. These moves against the Left culminated in the passage of the "emergen-

[16]*Rizospastis,* August 23, 1947.

cy measures" act that provided the Greek government with broad powers to arrest, detain, and punish (by death) those pursuing autonomist activity or leading armed bands. Finally, there apparently was dissension within the KKE and between the KKE and EAM which made effective policy formulation and implementation difficult.[17] So, in the months after the elections, Communist policy focused on legal activity and produced rapidly diminishing returns while armed bands arose of their own accord in the mountains of Greece.[18]

By mid-summer, however, the dual strategy reappeared once again. In July, *Rizospastis,* the KKE newspaper, began what turned into a steady stream of demands, proposals, and plans for "reconciliation" (*symfiliosis*).[19] In one article, Zachariadis presented not merely the KKE conception of reconciliation but a broader statement of overall Communist policy:

> as life in Greece goes ahead to this plebiscite [on the restoration of the monarchy], it concentrates around two poles; that of Reconciliation, whose banner is Republic and means work, rehabilitation, order, concord, freedom, and national independence and the other [pole] of Civil War which is organized and already practiced by British and monarchofascists under the banner of a monarchofascist dictatorship under King George[. The latter] means prevalence of the quisling spirit, mutual slaughter hunger and people's ruin, mopping up operations, deportations and selling out of Greece to foreigners.[20]

Interpreting this stark contrast between reconciliation and civil war, one can see the shadowy outlines of Soviet interests: reconciliation must take place in a context where there is no Western power present. Reconciliation, therefore, as conceived by the KKE, could not take place in the presence of Western powers. The policy of reconciliation implied that

[17]Ole L. Smith, "A Turning Point in the Greek Civil War 1945–1949," *Scandinavian Studies in Modern Greek,* no. 3 (1979), 37; DSR 868.00/4-2546, no. 2561; Hagen Fleischer, "The 'Third Factor': The Struggle for an Independent Socialist Policy during the Greek Civil War," in *Studies in the History of the Greek Civil War, 1945–1949,* ed. Lars Baerentzen, John O. Iatrides, and Ole L. Smith (Copenhagen: Museum Tusculanum Press, 1987), pp. 189–212; idem, "EAM 1941–1947: An Approach for Reconsideration" (paper presented at the Lehrman Institute Conference on the "Third Round" of the Greek Civil War, 1945–1949, Copenhagen, June 1987).

[18]Giorgis Vontitsos-Gousias, *Oi Aities gia tis Ittes, ti Diaspasi tou KKE kai tis Ellinikis Aristeras* (Athens: Na Iperetoume to Lao, 1977), 1:144–45.

[19]This was a constant theme in the Greek Communist press; for a typical example, see *Rizospastis,* July 13, 1946.

[20]This translation is found in DSR 868.00/7-2446, no. 2945.

while the KKE had clearly not abandoned the legal pathway, political activity constituted part of a broader strategy that included the use of force.

July was also a portentous month for the other side of KKE policy. Sometime in the first half of the month, Zachariadis met with Markos Vafeiadis (who would become military commander of the DSE in the near future) and gave him orders for the creation of an armed force. Markos was to leave his post in the Macedonian party organization and proceed into the mountains to begin organizing what was to become the Democratic Army of Greece. A closer examination of his orders reveals how well they reflect Zachariadis' continued interest in retaining the legal aspect of his policy and avoiding the impression that the KKE had determined on civil war. According to Markos, the orders were as follows:

1) With the committee of the PB [Politburo] to study in all aspects existing resources and to act accordingly, taking as a basis the armed groups which had already formed.

2) The numerical increase [of KKE strength] is to be achieved on an entirely voluntary basis.

3) Organized sectors of the army who want to desert to [the KKE] are not to be accepted—only isolated individuals.

4) The activity [of the KKE] should be confined to attacks on armed reactionaries only and engagements with military formations should be avoided.

5) It was confirmed that [the KKE] continues to remain in a position of reconciliation and peaceful solution of [the] internal problem and that all of [the party's] work aims at this objective.[21]

These are not orders that would be given to officers if a military course of action had been irrevocably chosen. Instead, they reflect Zachariadis' interest in building an armed force while leaving his options open and presenting the development of armed resistance as a natural outgrowth of an unnatural internal situation. Only in this context do the orders make sense.

Of course Zachariadis was perceptive enough to realize that hoping for success solely from this "limited mobilization" would be naive. Eventually the Greek government would react to the growing Communist forces, and a civil war would ensue. To make the Communist military force more credible would require other arrangements, and it is here that the Yugoslavs assumed critical importance. According to Zachariadis, he had made agree-

---

[21]In Smith, "Turning Point," p. 38.

ments with Yugoslav leaders (probably in March or April on the return leg of his journey to Prague and Moscow) for 20,000 former members of ELAS to be organized and armed by Tito's government.[22] Zachariadis, as has been pointed out over the last forty years, may be a biased source; probably he subsequently alleged that such a mobilization was to have taken place in order to preserve himself from criticism. But while there is disagreement about the numbers to be mobilized, there appears to be general consensus among KKE leaders that the target figure for mobilization was in the vicinity of 50,000–60,000.[23] Furthermore, Blanas cites figures of 10,000 and 18,000 as targets for recruitment by the Yugoslavs.[24] Hence the possibility of Yugoslavia's playing a greater role in the internal Greek crisis was substantially enhanced by KKE plans for recruitment. The agreements apparently had some immediate impact; within several months, particulàrly in July, evidence of foreign assistance to the armed groups working in Greece became unmistakable.[25]

It is difficult to determine the Soviet response. On an official level, they began a press campaign directed at demonstrating that the Greek elections were largely falsified in the interests of the extreme right.[26] The campaign also included attempts to cast doubt on the conclusions of the Allied Mission for Observing the Greek Elections (AMFOGE), which in mid-April had presented its report, arguing that the elections were essentially free

---

[22]Ibid., p. 40. "Limited mobilization" is Smith's term, and it aptly reflects the effort to mobilize KKE military forces stopping short of full commitment to civil war. See also the relevant portion of Zachariadis' speech at the Seventh Plenum of the KKE Central Committee (February 1957), in Panos Dimitriou, ed., *I Diaspasi tou KKE* (Athens: Themelio, 1978), 1:95.

[23]Vontitsos-Gousias, *Aities gia tis Ittes, ti Diasposi* 1:154. Markos asserts that the numbers could be as high as 60,000–70,000; Dimitris Gousidis, ed., *Markos Vafeiadis: Martyries* (Athens: Epikairotita, 1983), p. 18 (hereafter *Vafeiadis*). Markos Vafeiadis is at this writing working on the fourth and crucial volume of his memoirs.

[24]Giorgis Blanas, *Emfilios Polemos, 1946–1949: Opos ta Ezisa* (Athens: n.p., 1976), pp. 95–96. Gerasimos Maltezos echoes Blanas' estimates but fails to provide any new evidence; see Maltezos, *DSE: Dimokratikos Stratos Elladas* (Athens: n.p., 1984), pp. 33–34. An interesting and unresolved aspect of Greek-Yugoslav relations appears in Blanas, who recounts how Zachariadis gave the order to Markos to raise weapons for an army of 18,000, a number not inconsistent with what the KKE general secretary requested of the Soviets in autumn of 1946. According to Blanas, Markos alleged he was forced to change the level of weapons to only 4,000–5,000 men at the insistence of Ioannidis, with whom the DSE chief met in Belgrade. Blanas suspects that Ioannidis was acting on the initiative of the Yugoslavs (pp. 94–95). More than likely, Ioannidis had little more to give Markos at that time, a conclusion strengthened by the fact that in September the KKE had to direct its appeal to the Soviets.

[25]Stephen G. Xydis, *Greece and the Great Powers, 1944–47* (Thessaloniki: Institute for Balkan Studies, 1963), pp. 254–55.

[26]See, for example, DSR 868.00/4-846, no. 1095; DSR 868.00/4-1246, no. 1167.

and fair. *Pravda* responded to the AMFOGE report on April 14 by using AMFOGE statistics to conclude that only 42.6 percent of registered voters actually voted. Otherwise, there appeared to be little public Soviet activity in the months immediately after the elections.

Privately, however, Stalin endeavored to keep the KKE on its dualist strategy. Although when Zachariadis met with him after the elections, the Soviet leader reportedly endorsed Zachariadis' plans for the gradual development of an armed struggle, Stalin cautioned that military force be used as a means of finding a political compromise rather than as a prelude to a wider insurgency. Stalin did not, however, wish to go into the details of supporting the gradual military build-up and allegedly advised Zachariadis to take them up with Tito before returning to Greece.[27] If true, this raises an important question: if Stalin was suspicious of Tito's intentions, why did he instruct Zachariadis to arrange matters with the Yugoslav leader? Unfortunately, there is no evidence on this point, but several interpretations are possible.

Conceivably, Stalin may not yet have been aware of the danger that Tito represented to his postwar aims in the Balkans. By mid-1946, however, it would be difficult to argue that Stalin could still be ignorant of Tito's activities. Furthermore, the Soviets had agents in northern Greece able to provide information on relations among the Balkan Communist parties. A second possibility is that Stalin gave Zachariadis this advice because he believed it would have a restraining effect on the KKE. The Soviets were obviously aware of the tension in the KKE-Yugoslav relationship as well as Zachariadis' anxiety about excessive dependence on Tito for support. Stalin probably calculated that the advice to turn to Tito would compel the KKE leader to be circumspect in his demands.[28] If this second interpretation is true, then the Soviet leader overestimated the extent to which this tactic would restrain Zachariadis; for by the end of the year, the Soviets were compelled to find another means of dampening the development of the civil war.

In the closing months of 1946, correspondences among the KKE, Tito, and Dimitrov, combined with diplomatic activity, indicated that Soviet policy in Greece had changed in one significant respect. Now, instead of

---

[27]Lefteris P. Eleftheriou, *Synomilies me ton Niko Zachariadi* (Athens: Kentavros, 1986), pp. 34–35. Eleftheriou implies that Stalin gave this advice at his first meeting with Zachariadis, when both Zhdanov and Molotov were present; when Zachariadis met privately with Stalin (according to Eleftheriou's account), there is no evidence that the same advice was reiterated.

[28]Ole L. Smith suggested this possibility to me in a personal communication, May 31, 1986.

encouraging the KKE to continue in its dual strategy, the Soviets intentionally attempted to hold back the development of armed resistance in Greece while maintaining diplomatic pressure on the Greek and British governments. Zachariadis persisted in the dual policy, but the momentum toward civil war could no longer be reversed, as activity now greatly increased in northern Greece. Since the prospect of a force of fifty-to-sixty thousand men required more weapons than the KKE could provide, appeals to other Communist powers were necessary. The two most logical candidates were Yugoslavia and the Soviet Union.

It appears that Zachariadis first tried the direct approach of simply requesting greater assistance; Politburo members Ioannidis and Rousos went with a set of KKE proposals to Belgrade and then on to Moscow.[29] This was the beginning of a months-long process of transferring the key members of the KKE Politburo from Greece to Belgrade, which culminated in Zachariadis' arrival in Yugoslavia in early April 1947.[30] In September 1946, however, only Ioannidis and Rousos had as yet set up residence in Belgrade. They brought with them a report, "The Situation in Greece and the Urgent Problems of Our Movement," that summarized the condition of the insurgent activities and offered a set of proposals for Soviet response.

The proposals continued Zachariadis' commitment to a dual strategy: (1) that Greece be declared a neutral power under the guarantee of the Great Powers; (2) that, because many weapons concealed after the Varkiza Agreement had been lost, the Soviets should provide material assistance to increase the number of armed *andartes* to fifteen-to-twenty thousand; and (3) that the KKE, as well as EAM and cooperating parties, should receive financial assistance. Soviet help was also requested in disseminating propaganda about the Greek "struggle" and in creating a radio station.[31] The report was delivered to Dimitrov in Bulgaria on September 12, and while there, the KKE delegates inquired as to the Bulgarian leader's opinion of the "neutralization" proposal. Dimitrov's

[29]In December 1979 the Greek Communist (Interior) newspaper, *Avgi,* ran a series of excerpts from the archives of the KKE, edited by Filippos Iliou. Although the material contains a great many gaps, there is still enough information there to make fascinating reading. Since the series was numbered and continued through January 1980, each time the archives are cited, the citation bears the name of the paper, the number in the series, and the date. Unless otherwise noted, the citations refer to the actual archival material and not editorial comment. This citation is therefore: *Avgi,* no. 1, December 2, 1979.

[30]*Avgi,* no. 6, December 8, 1979.

[31]*Avgi,* no. 4, December 6, 1979. The complete text of the KKE's report to the CPSU is contained in *Avgi* nos. 2, 3, 4; December 4–6, 1979.

reply came some five weeks later, when on November 10, Ioannidis informed Zachariadis, "On the subject of neutrality Pappou [Dimitrov] agrees and asked if we received the opinion of the above [the Soviets] via other means. Telegraph us immediately."[32]

The Soviet response was longer in coming, but one event indicated that when it did arrive, it would not be favorable to KKE interests. In the beginning of October, Ioannidis received word from the Soviets that his trip to Moscow was canceled. Instead, a special envoy would be sent to pick up the KKE's report, and Ioannidis would have the opportunity to brief him orally.[33] Once the report had been collected and the CPSU presumably had time to study the proposals, it gave its answer. The decision, transmitted through Dimitrov, was disappointing to the KKE leadership. It was summarized in a telegram from Ioannidis to Zachariadis:

> Niko
> We met [with] Pappou [Dimitrov] Sofia.
> He stressed the following as his opinion and of the above [Soviet Union].
> FIRST: The period of winter and the international situation dictate that extensive measures in the armed struggle not be taken.
> SECOND: The central effort should be the mass popular political struggle and also the maintenance of the most minimal legal means, consequently you should maintain the connection of the party with the masses.
> THIRD: We should carefully preserve the party cadres and not expose them to the dangers of their annihilation.
> We stressed that the party line corresponds to suggestions. . .
> 10/11/46 [November 10, 1946] Dionysis [Ioannidis][34]

The Soviets thus continued to insist the KKE stick to its policy of dualism. The only point left unclear was the neutrality of Greece. Ten days later, on November 20, it was Zachariadis' turn to inform Ioannidis on Soviet opinion. In a message about the neutralization proposal,

[32]*Avgi*, no. 1, December 2, 1979.

[33]*Avgi*, no. 2, December 4, 1979. There is some evidence to indicate that the envoy might actually have been Dimitrov himself. The British Embassy in Moscow informed the Foreign Office it had been "credibly informed" that on October 21, 1946, Dimitrov was in Moscow: FO 371-59525 R15517, October 23, 1946.

[34]*Avgi*, no. 1, December 2, 1979. An excerpt from the U.S. ambassador's report to the State Department supports the conclusion that the KKE request was refused: "Significantly, nothing is said of rumors (which conservative persons here all desire to believe) to the effect that Soviet orders for the cessation of outside support of the bandit movement in Greece have caused consternation in local communist ranks. (The King told me [MacVeagh] the other day that he has heard that Mr. Zachariades is practically hysterial over being thus let down by Moscow)": DSR 868.00B/1-2847, no. 3579.

Zachariadis noted, "The answer [from the Soviets] was the opposite [negative]." Not content with this reply, Ioannidis asked the Bulgarians on November 21 to obtain a more definitive reply: "Relative to the problem which was considered regarding the neutralization of Greece, under the guarantee of the Great Powers, comrade Zach[ariadis] informed us that he received from M[oscow] the opposite reply [i.e., the reply was the opposite of Dimitrov's]. Having our discussion with c[omrade] Pappou [Dimitrov] in mind, we invite you to inquire once again in behalf of Pappou, the opinion of the comrades from M[oscow] and to inform us." Despite this request, the matter seems to have been ignored by the Soviets; for on December 31, Zachariadis telegraphed from Athens, "We still have not received a reply regarding neutralization."[35]

By the end of 1946, then, the KKE found itself in a difficult position as regards the Soviet Union. Greek Communist proposals had met complete rejection, which now appears to have been a Soviet mistake, given the rising unrest in Greece and the American aid that was soon to materialize. The neutralization scheme, essentially an extension of Zachariadis' two-poles theory, sought to achieve neutralization within the context of the dual policy to which the KKE was committed. Without Soviet diplomatic intervention, success in legal activity seemed impossible. Stalin's refusal to support this plan and his reluctance to support the growing insurgency drove the KKE to rely increasingly on its military force and the good graces of the Yugoslavs.

Soviet diplomacy in 1946 is especially useful in the way it reveals a dramatic reorientation of Stalin's objectives in Greece. Through the autumn, the Soviet leader apparently felt comfortable in his efforts to pressure the British to leave Greece and in his ability to control the development of the KKE's dual strategy. In August, Manuil'skii, Ukrainian delegate to the United Nations, renewed the verbal offensive against Greece and Britain in the Security Council. His speeches, which received the strong support of Russian representative Andrei Gromyko, reflected the three key areas of Soviet interest.[36]

First, the "Ukrainian complaint" was timed to highlight the instability in Greece at the precise moment (September 1) a plebiscite was scheduled on the return of the Greek monarchy. The Ukrainian representative used

---

[35]*Avgi*, no. 1, December 2, 1979. Gousias maintains the Soviets considered Zachariadis' stand on neutrality to be "erroneous"; Vontitsos-Gousias, *Aities gia tis Ittes, ti Diaspasi* 1:134.

[36]This discussion of Soviet behavior at the United Nations is taken largely from Xydis, pp. 335–46, 349–55.

the U.N. debate to impugn the legitimacy of the plebiscite. To emphasize Soviet displeasure, and possibly undermine confidence in the feeble Greek government, Ambassador Rodionov left Athens on "official business" immediately before the vote and did not return until late February 1947. Soviet concern for the integrity of Albania was a second prominent feature in the analyses of the Soviet delegates. In fact, Albania, and not Yugoslavia or Bulgaria, received the lion's share of the Soviets' attention, on the grounds that it was the central objective of Greek ruling circles. Third, as in the earlier Security Council debates in February 1946, the British military presence came under attack. The substance and timing of the Ukrainian complaint suggest that the deterioration within Greece since January was not inconsistent with Soviet interests, for it gave them the chance to gain propaganda advantage at the expense of the West while simultaneously increasing diplomatic pressure. This was underscored by Gromyko's veto on September 20 of the American representative's proposal to establish a commission to investigate incidents on the Greek border.[37] At that time, there was no apparent benefit from direct involvement in Greece that outweighed the propaganda victories the Soviets could score by publicly blaming the Western powers for the disaster that had befallen Greece.

Yet by the end of the year, developments in the Security Council reflected that the Soviets' assessment of the Balkan situation had shifted significantly, indicating that Stalin had overestimated his capacity to control and channel instability in Greece in a direction favorable to Soviet interests. On December 19, in what appeared in the West as a surprising volte face, Gromyko accepted the American proposal to form the Commission of Investigation Concerning Greek Frontier Incidents. Given relations among the Communist Balkan states, the Soviet Union, and the KKE in recent months, this action clearly represented, as some have argued,[38] a Soviet attempt to put a brake on the Greek insurgency and the independent activities of the Yugoslavs. Not only did this Soviet decision

[37]Xydis, pp. 117, 643 n, points out that the notion of creating such an investigative body has a fairly lengthy history. In July 1945 the United States proposed to the Yugoslav government the appointment of an international commission to investigate border incidents and the status of Slav-speaking elements in the region of Macedonia. With the Potsdam Conference underway at the time, it would have been possible to bring this matter up, but neither the Yugoslavs nor the Soviets warmed to the idea. The pattern of proposals and rejections makes the Soviet acceptance in December 1946 all the more surprising. Woodhouse also mentions the earlier American proposal; see his *Struggle for Greece*, p. 157.

[38]Lawrence S. Wittner, *American Intervention in Greece, 1943–1949* (New York: Columbia University Press, 1982), p. 59.

(the instructions were given to the Soviet U.N. delegation by Molotov) place Yugoslavia in an exposed position; it would quite obviously have a detrimental effect on any supply programs for the Greek Communists.[39]

Soviet assent to the Commission of Investigation meant a realization of the insufficiency of their efforts to manage policy in the Balkans at a distance. The situation was serious enough that, in an action nearly unique in postwar history,[40] the Soviet Union consented to an international inquiry on Eastern-bloc soil. Although as early as March 1946, the KKE's dual strategy had begun to degenerate into civil war, despite Zachariadis' professions of a balanced policy, the Soviet shift in their U.N. stand implies that it was only in December that Stalin realized his inability to control the evolution of policy.

In retrospect, other evidence suggests that Stalin underestimated the speed at which events were unfolding in the Balkans. It seems incredible that Stalin would have accepted plans to raise a Greek Communist army of fifty thousand, as Zachariadis apparently suggested in his meeting with Tito in April 1946. Whatever the KKE general secretary might have believed was still within the limits of a dual policy, an army of such proportions clearly was not, since it could not fail to serve as proof of the KKE's aggressive intentions. The crucial point is that this figure was discussed between Zachariadis and *Tito,* on the former's *return* from Moscow; there is as yet no evidence to indicate that Stalin was aware of such high figures in early 1946. But since in November he vetoed KKE plans to increase partisan strength to a mere twenty thousand, Stalin would surely have opposed a figure as high as fifty thousand. Quite possibly, this information only reached Stalin by the end of the year, impressing upon him the need to act to contain the armed struggle and the militant Yugoslavs. In that case, Soviet representation on the Commission of Investigation could serve a useful function by transmitting directly to the Greek Communists the Soviet interest in restraining the growth of the insurgency.

But the Greek Communists did not have the luxury of procrastination. Zachariadis' proposals for military assistance meant an expansion of KKE military strength was essential, if not with Soviet aid, then with aid from

[39]Ibid.
[40]In 1987 the Soviet Union permitted Western military officials to observe Warsaw Pact exercises. The Balkan Commission of Investigation, however, still represents the only instance in which Soviet, Albanian, Yugoslav, and Bulgarian consent was obtained for an international body to conduct investigations within these countries.

elsewhere. Indeed, given the KKE estimates of the fighting force they desired, events had to move quickly. Once civil war seemed inevitable, the Communists could logically assume that their adversaries would move as rapidly as possible to defeat them. Consequently, the creation of the DSE had to proceed apace, but its ability to recruit men and provide adequate arms lagged behind. The first task was to establish control over the armed groups scattered throughout the country. By late summer, according to Giorgis Vontitsos-Gousias, groups of seventy-to-one hundred men were formed and armed with light weaponry. On October 28, the DSE General Staff was created, then the regional commands in western and central Macedonia, Thessaly, Epirus, and Roumeli.[41]

Given the rapid development of the DSE (except in number of recruits), it must have been disconcerting when the KKE's appeals fell on deaf ears. The Yugoslav welcome was quite different, as was evident from the reception the Yugoslavs accorded Ioannidis and Rousos on their arrival in Belgrade:

[August 30, 1946]

. . . We arrived in Belgrade on August 25, we presented the objective for which we came and found complete understanding and comradely hospitality.

On the 28th we arrived in Sofia for the presentation to Pappou [Dimitrov]. . . . Unfortunately Pappou was absent. We telegraphed him but have not as yet received a reply.

We returned today [to] Belgrade . . .

Dionysis [Ioannidis][42]

Two other telegrams reveal the contrast in KKE attitude toward the Bulgarian and Yugoslav Communists, most likely reflective of a growing division between Yugoslavia and the Soviet Union:

10.2.47. [February 10, 1947] . . .

Dear C[omrade] Dimitrov

We thank you and the C[entral] C[ommittee] of the party for the aid which you gave us in reply to the appeal of our Central Committee.

With C[omradely] g[reetings]

In the name of the CC of the KKE

(Iannis Ioannidis)

[41]Vontitsos-Gousias, *Aities gia tis Ittes, ti Diaspasi* 1:153.
[42]*Avgi*, no. 2, December 4, 1979.

[February 10, 1947] . . .

Dear C[omrade] Tito

We consider it our imperative duty to thank you heartwarmingly as well as all of the C[entral] C[ommittee] for the serious help which you gave us in reply to the last appeal of our Central Committee, as well as all of the aid which the fraternal Yugoslav party gave us.

This help arrived at a moment of new intense struggle of the Greek people for independence and democracy and strengthened still further the bonds between the peoples of Yugoslavia and Greece.

In the name of the CC of the KKE

. . . . [omission in original text][43]

The rough draft of this telegram (according to Filippos Iliou), has one more phrase the KKE representatives had erased: ". . . strengthens still further the bonds between the peoples of Yugoslavia and Greece, which is a condition for the full deliverance of the Balkan peoples from the yoke of imperialism and the strengthening of Popular Democracy in all the Balkans."[44]

Thus, while relations were good between the KKE and Tito, there appeared to be some concern that the KKE might be too easily perceived as a subordinate. This view is further strengthened by a report that indicates Zachariadis had agreed to the formation of a Macedonian "state" at the spring 1946 meeting of Communist party leaders in Prague but then reneged on the agreement and notified his Communist partners that he was opposed to the cession of Greek territory.[45]

The impression that emerges is that the KKE, by virtue of Soviet opposition, was forced into increasing reliance on Tito in order to pursue a more militant policy. This relationship had the effect of increasing divisions between the Yugoslavs and the Bulgarians and, by implication, the Soviets. As armed activity continued to increase, the stage was set for the developments of the coming year: Zachariadis would have to extract Soviet support, and the Soviets would have to find a means of containing the rebellion in Greece and the dangerous growth of Yugoslav influence and initiative in the Balkans.

[43]*Avgi*, no. 5, December 7, 1979.
[44]Ibid.
[45]DSR 868.01/12-3047, no. 1697.

1947: The End of Dualism—Soviet Consent to Aid the Greek Communists

In his continuous efforts to obtain aid from other Communist states, principally the Soviet Union, Zachariadis must have been forced to conclude that merely requesting aid simply did not suffice. Early in 1947 he apparently adopted a different approach, which ultimately proved much more successful. Sometime in February the KKE leadership altered its dual policy: henceforth, primary emphasis was to be placed on the military struggle. This is a crucial change, yet there is no information presently available with which to determine whether the decision was taken on Greek Communist initiative or as an accommodation to Soviet wishes. A message of Zachariadis' to Stalin on May 13, 1947, establishes that such a change in policy had taken place: "The Politburo of the Central Committee of the Communist Party of Greece in its conference in February 1947, after examining the situation, arrived at the conclusion that the democratic movement, continuing the full exploitation of all legal means, must consider that the armed struggle has become dominant, and in this regard has taken a series of practical measures."[46] Precisely what those "practical measures" were is not known, but Iliou is probably correct when he argues that in February and March there was a KKE consensus for a large increase in military aid, a conclusion he bases on the following telegram from Ioannidis to Markos on April 2, 1947:

Num[ber] 32

Marko[s]
    Telegraph to me urgently needed quantities of different weapons and war materials which are needed for all of the army.
    . . . [Designate] quantities which must be surrendered at each point. . .
    I invite your thoughts [on the various points discussed in the preceding paragraph]; send me [a list of] places which can become landings and drop-off points. These places will become reserve for time of need.
    2)4)47   Dionysis [Ioannidis][47]

These new orientations of the KKE took on added significance immediately preceding Zachariadis' arrival in Belgrade.[48] On April 17, five days

[46]Avgi, no. 7, December 9, 1979; no. 11, December 14, 1979.
[47]Avgi, no. 7, December 9, 1979.
[48]Although the KKE had clearly oriented itself toward civil war, the decision was not made official until the Third Plenum in September, perhaps because Zachariadis had to

before meeting with Tito and more than one month before meeting with Stalin, the Greek Communist general secretary gave a set of orders to the DSE commander which, in effect, oriented the DSE toward civil war. In his "absolutely confidential" orders to Markos, Zachariadis charged him with preparing a plan of action for the DSE with its primary goal the liberation of a region of Greece with its center at Thessaloniki. To achieve this goal, Zachariadis argued, the DSE was to be transformed into a regular army in the liberated areas of Greece, while guerrilla groups could operate in "occupied" areas.[49]

For some reason, Zachariadis continued to cling to a policy of "popular unity and reconciliation," although that objective no longer appeared a dominant part of his strategy.[50] Quite possibly it was the result of Zachariadis' persistent desire to leave his options open, or it could have been a consequence of his accommodating Soviet interests. Whatever the reasons for his position, Zachariadis had created the basis for presenting a fait accompli when discussions of assistance arose: the DSE was under orders to plan the seizure of northern Greece, and the military struggle had become dominant. Starting an insurgency was no longer the issue, Zachariadis could claim, because one was already underway. As in the abstention from the Greek elections a year earlier, Stalin would face a set of circumstances in which the only reasonable path was that desired by the KKE general secretary; and to buttress his case, Zachariadis could point to the crescendo of rightist terror that had left "progressive" forces in Greece with no choice.

These issues Zachariadis discussed in a subsequent meeting with Tito on April 21, from which emerged two further points worthy of mention. First, Zachariadis expressed an interest in developing a strong military presence in the cities,[51] evidence that clandestine and military methods

---

guarantee a steady flow of material assistance, something he mistakenly thought he had achieved only in August. Zachariadis sent his April 17 telegram to Markos after he had already arrived in Belgrade. On March 31 he had sent his last telegram from Greek soil, and on April 6 he had illegally crossed the frontier into Yugoslavia. That same day Ioannidis telegraphed Markos that "Koukos [Zachariadis] arrived today": *Avgi*, no. 6, December 8, 1979.

[49]*Avgi*, no. 8, December 11, 1979.

[50]Ibid. On January 19, EAM, the KKE political front, issued a well-publicized appeal for cessation of hostilities between the DSE and the Greek National Army. This appeal was quite definitely tied to Soviet policy; for it coincided with the arrival in Greece of the Balkan Commission of Investigation, but the British also speculated that it was timed to take advantage of a cabinet crisis in the Tsaldaris government. The British thought the peace offer would improve the position of Themistoklis Sofoulis and possibly split Konstantinos Tsaldaris' Populist party: FO 371-66997 R858, January 21, 1947.

[51]*Avgi*, no. 7, December 9, 1979.

had now become dominant, since the bulk of KKE activity in the cities would thus have to be illegal. Second, although the KKE received substantial material aid from Yugoslavia, and Tito apparently encouraged Zachariadis' new plans, there was no mention of the recruits supposedly being gathered in Yugoslavia for future action in Greece. Given that April was a pivotal month for the development of KKE policy and that Zachariadis must have discussed the relevant aspects of Yugoslav assistance with Tito at this time, it is odd that no mention of the mobilization of recruits appears. Earler evidence indicated that Zachariadis had gained Yugoslav consent for using Yugoslavia as a source of recruitment; yet in April, Zachariadis informed Tito of DSE needs without recalling earlier assumptions about the recruitment project.[52] The puzzle is, assuming Zachariadis' account of the recruitment agreement is accurate, why he did not review it with Tito in the spring? This potential manpower problem, because of its critical importance to the success of KKE plans, might have inclined Zachariadis to decrease his reliance on Yugoslavia. This problem notwithstanding, Zachariadis next traveled to Moscow in May for discussions with Stalin.

Although no actual records of the meeting with Stalin have come to light, there are sufficient indications that these talks resulted in an outcome that conformed to the new KKE policy orientation. Immediately after Zachariadis' meeting with Stalin (he was apparently still in Moscow at the time), the Soviets asked the KKE to send them a statement of the outstanding DSE armaments needs (this was transmitted on May 24). A June 4 telegram from Ioannidis in Belgrade to those Politburo members still in Athens confirmed a positive outcome of the talks: "These last few weeks Koukos [Zachariadis] met with grandfather [Stalin] where our matters were effectively discussed. From the results of these meetings we must be completely satisfied."[53] Finally, KKE policy in the months after the Moscow meetings suggested that Stalin had consented to KKE plans.

In retrospect, Stalin had little choice but to consent unless he was willing to risk losing his influence on the KKE to Tito. Zachariadis came to Moscow in 1947 with his hands effectively tied: "monarchofascist" terror forced the KKE to make use of the DSE; this became the mainstay of its policy, though legal activity was not abandoned; insurgent activities were being planned in the cities; and all of this had been transmitted to the head of the DSE in the form of an order. Stalin must have realized it was now out of the question to speak of preventing a civil war. To suggest

[52]Ibid.
[53]*Avgi*, no. 9, December 12, 1979.

folding up the insurgency at such a point would have meant handing the initiative to Tito. The best Stalin could do was to try to control the tempo at which KKE policy unfolded, hoping thereby to restore a situation in the Balkans conducive to Soviet objectives.

A final point about the change in Soviet attitude deserves mention. It is conceivable that by the closing months of 1946 Stalin was aware of the increasing likelihood of U.S. intervention in Greece. By the beginning of 1947, however, it must have been clear to him that the possibilities of preventing Western involvement in the eastern Mediterranean had vanished. The Soviet leader may nevertheless have thought it conceivable that, at the very least, Western influence could be minimized and a token Communist presence retained in Greece, a result obviously only possible through negotiations. Thus, while the eventual enunciation of the Truman Doctrine freed Stalin from his constraint with respect to Yugoslav activity, it did not completely eliminate the utility of diplomatic efforts. The diplomatic route also held an advantage for the Soviets in that only they, and not the Yugoslavs, could effectively negotiate with the West.

What remains unclear is whether the manipulation of policy to KKE advantage is something Zachariadis consciously strove to achieve or whether he was unwittingly the beneficiary of favorable circumstances. The KKE leader was certainly sensitive to the problems posed by excessive dependence upon the Yugoslavs, but there is little evidence to indicate that at this time he was privy to information that would allow him to gauge the extent of discord between Stalin and Tito. There were, however, good reasons for seeking out Soviet assistance. Besides the greater political flexibility two sources would provide, the KKE needed more material assistance than Yugoslavia could give. The reserves of the Soviet Union must have been a strong lure to an army in search of weapons. Another reason was that several arrangements with the Yugoslavs were apparently not working out well, chief among them, the training of men. While there were certainly training camps in Yugoslav territory, they failed to meet the optimistic expectation of twenty thousand men. Several sources have reported that Boulkes, the main camp for Greek Communist military recruitment, was incapable of producing trained soldiers in substantial numbers.[54] Finally, Zachariadis may have known, as in the ab-

[54]Dominique Eudes, *The Kapetanios: Partisans and Civil War in Greece, 1943-1949* (New York: Monthly Review Press, 1972), pp. 250-51, 288-89; Vontitsos-Gousias, *Aities gia tis Ittes, ti Diaspasi* 2:58-64; DSR 868.00/11-245, no. 148; FO 371-67133 R61244, September 30, 1947; Kenneth Matthews, *Memories of a Mountain War: Greece, 1944-1949* (London: Longmans, Green, 1972), pp. 140-43. The most interesting source is the Department of State document that is an account of a *Newsweek* journalist's trip to the camp; DSR 868.00/11-245, no. 148.

stention from the Greek elections a year earlier, that he could exploit Stalin's limited control over the Balkans, particularly in 1947, when Stalin was concerned that too much control be given to Tito, yet still not in a position to neutralize the Yugoslav leader.

Hence, the strong inclination of the KKE to obtain Soviet support combined with the inability of the Soviet leadership to undo a rebellion without risking a loss of political influence in the Balkans to make Soviet support to Greece inevitable. Miltiadis Porfyrogenis' announcement at the French Communist Party Congress in Strasbourg on June 27 that the KKE planned to create a "free" Greek state thus came as a surprise only to observers in the West. Not only did the Soviets have foreknowledge of the new policy, but KKE archives also indicate that Porfyrogenis went to the Soviet Union before attending the French Communist party's congress.[55] The Soviets were thus well informed (and the KKE saw to it that the CPSU remained informed) of all Greek Communist activities.

Stalin therefore acquiesced to policy over which he had little control. If this disturbed him, then the fact that the key members of the KKE Politburo resided in Belgrade must have disconcerted him even more because it underscored the considerable advantage Tito held in accessibility. But this acquiescence did not mean the Soviets were powerless to affect events. While they consented to the content of KKE policy and its new orientation, powerful factors gave them significant control over the pace of policy implementation.

Strategic factors were now less important than the problem of Yugoslavia, so the unsettled situation in Greece lent itself to propaganda advantage. As the Soviet Union consolidated its control over Eastern Europe, the world's attention was diverted to conditions in Greece. The Soviets could thus gain from allowing the Greek Civil War to play itself out slowly for maximum propaganda value. The KKE, with its dependence upon Soviet support, could only urge the Soviets to make good on their promises as rapidly as possible. The effectiveness of a fighting force is determined not by how many men are in the army but by how many are actually *under arms;*[56] the size and rate of growth of Greek guerrilla forces depended directly upon the amount of weapons available. It simply would do no good to have an army of unarmed soldiers arrayed against forces supplied by the United States. Gousias, who had several times complained about the lack of arms, also made the point that the DSE could

[55]*Avgi*, no. 12, December 15, 1979.
[56]Wittner, p. 255, mentions that American officials believed there to be a deliberate manpower ceiling created through the shortage of arms; this would be in keeping with Soviet policy and greatly complicate matters for the KKE.

not continue to rely on captured weapons as the source of arms. The massive levels of recruitment that would make the DSE a serious challenge to the National Army required an equally massive and constant source of weaponry. Furthermore, the DSE relied on its mobility, which would be greatly reduced (as Gousias confirms), were it forced to move columns of unarmed men over great distances.[57]

Two other points underscored the seriousness of the arms problem. Although immediately after the Varkiza Agreement the KKE had hidden a large quantity of weapons, and several ELAS and DSE officials have argued that these caches could have been used in an armed uprising, the proponents of this option have also acknowledged that by mid-1946, the time for using these caches had passed because many of the weapons had either been discovered by the Greek government forces or were in disrepair. The change in government support from Britain to the United States also had an impact. According to Gousias, the National Army's change from British to American equipment rendered useless that part of the DSE's arsenal that came from captured British weapons.[58] The only solution was a source of weapons and ammunition that did not depend upon enemy forces, and here the Soviets could exert control. It was only in August, six months after the KKE had resolved to pursue a military option and three months after Stalin gave his consent, that Ioannidis and Zachariadis reported their material needs were satisfied; and that assessment they soon realized was premature, as the trickle of material assistance failed to increase in accord with KKE plans.

In the meantime, the slowness with which the aid arrived created the impression that the KKE was going about things in an illogical manner. The decision for a military policy was based on conditions in Greece as of February 1947 (some KKE Central Committee members have argued, not without reason, that the KKE's assessment of the military situation was actually based on estimates as old as February 1946), and the KKE announced its intention of striving to liberate northern Greece and create a separate state before it had made sure that its cadres were not in an exposed position. In effect, Greek Communist policy decisions forewarned the Greek government of its actions and left its organizations exposed. Consequently, on July 9 and 10, the Greek government carried

---

[57]Vontitsos-Gousias, *Aities gia tis Ittes, ti Diaspasi* 1:170, 192, 253.
[58]Ibid. p. 506. Zachariadis wrote a letter to "comrade Baranov" in the CPSU in which he requested English arms and ammunition for English weapons: *Avgi*, no. 33, January 13, 1980.

out mass arrests, gathering in suspected Communist sympathizers and depriving the KKE and DSE of much-needed manpower.

While there continues to be much debate about failure to recruit sufficient cadres,[59] it seems a major cause was this inability to secure munitions support in time. Instead of first securing a force and then bargaining from strength, the KKE leadership succumbed to pressure from the Greek government and declared its policy while it still awaited supplies. Once the supplies did arrive, initiatives could be taken more quickly, but by then the Greek government had made significant headway in depriving the KKE of its source of recruits.

In a letter from Ioannidis to Markos on August 7, there appears the first indication that the KKE had finally begun to receive its long-awaited support from external sources. Markos was informed that the KKE Politburo agreed "there should be a mobilization everywhere. The only problem is how you [Markos] will be supplied with arms. [The KKE] naturally has at its disposal great quantities of material which, however, you are not able to receive. With the material that [the KKE has, it] is possible to more than completely double the strength of the DSE."[60] Further indication that some form of Soviet assistance had finally arrived came in Zachariadis' September 1 letter to Zhdanov, in which he informed the Soviet Politburo member, "We have received the materials and we thank you very much." The KKE had also received financial support from the Soviets. Zachariadis noted: "You would assist us very much if you sent us the same amount of money [that] I received when I was with you [in Moscow]."[61] At last, with financial and material assistance beginning to materialize, the KKE was apparently in a position to move forward in a credible fashion.

[59]This is a subject on which former DSE officers and KKE officials have produced a voluminous literature; see Blanas; Vasilis Bartziotas, *O Agonas tou Dimokratikou Stratou Elladas*, 2d ed. (Athens: Sygchroni Epochi, 1982); Vontitsos-Gousias, *Aities gia tis Ittes, ti Diaspasi; Vafeiadis*. Many more have their own arguments about the failure to recruit cadres and reserves.

[60]*Avgi*, no. 20, December 25, 1979. Ioannidis obviously must have had the material at his immediate disposal; for he also felt confident enough to send Markos another telegram requesting that he take the time to designate some landing strips, presumably to serve as drop-off points: *Avgi*, no. 22, December 29, 1979. See FO 371-72342 R4191, April 2, 1948, for evidence that the KKE had established an improvised landing field at Prespa. Vontitsos-Gousias (*Aities gia tis Ittes, ti Diaspasi* 1:206, 209), confirms that in August he received a telegram from DSE headquarters inquiring how long it would take him to construct a landing strip for dropping off supplies.

[61]*Avgi*, no. 23, December 30, 1979. Zachariadis is here referring to his May 1947 meeting with Soviet leaders.

This optimistic assessment of the new situation was echoed by Zachariadis five days later in a letter to Tito. Zachariadis assured the Yugoslav
leader the required supplies had been secured and the only difficulty was
its transport. The KKE leader was in fact optimistic enough to add:
"Without exaggeration, we can say that [the] prospects for the forthcoming winter and the spring of 1948 are positive."[62] The Politburo (or more
precisely, Second Subcommittee of the Politburo, which consisted of
those KKE Politburo members residing in Belgrade) thus assumed it could
sanction its policy officially at the Third Plenum of the KKE Central
Committee in September. But Zachariadis' optimism proved premature,
for the DSE now found itself forced to act on a policy that corresponded to
conditions that had existed more than six months earlier, and this despite
serious deficiencies in personnel.

Thus did the twin objectives of restraining the expansion of the Greek
Civil War and preventing the ascendance of Yugoslavia in Balkan affairs
dominate Soviet-KKE relations. The Soviet diplomatic record also reveals
these same concerns. First, the Soviets sought more direct intervention in
Greece in order to hamper efforts to widen the insurgency, the principal
means being the U.N. Commission of Investigation, which, by exposing
Greece to international scrutiny, would make supplying the Greek Communist forces difficult. A second thrust of Soviet policy from 1946 to
1949 was in presenting diplomatic initiatives aimed at a negotiated solution to the civil war. This was a reasonable tactic because, if successful, it
would prevent the Yugoslavs from playing a larger role than the Soviets.
Furthermore, negotiations had the added advantage of thrusting the Soviet
Union into the spotlight, at the expense of the Yugoslavs. Stalin could
then capitalize on a successful agreement to enhance his position relative
to both the West and Tito.

Third, there was the Soviet campaign to exploit the difficulties in
Greece for propaganda. (Previous analyses have stressed propaganda as
the primary or sole purpose of Soviet policy, completely neglecting the
importance of the Yugoslav factor.) Throughout 1947 the Soviet delegation in the United Nations provided as much exposure as possible to the
negative aspects of Western involvement and the benefits of Soviet proposals. Gromyko, Manuil'skii, and Vyshinskii stood up in turn to denounce the presence of foreign troops and warn of the threat Greece posed
to world peace. On occasion, there would be interesting variations, all
geared to give the DSE maximum press exposure. In the latter part of

[62]*Avgi,* no. 20, December 25, 1979.

September, for example, Vyshinskii told a group of reporters at the United Nations that the DSE should be invited to the deliberations in the General Assembly, since it was an "interested party."[63]

The propaganda drive was a constant throughout the entire period, but the most prominent diplomatic developments of 1947 surrounded the U.N. Commission of Investigation. The commission (also known as the Commission of Inquiry) arrived in Athens on January 20 and began work by the end of the month. The Soviet delegation, headed by A. A. Lavrishchev and assisted by the Polish delegation, focused its energies on promoting the Albanian, Yugoslav, and Bulgarian liaison officers at the expense of the Greek representative.[64] In addition, the Soviets used their presence in Greece to champion the cause of EAM, something on which the KKE was quick to capitalize. On January 19, one day before the commission's arrival and in the middle of a cabinet crisis in the Greek government, EAM published its latest truce offer, proposing the suspension of war operations between the DSE and the Greek National Army for the period of the commission's work in Greece.[65]

Contact with the Greek Communists through the commission was undoubtedly useful in transmitting Soviet opinion of KKE strategy. Although the content of the contacts is still unknown, Soviet Andrei Graur had the occasion for a long private discussion with Tzimas, and the entire delegation warmly received Bakirtzis.[66] On March 20, Soviet and Polish delegates remained behind in the mountains to meet with Markos, even though the main commission group, after several days' search for the guerrilla leader, had abandoned its efforts. Because a complete delegation

[63]*Rizospastis*, September 27, 1947.

[64]According to FO 371-66997 R937, January 22, 1947, the Soviet delegation was composed of A. A. Lavrishchev, representative; S. M. Beliaev, Andrei G. Graur, and S. M. Kudriavtsev, advisors; G. B. Kasparov, I. P. Shapovalov, and S. M. Tisbizov, experts; and N. F. Paisov, Secretary.

[65]United Nations Archives (hereafter UNA), DAG 13/4.0.0., Box 6, February 8, 1947; see also FO 371-66997 R858, January 21, 1947.

[66]FO 371-67073 R3457, March 14, 1947. Xydis, p. 675n, citing D. G. Zafeiropoulos, argues that Zachariadis visited Lavrishchev in Thessaloniki late in March, when the Soviet representative reportedly approved of the KKE leader's decision to orient policy toward the armed struggle. Apparently, he cautioned only that the KKE wait until the failure of the Greek government's efforts to carry out counteroffensive operations; see Zafeiropoulos, *O Antisymmoriakos Agon, 1945–1949* (Athens: n.p., 1956), p. 47. If true, this would be an important piece of evidence supporting the general interpretation. Lavrishchev's advice came *after* the declaration of the Truman Doctrine, when the Soviets could afford to appear more aggressive to the KKE. Zachariadis was also in Thessaloniki at the time, preparing to cross over into Yugoslavia in early April. The timing of events is consistent, but there is as yet no supporting evidence for this intriguing piece of information.

never met with the DSE commander, the substance of this meeting was not admitted in the final commission proceedings, but the Soviets no doubt took the occasion to discuss policy with the DSE chief.[67]

Finally, the Soviets had a decided advantage within the commission because Konstantin Volokhov, the assistant secretary of the commission, and Gustav Gottesman, deputy principal secretary, were evidently Soviet agents.[68] The unreliability of the secretariat staff was a major reason the United States and Britain remained suspicious of the commission staff. The Soviet delegation was generally able to create a public facade of unity among the Communist representatives and to obstruct consideration of issues that might place the responsibility for conditions in Greece on the Slav states.[69]

An equally important aspect of the U.N. Commission of Inquiry is the correlation of the behavior of the Soviet delegation with other important developments. Despite their obstructionism, the Soviets apparently accepted the utility of the commission—until the Truman Doctrine. The main body of the commission had completed its work in Greece by March 22, 1947, but a majority of the members proposed to retain a subsidiary group in Thessaloniki to continue investigating frontier incidents. Lavrishchev initially resisted but later consented, with reservations, to avoid being isolated as a minority (with the exception of the Polish delegate).

Quite possibly, the Soviets switched from supporting to opposing the commission's activities because of the American commitment to Greece. Since a major objective of Soviet policy had been to prevent such a

[67]Andrei Graur was the Soviet who met with Markos in the mountains, accompanied by the Polish delegate and representatives of Albania, Bulgaria, and Yugoslavia. According to the Soviets, they met in the village of Chrisomilia, in the Trikala District, where Markos gave many documents to the Soviet representative: UNA, DAG 13/4.0.0. Box 4, S/AC.4/177, March 28, 1947. These documents, although not admitted in the commission's official report, were brought along to Geneva when the commission left Greece. I was unable to locate them in the United Nations Archives or published records.

[68]James Barros, personal communications, October 15, 1984, and January 5, 1988. Barros also pointed out that the commission's press attaché, Stanley Ryan, was a Canadian citizen but was born in Russia and had changed his surname in Canada legally. It is unclear whether Ryan was a Soviet agent at the time, but apparently he did serve Soviet interests in later years. For more on the Soviet presence on the Commission of Inquiry, see James Barros, *Trygve Lie and the Cold War: The U.N. Secretary-General Pursues Peace, 1946– 53,* (DeKalb: Northern Illinois University Press, forthcoming), chap. 4.

[69]Lavrishchev was especially insistent on restricting the discussion of Macedonia, particularly when it was treated in isolation from other subjects. When U.S. representative Mark Ethridge persisted in trying to put the Macedonian issue on the agenda, Lavrishchev responded by claiming that Bulgaria's claim to Western Thrace should also be considered. He and the other Communist representatives also attempted to block any discussion of the refugee question: UNA, RAG 1/108, nos. 65–67, March 26, 1947.

development, once it occurred, the Soviets were freed of the need to restrain the insurgency for strategic reasons. Stalin was then able to speak to the KKE with two voices: in private contacts he could sympathize with Greek Communist policy while counseling negotiation and compromise; in relations that included the Yugoslavs, he could devote his energies to containing Tito's independence by appearing more supportive of the military option. In any event, there was another means by which Lavrishchev could neutralize the work of the Subsidiary Group. The group was created on April 18 but it soon found it impossible to discharge its duties because the Communist Balkan states now refused permission to enter their territory.[70] Lacking access to key areas, the group languished until it was finally dissolved on September 15—the exact date the KKE Third Plenum finalized plans for the seizure of northern Greece.

Other evidence pertaining to the activities of the Commission of Inquiry were indicative of the tensions in relations among the Soviets, the Yugoslavs, and the KKE. Lavrishchev in particular exhibited a tendency to lecture his Greek comrades in private while applauding them in public. The British consul in Thessaloniki noted that the Soviets were irritated with developments in Greece and were annoyed at the incompetence of the Yugoslav liaison officer. More important, the consul reported that "top secret sources" had informed him of strain between the Soviet delegation and EAM/KKE.[71] But problems with the Greek Communists must have

[70] On Lavrishchev's resistance to the creation of the Subsidiary Group, see UNA, RAG 1/108, 1205-2, "Commission of Investigation of Greek Border Incidents," no. 61, March 21, 1947. G. B. Kasparov was the Soviet representative on the Subsidiary Group: ibid., DAG 13/4.0.0. Box 1. Each Balkan state apparently had its own style of rejecting requests by members of the Subsidiary Group to enter their soil. After an incident on the Bulgarian frontier on May 28 in which Greek partisans were said to have crossed over into Bulgaria, the Bulgarian government refused entry to the Subsidiary Group on the grounds that it had not had time to "prepare" the area. The Yugoslavs resorted to a different tactic: upon requesting entry into Yugoslav territory, the sentry on duty replied that he had no authority to permit it. Predictably, it proved impossible for the sentries to contact Belgrade and obtain such authority. The Albanians simply did not acknowledge the group representative's request. When the representative got out of his jeep and shouted across the border in the direction of the Albanian frontier post that he wished to carry documents to Tirana, all he heard in reply was a disembodied "no!" The representative persisted and then was told, "If you want to walk to Tirana to deliver documents, do it yourself." His automobile was not permitted to cross the frontier. He abandoned his efforts: ibid., RAG 1/110, 1205-2-12, "Subsidiary Commission on Inquiry for Greek Frontier Problems" (file).

[71] FO 371-67063 R3663, March 12, 1947. The consul added his own interpretation: "There is an unwillingness on the part of [EAM/KKE] to allow Markos to be interrogated by the Commission for fear of searching questions being put to him." The commission never did succeed in meeting with Markos (but the Soviet delegate did, although it was not Lavrishchev), so it remains unclear whether the consul's analysis was valid.

been secondary to tensions between the Soviets and Yugoslavs. Soviet efforts to the contrary notwithstanding, testimony before the commission succeeded in convincing the majority of its members that Balkan states were providing assistance to Greek Communist forces. Parts of the testimony also revealed, however, that it was the Yugoslavs (and to a lesser degree the Bulgarians) who had taken the lead in the civil war. This was strikingly demonstrated by the statement of a witness brought by the *Greek* government: "In contradiction with Greek documents . . . which spoke of 'several['] visits [to] Rubi[q] and B[o]ulkes camp by Russian, Bulgarian and Yugoslav officers [Fotios Kontopanos] state[d] no Russians visited camps, one visit by commander of Yugoslav Army Corps Novisa[d] and one Bulgarian visited camp. Of Greek Leftwingers, Sec[retary] Gen[eral of the] Greek Communist Party Zachariades visited."[72]

Furthermore, while the Yugoslav attitude in the United Nations generally conformed to that of the Soviets, the disparity between their views on Greece continued to grow during 1947. In particular, the Yugoslavs were angered that they had been left to "face the music alone"[73] when the Soviets went along with the creation of the Balkan Commission of Inquiry in December 1946. Yugoslav officials also evinced little or no desire to see a negotiated solution in Greece and actually appeared to become more confident about the success of the DSE. In response, the Soviet delegate on the Balkan commission became increasingly irritated with the Yugoslav liaison's tendency to "overdo his case."[74] Some months later, the British Foreign Office commented that the chances for a rapid Soviet recognition of a rebel government were as yet premature and noted that the Soviet Union believed the solution to the problem lay in getting Greece to establish better relations with the governments of her northern neighbors.[75] This view certainly was not shared by the Yugoslavs in the

[72]UNA, RAG 1/108, 1205-2, "Commission of Investigation of Greek Border Incidents (Part II)," no. 41, February 26, 1947. Markos also seems to imply that it was the Yugoslavs that were giving the military advice. In criticizing Zachariadis for attempting to create a regular army, the former DSE commander-in-chief argued, "Our movement could prevail only through partisan struggle. Friends with international experience, experts in partisan warfare advised us of this": *Vafeiadis,* p. 20. Although he stops short of providing names, Markos must be referring to the Yugoslavs, given that they succeeded in partisan tactics and Stalin manifested nothing but distaste and contempt for this type of warfare. Boulkes never turned out to be much of a contribution to the KKE cause. Most of those who passed through there stressed that they were treated poorly, segregated from the Slavo-Macedonians, heavily propagandized, and used to perform manual labor in Yugoslavia. The contribution of 20,000 men that Zachariadis planned on certainly never came from Boulkes.
[73]Djilas, *Conversations with Stalin,* pp. 131–32.
[74]FO 371-66294 N3581, March 25, 1947.
[75]FO 371-67157 R11230, August 15, 1947.

early autumn of 1947. On the contrary, when the British ambassador had a conversation with Deputy Foreign Minister Aleš Bebler in September, he found him remarkably expansive and confident about the situation in Greece. Bebler admitted that in the past the Greek rebels had received arms and munitions from the satellites, and he added that the rebel movement in the Peloponnese seemed to be making quite good progress. On the near future, the Yugoslav deputy foreign minister mused that the U.S. loan to Greece was not sufficient, and since the United States was on the brink of an economic collapse, further aid to Greece was not expected. The British ambassador concluded that the Yugoslavs expected Greece to tumble into the hands of the satellites as soon as conditions matured.[76] Obviously, these remarks do not reflect an interest in negotiation. Thus Soviet activity on the Commission of Inquiry reflected Stalin's weak position relative to the Yugoslavs in Balkan affairs as much as it did his effort to redirect policy and gain propaganda advantage at Western expense.

Despite the growing disparity of views between the Yugoslavs and the Soviets, Stalin continued his attempts to keep the diplomatic route, and consequently his options, open. The reason for this, which becomes apparent only later in the civil war, was that Stalin still held out the rather murky and long-term goal of preserving some pro-Soviet influence in Greece. Once the Yugoslav initiative was turned back, Stalin's only chance of retaining the KKE in Greece was to achieve a negotiated solution. The KKE echoed this theme in its numerous offers for such a solution through the duration of the war.

The Soviets were also engaged in making offers of their own. In February, general and former Greek prime minister Plastiras was invited to the Soviet Embassy, where Ambassador Rodionov proceeded to suggest the general lead a "great anti-British campaign" to get rid of the British and prevent Greece from doom. Plastiras refused and the matter appeared to rest at that.[77] Less than one month later, however, the Soviets reemphasized their opinions on the need for a diplomatic resolution, and this time the occasion was a meeting between members of the EAM delegation attached to the U.N. Balkan commission and the Soviet delegate, Lavrishchev. According to Michalis Kirkos, a member of the EAM delegation, "Lavris[hch]ev did not want to [comment on] the Truman Doctrine. He told us only that understanding and compromise is always better and

---

[76]FO 371-57157 R13254, September 19, 1947.
[77]DSR 868.00B/2-2447, no. 268.

that the steadfast policy of the Soviet Union in every international political matter is the support and promotion of agreements and negotiations in order to attain a compromise solution. Lavris[hch]ev knew a little Greek and told us in Greek: 'Whoever does not want agreement is . . . a horse!!!' (He meant to say, 'is talking nonsense!!').["78]

Finally, in July the KKE secretly contacted Sofoulis (who had been prime minister at the high point of the Soviets' gradualist strategy in November 1945) with proposals for the formation of a new Greek government. The basic points in the KKE offer were a change of government and dissolution of parliament, with consequent formation of a pure Center government, including such figures as Plastiras and Tsouderos. After the formation of such a government, an agreement would be signed between the KKE and the government allowing for a general amnesty, guarantee of security to those giving up their arms, and the promise of new elections.[79] Whether this agreement would have borne fruit is impossible to say, for it occurred at a time when the government had begun carrying out massive arrests of suspected Communists and long after the KKE Politburo members located in Belgrade had decided that the central thrust of KKE policy would be toward the insurgency.

In any event, on the eve of the Third Plenum of the KKE Central Committee, the strategy of dualism was a mere shadow of what it once was. KKE policy was oriented toward civil war, and Zachariadis had succeeded in eliciting Stalin's assurance of support. In return, Stalin succeeded in retarding the application of this policy to a point where the ability of the DSE actually to succeed was objectively in doubt. For the moment, however, the Greek Communist leadership felt confident that the policy goals marked out seven months earlier could now be effected.

The KKE Third Plenum and After: The Critical Months

The Third Plenum of the KKE Central Committee convened in Belgrade on September 12–15, 1947. It was the first such meeting of the KKE in more than eighteen months, and its purpose was to ratify and implement the plan to liberate a large region of northern Greece, including Thes-

[78]*Avgi*, no. 38, January 20, 1980.
[79]DSR 868.01/7-1647, aide memoire.

saloniki, in order to form a "free" Greek state. The military schedule drawn up reflected the optimistic assessments of Ioannidis and Zacharia-dis of the previous month. According to the plan (code-named *Limnes*), "conditions have matured for the fulfillment of the basic, strategic duty which stands before our Democratic Army, namely, the creation of a free territory in the expanse of Macedonia and the liberation of all of Mac-edonia-Thrace, with the center [at] Thessaloniki."[80]

Success depended upon several factors, primarily the ability of the DSE to raise the strength of the army to approximately 50,000 men and to provide for their adequate supply with armaments and provisions. Conse-quently, the plenum ordered that the pace of mobilization be increased so that it would triple by the spring of 1948 (the military plan of the plenum estimated the number of available forces to be 24,000, of which 18,000 were battle ready). In addition, measures were to be taken to facilitate the transport of materiel for complete arming of forces and the formation of a regular army, also by early spring of the next year.

Another key element of the strategy was to make use of Communist cadres in the larger cities, especially Thessaloniki, to create unrest and sabotage. A resolution of the Second Subcommittee of the Politburo (the Belgrade-based section of the KKE leadership) stated that the essential requirement for success was the "creation (in the cities) of armed groups of fighters who will ceaselessly carry out armed activity and sabotage and who, at the corresponding moment, will decisively assist the DSE in the seizure of cities."[81] On the assumption that all aspects of the plan would be fulfilled, the prospects for a decisive success in 1948 were deemed very good.

The fundamental difficulty was that as time went on, it became appar-ent that the preconditions for the DSE's military plan were not being fulfilled, thereby jeopardizing the entire operation. Available evidence indicates several reasons. A major problem was the unjustified optimism of Ioannidis and Zachariadis. Contrary to expectations, deficiencies in materials (both military and otherwise) continued to be enormous. In a letter to Tito on September 20, after the decisions of the Third Plenum and more than a month after the KKE general secretary had assured Tito that

[80]This quotation and the figures in the next paragraph are found in *Avgi,* no. 28, January 6, 1980. Contained in this issue is the entire plan for the seizure of northern Greece, including Thessaloniki. There is a comparison of enemy and DSE forces; especially striking is the almost complete absence of transport facilities for the DSE.

[81]*Avgi,* no. 34, January 15, 1980.

sufficient assistance had been secured, Zachariadis resumed requesting assistance from the Yugoslavs. Although the DSE was rapidly being transformed into a regular army and there was progress in the liberation of territory, Zachariadis nonetheless stressed the need for Yugoslav assistance in several areas: support for the victims of fascist terror, promotion of the Greek Communist cause in world opinion, and material aid. Zachariadis' lengthy list of needed items revealed that the DSE required urgent assistance in almost every aspect of its military organization.[82] Other information confirms this serious lack of munitions. In late October, Gousias recalled that the men he had recruited to go into the mountains numbered enough to form two brigades. Because they had to be transported across long stretches, Gousias requested help from the DSE General Staff; as he put it, it was "difficult to be moving columns of unarmed men over such great distances."[83]

Also in October, Zachariadis addressed himself to the Soviet Union once again. In two letters to "comrade Baranov" dated October 6 and November 10, respectively, the KKE leader took up the question of assistance from the Soviets. The October letter reveals that Soviet aid was exceptionally slow in arriving, and the amounts that did arrive were still unsatisfactory. The letter also indicates that the Soviets could not be cajoled into stepping up the pace of deliveries and that the preceding month's letter to Tito had met with a negative response: "We do not have information regarding the arrival of other material. . . . Since you have informed us that you cannot do anything regarding defraying the cost of the clothing and foot-gear, we ask you to help us, to the extent that you can, to find these things in other fraternal countries. . . . The Yugoslav comrades do what they can, but their reserves have been exhausted. Comrade Zhivkov will remain with us."[84]

In the November 10 letter, written two days before Zachariadis left Belgrade to go into northern Greece and join the DSE General Staff, the general secretary again requested aid and then discussed the poor relations between the Bulgarians and the KKE. The contrast of good relations with Albania and Yugoslavia as opposed to poor relations with Bulgaria is striking, for it serves to underscore the tension between the Yugoslavs and the Soviets (whose confidence in their capacity to influence Dimitrov must have been higher than Tito's). The letter is revealing in other respects and so merits substantial attention:

[82]*Avgi*, no. 31, January 11, 1980.
[83]Vontitsos-Gousias, *Aities gia tis Ittes, ti Diaspasi* 1:253.
[84]*Avgi*, no. 32, January 12, 1980.

10.11.47 [November 10, 1947]

Dear C[omrade] Baranov,

You received today certain materials from the Politburo in Athens regarding our organization in Thessaloniki, the EPON, copies of the letters of Denisov [Ioannidis] and Markos.

I ask you to pay special attention to the materials which refer to Bulgaria and which reveal a bad [*ochi kali*] situation in the area of understanding and assistance in our struggle by the Bulgarian comrades, in contrast to that which exists with the Yugoslav and Albanian comrades.

I would also request, if possible, your support in this area.

It would help if a relevant directive could be made by you. . .

All of the material in your last shipment arrived, as also the Pakar [Packard?].

In two days I will leave for the G(eneral) S(taff) of the DSE. . .

Below I provide a list of the military and other material which is indispensable for the DSE and which only you can supply us.

I would ask you to dispatch this matter as quickly as possible because the seasonal conditions in the mountains constitute a serious factor regarding the transport of material.

The greatest difficulties in this respect are present in January and therefore it is necessary for us to try to use intensively the few weeks which remain for us.

—Bullets 9MM 10 mil[lion]
—Sheaves for automatic [rifles] 5,000
—Mines for sand 10,000
—Mines for train 5,000
—Mines for tank 2,000
—Panzerfaust 10,000
—Dynamite 50 tons
—Instantaneous fuse 50,000 meters
—Slow-burning fuse 50,000 meters
—[Requests for munitions for mortar of varying sizes]
—Bullets for English weapons and English machine-guns (the same) 5,000,000 . . .

The list goes on for some time, covering other aspects of war materials such as medical supplies and radios. In a final section of the letter, Zachariadis provides an inventory of the materiel contributions of other Communist parties:

The Czechs have not given anything. . .
The Czechs some 8 months ago promised 5,000 boots but they have not done anything.

The Romanians send little.
The Poles have helped a great deal.
The Hungarians have promised.[85]

The needs of the KKE appeared great indeed, and apparently the only major sources of support were the Yugoslavs, the Albanians, and the Soviets—the latter, little and slowly. In addition, the letter reveals the need to get the supplies before the winter, which suggests that the subsequent declaration of a provisional democratic government and the attack on Konitsa were hastily prepared because the KKE could not afford to wait through the winter and allow government armed forces to gain the advantage of time. Thus pressed for time, the KKE had to proceed to the offensive with or without the necessary aid. The implication is that the outside assistance received before the close of the year was insufficient to assure a DSE victory, which was confirmed by the defeat of Democratic Army forces at Konitsa.

A second key area in which the DSE encountered problems was in the recruitment of cadres and reserves, both for the cities and in the mountains. In large part, this had been because of the unwillingness of the KKE leadership to mobilize as rapidly as possible while they still pursued the dual strategy; the Soviet policy preference had thus contributed to the inability to raise recruits. Time only made the problem worse, and an earlier decision to mobilize rapidly would have helped, given the Greek government's subsequent program of removing the population from affected areas, depriving the DSE of its resource base. The KKE, in not deciding to mobilize until long after the Greek government had begun gathering the population in urban centers, continued, in the middle of 1947, to follow the same old pattern of making decisions and taking actions long after the conditions supporting their validity had passed. Irrational as this may have appeared, it was the logical consequence of Stalin's dilatory tactics. Had the Soviet leader not cautioned restraint in 1945–46 nor sought to slow and reverse the momentum of the civil war in 1947–48, the Greek Communist position would have been considerably stronger.

In the cities, the recruitment problem had different causes. While the KKE Politburo in Belgrade (the Second Subcommittee) was critical of the inactivity of urban cadres, the KKE Politburo in Athens was reluctant to castigate the urban apparatchiki. The reason for this, as Chrysa Chatzi-

---

[85]*Avgi*, no. 33, January 13, 1980. The little information available on Baranov is discussed in chap. 5.

Vasileiou pointed out some time later, was that no one in the KKE leadership had given party cadres explicit instructions as to where and how they should proceed to the mountains.[86] Furthermore, the Greek government, according to U.S. documents, had done a fairly successful job of dismantling the KKE's covert organizations in the cities. Operations against KKE cells were said to be especially successful in Thessaloniki,[87] which was particularly damaging for the Communists, as their plans centered on the seizure of the port city.

By the end of 1947, it was apparent that despite the decisions of the Third Plenum, the KKE and DSE were not in a position to carry out their own plan because of a serious failure to fulfill basic tasks. The gravity of the situation was compounded by the fact that winter would impede the delivery of supplies from abroad. Seen from this perspective, the declaration of the provisional democratic government on December 23–24 and the attack on Konitsa several days later appear as a hasty and ill-prepared attempt to achieve some kind of success before the "objective correlation of forces" moved even further to the KKE's disadvantage.

Greek Communist strategy during 1947 suffered from the debilitating hesitancy that crippled its policy three years earlier during the second round of the Greek Civil War, and once again the necessity of accommodating Soviet interests was a root cause. Just as in December 1944 the KKE waited until after the optimal moment for employing force had passed, so in 1947 it adopted a strategy more than a year out of date. Giorgis Erythriadis, a participant at the Third Plenum, provided an accurate assessment of the situation: "Regarding the decisions of the Third Plenum[,] I am of the opinion that . . . we did not have a *complete picture* of the new situation which was created in our country (April–September 1947), with the American intervention in support of monarcho-fascism."[88]

The dilemma of obtaining support in the face of Yugoslav predominance continued through 1947, but there were now indications that KKE leaders, Zachariadis in particular, were aware of friction between the Yugoslavs and Stalin. In a letter to Zhdanov on September 1, Zachariadis closed with a statement bound to cause the Soviets anxiety: "I would very much like it if each time I could be informed verbally by comrade [A. I.]

[86]*Avgi*, no. 31, January 11, 1980.
[87]DSR 868.00B/12-2647, no. 5784; DSR 868.00B/5-848, no. 145.
[88]As cited in Bartziotas, *Agonas tou Dimokratikou Stratou Elladas*, p. 84; emphasis in original.

Lavrent'iev [the Soviet Ambassador to Yugoslavia] regarding that which you are sending us, because I am often in a position of ignorance regarding matters which concern us directly."[89] Given that relations between the Soviets and Tito were not cordial, it must have unsettled the Soviets to learn that information intended for the KKE did not always reach them. The fact that Zachariadis informed the Soviets indicated his discomfort.

The events in Greece in the latter part of 1947 and into 1948 correspond well with developments throughout the Balkans that reflected a heightening in the crisis between Stalin and Tito. In early 1948 the position of pro-Yugoslav forces in the Albanian Communist party improved, and there followed attempts to eliminate Hoxha and Mehmet Shehu.[90] In Bulgaria, Dimitrov, although remaining accessible to Soviet influence, was trying with some success to coordinate the policies of Yugoslavia and Bulgaria, as reflected in the generally favorable outcome of the Bled meeting in August 1947.[91]

From the Soviet perspective, either the independent activities of the Yugoslavs had to be reined in or Moscow would have to break with Belgrade. For events to continue as they had for the previous months meant a risk to Soviet control of the Balkans. The Soviets needed somehow to deflect the Yugoslavs from their adventurous projects and force them to think about their own security. The DSE campaign provided just the opportunity; for Stalin knew that if the situation became too dangerous, the United States would respond, which is what occurred.

Upon the formation of the provisional government, the United States became gravely concerned that Yugoslavia (and other Communist states) would recognize the government. The U.S. ambassador to Yugoslavia,

[89]*Avgi*, no. 23, December 30, 1979.
[90]Griffith, pp. 19–20.
[91]*Rizospastis*, August 5, 23, 1947. A long-standing interpretation of the Bled Conference results is that Zachariadis assented to the cession of Greek territory to Yugoslavia and Bulgaria in exchange for support in the armed struggle; see Philip E. Mosely, *The Kremlin and World Politics* (New York: Knopf, Vintage, 1960), p. 231; R. V. Burks, *The Dynamics of Communism in Eastern Europe* (Princeton, N.J.: Princeton University Press, 1961), pp. 99–102. Kondis, however, correctly points out that no corroborating evidence for this interpretation has surfaced; see his *Angloamerikaniki Politiki*, p. 337. Such an agreement doubtless corresponded with Yugoslav and Bulgarian ambitions, but given the uneasy relationship between the KKE and Tito presented here, it is doubtful that Zachariadis would have consented. A second problem with the earlier analysis is that it fails to take into consideration that the Yugoslavs and Bulgarians simply could not provide the kind of assistance the DSE needed in order to prevail. Only the Soviet Union had the necessary materiel, and this is why the KKE repeatedly addressed itself to Stalin. It made no sense to cede territory to Tito and Dimitrov when they were unable to provide what the KKE needed. The Bled Conference is therefore of more interest in analyzing the Yugoslav-Bulgarian relationship than the policy of the Greek Communists.

Cavendish Cannon, secretly warned the Yugoslavs on Christmas Day just how seriously the American government regarded the situation. While the British ambassador visited the Yugoslav deputy foreign minister two days later and gathered the impression that his (Bebler's) position was unchanged,[92] the French ambassador spoke with Bebler and gained a quite different impression. In contrast to the confidence Bebler had displayed three months earlier, the French ambassador found him "hesitant and depressed," and to the question of whether, if Markos should succeed in gaining a foothold in Greece, the Yugoslav government would regard his regime as extending over the whole of Greece, Bebler replied, "Very decidedly no"; the Yugoslavs would merely acknowledge his authority over the territory controlled. Bebler then went on to say that Yugoslavia had not lost sight of U.S. interests and thought it possible that the Yugoslav government would have diplomatic relations with both Markos and the Greek government. The deputy foreign minister concluded with the following words: "We are confronted by two tasks. We must give our moral support to the Markos government with whom we are in sympathy, but at the same time we must do nothing to compromise the interests of peace as a whole. We must not therefore take up too decided a position and we shall in consequence have to maneuver."[93] Less than one week later, the French Embassy in Athens confirmed that Bebler's attitude had indeed been greatly modified after Ambassador Cannon's representations.[94] This was obviously a major shift for someone who earlier felt at ease confiding to Western diplomats that Yugoslavia had provided assistance to Greek rebels.

Further confirmation of the change in the Yugoslav position came in early January 1948, when Bebler again reaffirmed that while Yugoslav sympathies were with the Markos forces, this did not mean the Yugoslav government was indifferent to world peace.[95] Cannon wrote on January 18 that he believed the arguments that most impressed Yugoslav leaders were warnings "that whatever [the] Soviet bloc does in aid to Markos, even if through Albanian or Bulgarian stooges, [the] western world will see Yugoslavia out in front as primarily responsible and most vulnerable."[96] Apparently, once exposed to the reality of the international setting, the Yugoslavs were shocked and decided to adopt a more cautious strategy.

[92]Wittner, p. 260; DSR 868.01/12-3047, no. 2374.
[93]FO 371-72236 R101, January 1, 1948; DSR 868.01/12-3147, no. 2376.
[94]DSR 868.01/1-548, no. 24; see also, Wittner, p. 261.
[95]FO 371-72237 R268, January 5, 1948.
[96]DSR 868.01/1-1848, no. 79.

By the beginning of January, enough events had converged for Stalin to take the offensive against Tito. The death of the anti-Yugoslav Nako Spiru,[97] the failure of the DSE to carry out its plans, and the recoil of the Yugoslavs at the thought of being in an exposed position vis-à-vis the United States all combined with circumstances more directly affecting Stalin's relations to Tito into a potent mix Stalin could use in his attack against the Yugoslav leader. Dimitrov was publicly rebuked in the Soviet press for his efforts to achieve a Balkan federation,[98] and the Bulgarian leader consequently found himself summoned to Moscow, along with the Yugoslav Communists, in February. There, in a meeting on February 10, Stalin could take the offensive. He had two primary objectives: to protect the integrity of Albania and to confuse, distort, or shatter any efforts on the separate East European states to pursue independent policies.

Stalin castigated Dimitrov for his stand on a Balkan federation and then turned his attention to the Yugoslav delegates: the uprising in Greece had to be stopped. When Edvard Kardelj attempted to argue that Greek Communist success was still possible, Stalin rebuffed him: "No, they have no prospect of success at all. What do you think, that Great Britain and the United States—the United States, the most powerful state in the world—will permit you to break their line of communication in the Mediterranean Sea! Nonsense."[99] In making this argument, Stalin could now point to both a decisive demonstration of U.S. resolve and a decisive Greek Communist defeat, evidence he did not have even two months before. Whether this argument affected the Yugoslavs is unclear, but they did emerge from the meetings convinced that they had to defend their vital national interests, even against Stalin.

The advice to the Yugoslavs suggests that Stalin was saying different things to the Yugoslav and Greek Communist parties in order to create two quite different effects. On February 9, just as Dimitrov and Kardelj were being attacked by Stalin for their adventurism, the Greek chargé in Prague informed the British ambassador of a meeting between Zachariadis and Molotov at which the KKE leader

> is said to have informed Molotov that the position of the guerrillas was desperate both from military and from economic point of view and that Markos gov[ernmen]t was dissatisfied with the diplomatic support it was receiving from supposedly friendly countries. Molotov is said to have replied

[97]Griffith, p. 19.
[98]Woodhouse, *Struggle for Greece*, p. 229.
[99]Djilas, *Conversations with Stalin*, pp. 181–82.

that it would soon be possible for the Soviet gov[ernmen]t and its friends [to provide] much stronger and more open support. But he was waiting for the Americans and British to give him an excuse by . . . adopting a more open and positive policy of support for the Greek gov[ernmen]t.[100]

While the KKE's dissatisfaction with the level of support is well-documented, the latter part of the document casts some doubt on the validity of the chargé's telegram, because it is hard to see how U.S. support could have been more open.

Other sources, however, suggest that at least part of the information is valid. Barker cites Markos to the effect that Zachariadis was in Belgrade in the spring of 1948, where he discussed the implications, for the Greek Communist cause, of the impending rupture between Tito and Stalin. Initially, Zachariadis and Markos, according to the DSE chief, agreed to adopt a neutral stand in the dispute, but when Zachariadis arrived in Moscow, he agreed to all Stalin's accusations.[101] Djilas says he met with Zachariadis in Belgrade *after* the Cominform resolution condemning the Yugoslav party and that Zachariadis implored the Yugoslavs not to cut off assistance.[102] In yet a third version, Gousias asserts that Zachariadis traveled to Moscow after the battle of Vitsi in August 1948, where he received assurances of material assistance from the Soviets.[103]

Two important conclusions can be extracted from this mass of information: first, whatever the schedule of the KKE general secretary's peregrinations, all accounts agree that at some point in 1948, Zachariadis was in the Soviet Union at least once to discuss KKE prospects; second, at no point does it appear that the Soviets explicitly told the KKE to fold up the insurgency, as they had the Yugoslavs. The second conclusion is further strengthened by Partsalidis' assertion that the Soviets never informed the KKE that armed struggle had to be terminated until spring of 1949.

[100]FO 371-72239 R1869, February 11, 1948. The United States received similar information but State Department officials, not knowing the original source, were unable to assess its reliability. The U.S. Embassy in Moscow was unable to confirm or deny Zachariadis' visit: FO 371-72239 R2241, February 17, 1948.

[101]Interview with Markos Vafeiadis in *Politika*, June 15–16, 1982; in Elisabeth Barker, "Yugoslav Policy towards Greece 1947–1949," in *Studies in the History of the Greek Civil War, 1945–1949*, ed. Lars Baerentzen, John O. Iatrides, and Ole L. Smith (Copenhagen: Museum Tusculanum Press, 1987), p. 276.

[102]Milovan Djilas, *Vlast* (London: Naša Reć, 1983), pp. 201–2; in Barker, "Yugoslav Policy towards Greece," pp. 276–77.

[103]Vontitsos-Gousias, *Aities gia tis Ittes, ti Diapasi* 1:440. Wittner, p. 267, also cites U.S. sources to the effect that KKE officials met with Yugoslav leaders in Belgrade during December.

Possibly the Yugoslavs conveyed to the KKE the negative Soviet reply they had received in February, but since Zachariadis was already suspicious of Yugoslav intentions and was in direct contact with Stalin, he would probably have believed Stalin. This episode emphasizes how Stalin successfully used developments in the civil war and exploited intra-Communist tensions to pressure the Yugoslavs while simultaneously bolstering the KKE.

Once he had destroyed the attempts of other Communist states to act on their own initiative and compelled them to concern themselves with their own survival, and Tito had had to respond to Stalin's verbal and diplomatic offensives, the Soviet dictator could proceed to further isolate and ultimately expel Yugoslavia from the Communist bloc. In mid-March, alleging local hostility, the Soviets withdrew their military and civilian advisors from Yugoslavia.[104] The lines were now clearly drawn, and a rupture in relations was only a matter of time.

By the end of spring, Stalin had succeeded in navigating the treacherous paths of Balkan politics to the point that he could break with Yugoslavia yet retain control of other key areas such as Albania and Bulgaria. As for Greece, the civil war was now in a phase that, barring a major catastrophe for the Greek government, would end in defeat for the guerrillas. Having succeeded in retaining the loyalty of the KKE thus far through the promise of aid, Stalin could get away with speaking out of both sides of his mouth. Regardless of what he had told the Yugoslavs, he could assure the KKE that he had supported them and would continue to do so.[105] Now, in the closing stages of the civil war, Stalin could concern himself with finding a negotiated solution and preserving the integrity of Albania from attack by the Western powers. In other words, the Soviet leader sought to restore conditions in which the influence of Yugoslavia would be minimized and a base of Communist influence could be preserved in Greece. In a way, it was a return to the dualist policy, only now, rather than building up the armed struggle, the Soviets had the task of gradually dismantling it. The long-term stakes were high; the Soviets knew that if the civil war was pushed to a military solution, Communist influence would be eliminated.

[104]Wittner, p. 263.
[105]It is by now almost common knowledge that (according to Djilas) Stalin told the Yugoslav delegation in February that the Greek Civil War had to fold up. When the KKE got wind of this sometime later (after the final defeat at Grammos), they asked Stalin, according to Zachariadis, whether he had in fact told the Yugoslavs the civil war had to be stopped. In this account, Stalin denied having said anything of the kind. Zachariadis concluded somewhat later (in keeping with the present analysis) that Stalin favored civil war but was unable to fulfill his promise of aid; see Vontitsos-Gousias, *Aities gia tis Ittes, ti Diaspasi* 2:250-52.

After the Break with Tito: The DSE in Decline

During the remaining two years of the civil war, communist forces continued to disrupt Greek society and inflict heavy losses on Greek government forces, but despite a fairly high level of morale, their capacity to win
a decisive victory rapidly deteriorated. The principle reasons were that
American aid had begun to make it possible for the Greek National Army
to carry out successful campaigns against the guerrillas, and the KKE
failed to solve its manpower problem. While the government benefited
from American aid, the KKE failed to obtain enough assistance at critically important moments. The massive KKE recruitment could not succeed when the population had been largely removed from affected areas
and many cadres had been imprisoned. The alternative, forcible conscrip-
tion of recruits, could provide only a marginally effective fighting force at
best. Finally, to compound the DSE's difficulties, the approaching rupture
between the Yugoslavs and Soviets would be disastrous for the Greek
Communists. Following Stalin's meeting with Yugoslav and Bulgarian
officials in Moscow in February, relations steadily deteriorated until June
28, when the Cominform expelled Yugoslavia.[106]

This development was important in several respects. In Albania, a key
source of Soviet anxiety, the break provided the anti-Yugoslav faction
under Hoxha and Shehu with an opportunity to launch a counterattack
against their chief rival, Xoxe. In Bulgaria, it gave Dimitrov, who had
spent the remainder of 1947 and the first month of 1948 pursuing independent initiatives with Tito, very little time to choose sides. In Greece, the

[106]The reasons for the formation of the Cominform and why certain Communist parties,
particularly the Greek and Albanian, were excluded from the founding meeting remain
unknown. Kardelj has provided a plausible yet unsubstantiated argument that squares with
the present account: Stalin used the Yugoslavs' ideological zeal to get them to attack the
French and Italian Communists, so that the resulting resentment would make it impossible
for Tito to turn to these parties for support in the next year; see Edvard Kardelj, *Memorie
Degli Anni di Ferro*, pp. 111–12; as cited in Paolo Spriano, *Stalin and the European
Communists*, trans. Jon Rothschild (London: Verso, 1985), p. 301. This account is consistent with what Eugenio Reale stated he was told by Kardelj some years after the break;
see Reale, *Nascita del Cominform* (Milan: Arnoldo Mondadori, 1958), p. 41. If forming the
Cominform was in fact one step in Stalin's plan to excommunicate Tito, it becomes possible
to explain the absence of delegates from the Albanian and Greek Communist parties. In
1947, Albania still had not been extricated from the acquisitive grasp of the Yugoslavs, and
Stalin could not yet guarantee that an Albanian delegation would support his views. As for
the KKE, it was then engaged in precisely the kind of strategy of which the Yugoslav
partisans would have wholeheartedly approved; it would thus have been impossible to get
the Yugoslavs to criticize the KKE. Hence, Kardelj and Djilas attacked the "accommoda-
tionist" French and Italian Communist parties, only to find themselves isolated a year later.
Spriano, p. 301, counters with the argument that Stalin wished to attack the PCF and PCI in
order to get them to commit themselves more strongly against the Marshall Plan.

Tito-Stalin split precipitated a severe crisis, for it thrust Greek Communists into the most delicate of political situations. The difficulty of their position was complicated by the fact that the battle of Grammos, by far the most crucial military operation of 1948, reached its most intense level in the months of July and August. The DSE, hard pressed by the government offensive yet still strong enough to avoid defeat, required arms more than at any other time in the war. A request phrased so it could be construed as taking a side in the Stalin-Tito dispute would surely finish any chances of success the DSE had.

The effects of the dispute did not take long to reach the KKE and the DSE. According to Gousias, all regional commanders (of which he was one) were summoned to DSE General Staff headquarters on July 8. There they were informed that subsequent to the denunciation of Yugoslavia published by the Cominform, all food and other forms of Yugoslav support were temporarily halted. This was a serious setback because, as Gousias acknowledged, Yugoslavia had been the country that provided the most aid. Nonetheless, the KKE Central Committee resolved to continue their struggle despite the added burdens they now faced in acquiring materiel.[107]

Two points of interest emerge from this information. First, the Yugoslavs apparently took the initiative in halting aid before the KKE had an opportunity to pass judgment on the issue. Tito must already have been convinced the KKE would not support him and would therefore side with Stalin.[108] Second, despite this setback, the KKE made an independent decision to continue the civil war. To Stalin, this meant that control of the Balkan environment was still insufficient to begin giving specific directives. The Greek Communists remained faithful to Stalin, but they had to respond independently to local circumstances. It was useless for Stalin to consider imposing rigid directives; for he knew that if a conflict developed in uncontrolled conditions between his orders and self-preservation, the KKE would choose the latter. The Soviet leader consequently found it prudent to continue for a time his efforts to appear supportive of KKE actions. The KKE, even before it had taken any action regarding the Yugoslav issue, thus found itself distrusted by both sides.

It was not for another three weeks that the Greek Communist leadership took any official action on their policy toward Tito. On July 28, the Fourth

---

[107]Vontitsos-Gousias, *Aities gia tis Ittes, ti Diaspasi* 1:381.

[108]Djilas, however, maintains that the Yugoslavs continued to remain supportive of the KKE until Markos was removed from his post in January 1949; see *Vlast*, pp. 201–2; in Barker, "Yugoslav Policy towards Greece," pp. 276–77.

Plenum of the KKE Central Committee convened to consider a number of matters, chief of which was the rupture between Tito and Stalin, but also to examine their current situation relative to the Greek government forces. Of the resolutions taken at the Fourth Plenum, one confirmed that because of weaknesses such as the failure to raise sufficient reserves and create a mass movement in the cities, it was not possible to achieve the goals set at the Third Plenum. Also, in a move designed to assuage the Macedonians fighting in the DSE, the plenum stressed the exceptional contribution of the Slavo-Macedonians.[109] As for the Yugoslav question, the plenum decided to support the Cominform resolution but not to circulate this decision publicly for fear of straining relations with the Yugoslavs. The final plenum decision acknowledged the KKE's heavy dependence on the Yugoslavs and that any public declaration of disagreement risked a complete aid cutoff.[110] In fact, there was no immediate and complete cessation of assistance from Yugoslavia (with the exception of the brief interruption immediately after the Cominform decision), as the DSE continued to be able to make use of the northern borders throughout 1948.

To increase their influence in KKE affairs, the Soviets had to find a way to decrease KKE reliance on Tito. Here, the remnants of the dual strategy were useful; for Stalin could use the international position of the Soviet Union to pursue a negotiated settlement to the civil war while simultaneously maintaining alternative supply routes to the DSE through Albania. Success in this endeavor would not only remove the Yugoslavs from the picture but return Stalin to a much more influential position in KKE affairs. Then it might even be possible to employ the disturbances in Greece to put pressure on the Yugoslavs; the most obvious means would be through activation of the Macedonian question, but as a threat to Tito, not a benefit. To proceed in this course, Stalin had first to gain control of the Slavo-Macedonians and then to find some means of political expression for his policy. Stalin's temptation to use the good offices of Zachariadis must have been great, but first it was necessary to "resolve" outstanding Balkan problems.

Evidence that the KKE (which had its own good reasons for seeking a favorable diplomatic settlement) and the Soviets pursued the diplomatic

[109]*Saranta Chronia tou KKE, 1918–1958* (n.p.: Politikes kai Logotechnikes Ekdoseis, 1958), pp. 561–66. The failure to raise a movement in the urban centers was probably the weakest spot. On this issue KKE leaders criticized each other needlessly: the Greek government had done a creditable job of destroying the mass movement in the cities, especially Thessaloniki. See also Vontitsas-Gousias, *Aities gia tis Ittes, ti Diaspasi* 1:389.

[110]*Saranta Chronia*, pp. 566–67; Vontitsos-Gousias, *Aities gia tis Ittes, ti Diaspasi* 1:377, 381, 389–90. Bartziotas, *Agonas tou Dimokratikou Stratou Elladas*, p. 86.

alternative is not hard to find. On April 7 the KKE approached former prime minister Tsouderos and presented its proposals for negotiation.[111] About the same time, the DSE radio began broadcasting peace proposals. In an especially prominent appeal broadcast on May 31, the DSE pledged to make every concession that "national and popular interest" allowed.[112] American officials, viewing the appeals as a mere "peace offensive" and not as genuine offers, rejected the rebel proposals.

American officials did not, however, immediately reject an offer that came from the Soviets. Back in late June, before the Cominform declaration, Foreign Minister Konstantinos Tsaldaris was approached "in strictest confidence" by a member of the Soviet Embassy in Athens, who proposed that conversations be initiated between the Greek and Soviet governments for the settlement of outstanding differences. The Soviet Embassy official imposed one curious requirement, however: the discussions were to be held personally and in greatest secrecy, without mentioning the matter to anyone else in the Greek government.[113]

Tsaldaris was unsure what to do, and U.S. officials were equally unsure what the Soviets intended. The U.S. officials welcomed any honest proposal, since they reasoned that a solution of outstanding difficulties necessarily entailed an exchange of views. But there was uncertainty as to why the negotiations had to be secret and personal.[114] In retrospect, it is difficult to comprehend how "personal" and "secret" talks with only one member of the Greek government could resolve differences between two governments, but one must remember the persistent Soviet avoidance of official involvement in Greece in any capacity. As early as 1946, the Soviets had rejected participation in AMFOGE; later they rejected Zachariadis' proposal for the neutralization of Greece under Great Power auspices. Given this established policy, it is most likely that the Soviets were seeking an informal means of getting a diplomatic foothold in Greece. Specifically, U.S. Embassy officials thought, this might allow the Soviets to act as intermediaries between the Greek government and the provisional democratic government.[115] While no further U.S. documentation appears on this matter, it is conceivable that some sort of effort was made in the end of June or early July.

[111]Wittner, p. 264.
[112]Barker, "Yugoslav Policy towards Greece," p. 277.
[113]DSR 761.68/7-748, Marshall to U.S. Embassy, July 16, 1948; DSR 761.68/7-748, Department of State memorandum, July 16, 1948.
[114]Ibid.
[115]Ibid.

Unfortunately, information on the genuine nature of the Soviet offer has been dissipated through the heated polemics among surviving KKE members. Because of the unusual nature of the Soviet approach, however, and its close correspondence with the rupture in relations with Yugoslavia, the competing versions of the contact with Tsaldaris bear at least passing mention. Markos recalls that there was an initiative on the part of Tsaldaris, thanks to the intervention of the Soviet Embassy. The "emissary" was an American reporter, Homer Bigart, who was brought to Grammos via Yugoslavia on July 15. When Markos spoke with Zachariadis about a meeting, Zachariadis, according to the DSE commander, refused to go at all and told Markos he could go, on the condition he tell Bigart the KKE was ready for negotiations only if it was declared that the Greek government was composed of criminals. Ultimately, Markos went to meet Bigart with Rousos, accompanied by Bartziotas' wife. Markos states that when he recounted Zachariadis' position to Bigart, the latter smiled and said, "That's one opinion," and with that the encounter ended.[116]

A quite different story is told by Bartziotas, whose wife served as the interpreter for Markos. The meeting with Bigart did indeed take place, but it was on June 29, and the American reporter was not a representative sent by Tsaldaris but a journalist exiled from Athens for writing articles about the DSE in U.S. papers. Bigart apparently wanted to meet with Markos, and his article recounting the experience appeared in the *New York Herald Tribune*. Bartziotas argues that Markos was trying to cast aspersions on Zachariadis, primarily because of the many errors committed by the DSE commander. A third version comes from yet another former high-ranking KKE member of that period. Dimitris Vlantas recalls that Tsaldaris did attempt some kind of action designed to start negotiations but that Zachariadis, Bartziotas, *and* Markos, without consulting their colleagues, rebuffed him.[117]

Little insight can be gained from this episode, save that surviving KKE members are more interested in using their interpretations of the past to attack their former colleagues than to reconstruct the historical record. This is a phenomenon that occurs quite frequently among Communist

[116]*Vafeiadis*, p. 33. It is unclear in Vafeiadis' account exactly *who* was to do the denouncing.

[117]Bartziotas, *Agonas tou Dimokratikou Stratou Elladas*, pp. 89–90; Vontitsos-Gousias, *Aities gia tis Ittes, ti Diaspasi* 1:373. Gousias does not say who it was that Markos was going to meet, but his date corresponds with that of Bartziotas. As for the results of the meeting, Gousias says nothing. Vlantas's version is in Woodhouse, *Struggle for Greece*, p. 253.

elites and is especially pronounced when a defeat must be explained. Despite the web of cross-cutting accusations, however, some later initiatives clearly were made both by the KKE and by the Soviets. As Bartziotas (who, while critical of the general secretary's errors, is nonetheless supportive of him and the party generally) argues, these attempts to start negotiations were an extension of the dual strategy pursued in 1946. Bartziotas states that even after the Third Plenum, Zachariadis did not totally abandon the idea of negotiations and that the desire to pursue them was again manifest in 1948–49, when the initiative for a peaceful solution was taken up by the Soviet Union.[118]

The Soviets did not give up on negotiations—they merely changed the forum from which such appeals were made. In the United Nations they pushed especially hard for solutions that would allow the Soviets a legal or quasi-legal right to participate in the negotiations or, at a minimum, to claim credit for them. The intensity of their efforts increased after the break with Tito. By the end of 1948, Prime Minister Sofoulis did accept a U.N. resolution that Greece and her northern neighbors should undertake negotiations to settle their differences through the mediation of U.N. secretary general Trygvye Lie. Sofoulis, under pressure to agree, did so only on the condition that there be no compromise with the DSE.[119] This stricture proved unacceptable, and the initiative came to naught.

The efforts of the Soviets to push through some form of negotiation did not, however, mean that Stalin had stopped giving material aid. The civil war went on, and the DSE continued to rely for support, though more precariously than before, on the Yugoslavs. There appears as well to have been no diminution in aid to the Greek Communists from either Albania or Bulgaria.[120] So Soviet policy continued to stress material assistance as well, and there is evidence to indicate that by 1948 the Soviets had established supply routes through Albania which could, if necessary, partially supplant the Yugoslav lines. In August the British ambassador to Yugoslavia, Sir Charles Peake, reported that the "French Minister at Tirana on July 3 had reported arrival of three Russian ships at Durazzo heavily laden with munitions which he believed destined for Korça [Korçë] dumps which [was the] supply base for Markos. French Minister . . . state[d] that 20 to 25 lorries each carrying approximately 2 tons passed near his Ministry daily. . . . No guns or M.T. [?] were seen and Minister believes all crates contained ammunition and light supplies."[121]

[118]Bartziotas, *Agonas tou Dimokratikou Stratou Elladas*, p. 91.
[119]Woodhouse, *Struggle for Greece*, p. 245.
[120]Ibid., p. 253.
[121]FO 371-72342 R9538, August 16, 1948.

This is precisely the kind of assistance one would expect if Stalin was interested in demonstrating that he was contributing to the KKE cause yet simultaneously trying to wind it down. If he were interested in expanding the war, or even keeping DSE prospects stable, heavier materiel would have been provided.

As the battles of Grammos and then Vitsi wore on, the KKE tried to muster the arms it desperately needed for survival. In late September, after the battle of Vitsi, Zachariadis went once again to Moscow for talks with the Soviet leadership. In addition to his title of KKE general secretary, Zachariadis was now the president of the War Council, a recent creation, the result of Markos's three months' departure from his command post. According to Gousias, Zachariadis spoke with Stalin and other members of the Soviet leadership and requested material assistance of all kinds: weapons, food supplies, clothing, medical assistance, care for the injured, and help in recruiting Greeks who resided outside of Greece.[122]

The Soviet leadership, according to this account, agreed to provide the required assistance. Apparently, the Soviets "set up a military factory to work on the account of the DSE." Up to the end of winter 1948–49, it was to deliver "to the DSE 1,000 cannons of varying sizes with 1,000,000 shells; 1,000 anti-aircraft guns with more than 1,000,000 shells; 1,000 antitank cannons; aircraft for supplying our groups in the Peloponnese, Roumeli, Thessaly. It was decided to help us transfer about 8,000 Greeks who would be enlisted from the Western countries." On his return to Greece, the news apparently so uplifted the spirits of the DSE personnel that they sent some of their cadres off for training in flying, began preparing landing strips, and informed their forces in the south of Greece that they should set up drop-off points.[123]

This kind of response from the Soviet Union seems too good to have been true, and indeed it probably was. Bartziotas strongly disagrees with Gousias and accuses him of anti-Sovietism, because Gousias goes on to argue that the Soviets made promises and did not keep them. In particular, Bartziotas calls the promise of cannons imaginary.[124] Bartziotas does not

---

[122]Vontitsos-Gousias, *Aities gia tis Ittes, ti Diaspasi* 1:440.

[123]Ibid., pp. 440, 441. Other evidence indicates that landing strips were either in existence or contemplated: FO 371-73432 R4191, April 2, 1948; *Avgi*, no. 7, December 9, 1979. The *Avgi* document reveals a tantalizing bit of information. In early April 1947, Ioannidis asked Markos for a list of possible landing strips, but on April 26, 1947, several days after the Zachariadis-Tito meeting, Ioannidis again telegraphed Markos: "Immediate possibility for drop-offs does not exist. Diversion of material in the usual manner begins at this time." What the "usual manner" of providing arms to the DSE was remains unclear, as does the reason for postponing the construction of landing strips.

[124]Bartziotas, *Agonas tou Dimokratikou Stratou Elladas*, p. 47.

deny, however, that Zachariadis went to Moscow, nor does he deny the promise of other forms of assistance. And, if the past was any guide, it is not unlikely that the Soviets made promises they did not keep. Generally, this strengthens the argument that Stalin promised aid yet did not deliver in sufficient quantities.

Stalin was getting his way in the rest of the Balkans. With Hoxha and Shehu ascendant in Albania, the Albanian government issued conciliatory statements in May, even though its aid to the Greek Communists was undiminished. In Bulgaria, Dimitrov soon began to echo the Soviet line, and other Bulgarian officials considered the reestablishment of relations with Greece.[125] But for those who had dabbled with Tito in unsanctioned activities, there was no hope. In September, Xoxe was denounced as a Titoist, and he was executed the following year. As for Dimitrov, while it will probably never be known whether he was purged by Stalin, it is safe to say that his death in Moscow certainly occurred at an opportune moment for Soviet policy.

Through offers of aid to the DSE, Stalin managed to keep pace with the momentum of dangerous independent activities in northern Greece. By failing to honor his promises on time, he crippled the Greek Communist insurgency and placed pressure on Tito. In continuing this process, the Soviet leader succeeded in retrieving the political loyalty and obedience of Albania, Bulgaria, and the KKE and was in an excellent position to try and retain some pro-Soviet influence in Greece while simultaneously pressuring Yugoslavia. Stalin may have lost Yugoslavia, but he did succeed in retaining the rest of the Balkans at a time when his physical ability to control events was limited.

The Final Phase

By the beginning of 1949, the DSE was no longer in a position credibly to claim it could "win" the civil war, despite its relatively high morale for an army in dire straits. Although the potential to produce a significant effect through hit-and-run tactics remained, the DSE could not achieve the victory it officially strove for, only plunge the country further into despair. In January the DSE continued operations with some success, but each of its victories typified its inability to control territory. On January 11–12 it attacked the town of Naousa and held it for five days; several days later

125Wittner, p. 263.

the National Army repelled a DSE attack on Florina. Finally, on January 19, the DSE began a major assult on the town of Karpenisi, seized the town, and occupied it for a week. On January 29, however, government forces launched counterattacks that dislodged the DSE from the town.

To the Soviets, it was evident that the KKE was no longer in a position to threaten the Greek National Army seriously. Woodhouse is thus partly correct when he asserts that Stalin lost interest in the KKE.[126] As a military threat and a potentially independent Communist entity, the KKE was now effectively neutralized; but as long as the civil war continued, the KKE was still a potentially disruptive force outside of Stalin's control which could be harnessed for political goals or imperil hard-won gains. In 1949, both occurred: Stalin capitalized on the KKE's weakened position to subvert Tito, and the Greek government, in its desire finally to terminate the war, suggested the invasion of Albania (geographically isolated from the Soviet bloc by Tito's defection) to clean out the "nests" of subversion.

In the case of Tito, two questions naturally arise: how did Stalin plan to use the KKE against Tito, and why was this policy not implemented earlier, immediately after the Soviet-Yugoslav split? The answer to the first question is that the KKE would attempt to use the familiar issue of "Macedonian autonomy" to fragment the Republic of Macedonia in Yugoslavia.[127] This in turn answers the second question: Stalin needed time to establish control over those Macedonian organizations not under Tito's control. Without this control, the Soviet plan could backfire and result in Tito's capitalizing on Macedonian sympathy. In short, Stalin operated with a simple formula: establish tight organizational control, then proceed to use the organizations as political weapons.

In the KKE, Stalin had a good choice; as the war progressed to the disadvantage of the DSE, the Greek Communists were compelled to rely increasingly on Slavo-Macedonian recruits for their fighting force. By mid-1949, an estimated fourteen thousand of the less than twenty thousand *andartes* in the DSE were Slavo-Macedonians.[128] This was a favorable basis from which Stalin could start his campaign for an "independent Macedonia" in the ranks of the DSE. The first step was to establish a "Macedonian" organization to rival Tito's Macedonian Republic, and this

---

[126]Woodhouse, *Struggle for Greece*, p. 264.

[127]In support of this proposition, Kondis uses British and American documents to conclude that the KKE's Macedonia policy was in line with Soviet efforts to undermine Tito; see Kondis, *Angloamerikaniki Politiki*, p. 379. Wittner, p. 268, concurs.

[128]Woodhouse, *Struggle for Greece*, p. 262.

was accomplished by the Bulgarian takeover of the SNOF organization (later renamed NOF). NOF had been cooperating with the DSE for some time, and in August 1948 it began a purge of pro-Yugoslav cadres.[129] By December, NOF began asserting "national claims" to Macedonia, which placed the KKE in yet another dilemma: it could denounce NOF and risk losing the support of much of its fighting force, or it could acquiesce to NOF and risk being branded "anti-Greek."

The second step was accomplished at the Fifth Plenum of the KKE Central Committee (January 30–31, 1949), at which several important developments occurred. The DSE military plan was analyzed; Markos was removed from the Politburo and denounced for defeatism; and massive uprisings were planned in the cities—all decisions that reflected the extent to which the KKE, and Zachariadis in particular, were removed from reality. But the key developments were the resolution in support of Macedonian autonomy and a related decision to allow Slavo-Macedonians into the provisional democratic government. These two decisions must have had the support of the Soviet Union because Petrov, the Soviet official from the International Department of the CPSU, and Shehu, representative for the Albanian Workers' party, were present at the plenum proceedings.[130] It is inconceivable that the KKE, now dependent on the CPSU, would enact measures contrary to Soviet wishes with Soviet delegates present.

The final step in the clarification of this new aspect of Soviet policy came on February 3, just three days after the close of the Fifth Plenum. Zachariadis made his appearance at the Second Plenum of the NOF Central Committee that day, the same day NOF decided to announce at its congress the following month that it would support the "union of Macedonia into a complete, independent, and equal Macedonian nation within the Popular Democratic Federation of the Balkan Peoples."[131]

Tito and the Yugoslavs perceived the thrust of KKE and Soviet policy; Vukmanović-Tempo was convinced it was aimed at detaching Yugoslav Macedonia from Yugoslavia proper.[132] The success of Stalin's plan would rest on his ability to dilute the loyalties of the Yugoslav Macedo-

---

[129]Ibid., p. 253.

[130]Vontitsos-Gousias, *Aities gia tis Ittes, ti Diaspasi* 1:481. The Soviet official's name might possibly be P. Petrov, or it may be a pseudonym. As with many Soviet officials, their full names are unavailable.

[131]Woodhouse, *Struggle for Greece*, p. 264.

[132]Svetozar Vukmanović-Tempo, *How and Why the People's Liberation Struggle of Greece Met with Defeat* (London: n.p., 1950), pp. 51–55.

nians and lure them away with the promise of an integrated Macedonia. What was once the basis of Bulgarian and Yugoslav machinations now became a part of Stalin's arsenal, and he could maintain this organizational weapon as long as the Greek Civil War continued. Once the war was ended and the border situation was clarified, parastate organizations like the NOF Central Committee would lose their legitimacy.

But between March and April, events took an abrupt turn that dictated the insurgency be terminated and the effort to fragment Yugoslavia abandoned. The unstable situation in the Balkans had always been a potential threat to the security of a pro-Soviet Albania, but through 1948, Stalin did not seem excessively concerned that the Greek Civil War might trigger a Western-backed invasion of that country. Now, events made the threat uncomfortably real. As the war swung in favor of the Greek government, a stalemate arose: the DSE could not destroy Greece (only undermine its morale), and the Greek government could not eliminate the DSE. Much to the dismay of the Greek military and political leaders, the mountain heights of Grammos were once again being occupied by the DSE. Now, however, the source of DSE support was Albania, not Yugoslavia. Faced with the prospect of yet another fall campaign where the guerrillas had the opportunity to cross the border to safety, the Greek government addressed itself to the Western powers.

In early April the Greek government believed conditions were ripe for the Western powers to take decisive action to end the civil war and with it, the threat to Greece and Yugoslavia posed by the Soviets' meddling in the "Macedonian question." A Greek Embassy memorandum to the Foreign Office in London put it bluntly:

If the Western Powers have really decided that their future line of action shall be guided by the determination to call a halt to Russia's policy of blackmail and intimidation . . . it is essential to make perfectly clear . . . that any aggressive act by Russia will be followed by deeds, not merely words.

7. The geographical lay-out in the Balkans is such as to offer the possibility, today, for taking bold actions of this nature. The state of Albania . . . is exceptionally critical both from the political and economic point of view . . . her isolation from direct contact with Russia as the result of Tito's apostasy, has reduced Albania to an impasse. . . . The Albanian armed forces would not be in a position to oppose any effective resistance to any vigorous measures that the Western Powers might resort to from the sea. On the contrary, it is extremely probable that . . . Enver Hodja's regime would crumble to pieces. . . .

Consequently, the Greek government are of the opinion that swift action by the Allies in Albania would be the best and most effective means of staving off the possible consequences of a Russian advance in Macedonia and Yugoslavia.[133]

Stalin's maneuvering in Macedonia through the KKE had the damaging effect of exacerbating the unsettled situation on the Greek frontier, thereby forcing the Greek government to consider invading the Soviet's only access to the Mediterranean in order to pacify the region. The Soviets apparently felt obliged to take some counteraction, yet were still unable to intervene militarily in the Balkans. On April 11, less than one week after the Foreign Office received the memorandum, Zachariadis was summoned to Moscow from the DSE General Staff on Grammos. He returned on April 19, to speculation by the DSE leaders that Stalin finally would make good on his promises. Instead, the news was the reverse: Stalin ordered the shutdown of all DSE operations by the beginning of May, as the invasion of Albania would surely result if the Greek Civil War continued in the indecisive fashion of the last several months.[134] The next

[133]FO 371-78398/4018, April 4, 1949, Greek Embassy memorandum; as cited in Kondis, *Angloamerikaniki Politiki*, pp. 465–72. Kondis' analysis of Albania's position and Soviet diplomatic maneuvering in the closing stages of the civil war (pp. 382–90) is similar to the present one. That Stalin realized the danger of such a development is supported by his interest in Albania even after the final defeat of Greek Communist forces: when the British government attempted a covert operation to infiltrate Albania in 1949–50, Kim Philby was able to forewarn the Soviets. On the alleged covert operation in Albania and Philby's role in it, see Nicholas Bethell, *Betrayed* (New York: Times Books, 1984). Greek Communist sources also reveal Soviet sensitivity to Albania's position after 1949. Partsalidis recounted in an interview that in his January 1950 meeting with Stalin, Hoxha, and other Soviet, Albanian, and Greek Communist leaders, poor KKE-Albanian relations were discussed. Hoxha, fearing invasion, had taken the initiative in disarming the Greeks. Stalin, while chiding the Albanians for their action, essentially agreed with Hoxha's position when he stated that at present it was better that the Greek Communists not be based in Albania. Partsalidis closes his reminiscences of this part of the meeting with: "Really, if anyone recalls the situation which then prevailed in the Balkans, the mere presence of the leadership of the KKE and the Democratic Army could create difficulties and dangers for the People's Republic of Albania. And I think that . . . that which had the greatest weight in the Albanians' decision when they asked us to leave was the estimate of these dangers": *Avgi*, February 29, 1976. Clearly, if the danger to Albania was such an important consideration in January 1950, Stalin must have been aware of it even earlier. He also had reason to fear the Yugoslavs, as he knew in early 1948 that two Yugoslav divisions had entered Albania. According to Djilas, Stalin did not take this news well: "Moscow vigorously protested, refusing to accept as a reason that the Yugoslav divisions were needed to defend Albania from possible attack by the Greek 'monarcho-fascists.' In his dispatch to Belgrade, Molotov threatened an open breach"; see Djilas, *Conversations with Stalin*, p. 172.

[134]Vontitsos-Gousias, *Aities gia tis Ittes, ti Diaspasi* 1:500–3. Dimitris [Mitsos] Partsalidis, *Dipli Apokatastasi tis Ethnikis Antistasis* (Athens: Themelio, 1978), p. 199.

day, April 20, the provisional democratic government, addressing itself to the United Nations, announced that in order for peace to triumph, it (i.e., the KKE) was ready to make the heaviest sacrifices.[135]

Apparently, the Greek Civil War was finally nearing its conclusion. In response to the directives from Moscow, the KKE and DSE began preparing the withdrawal from the country. Zachariadis arrived on Grammos on May 1 to discuss how the withdrawal could be carried out. On May 2, Zachariadis concluded his discussions and returned to Vitsi. Two days later, the military leaders at Grammos, Bartziotas and Gousias, were stunned to receive a telegram from Zachariadis in which he stated that the situation had temporarily changed and instead of retreat, there must be vigorous offensive activity.[136]

What had happened between April 20 and May 4? The explanation is to be found in a close reading of the diplomatic activities between the United States and the Soviet Union. The threat of invasion had apparently succeeded (unintentionally, as it turned out) in making the Soviets choose to shut down the entire civil war; the implicit threat had come from a Western position of strength. On April 26, however, U.S. assistant secretary of state Dean Rusk took the occasion of a dinner with Gromyko and U.N. secretary general Lie to inquire whether the governments of the Soviet Union, United States, and Great Britain might not be able to do something to bring about a settlement of the Greek situation.[137] Gromyko sensed the shift from a military solution to a political one implicit in this question. It meant that the possibilities for negotiations might still be open (or that they had reopened), and the Soviets might yet have a chance to recoup some influence in Greece. After all, the Macedonian issue had brought on the fear of the invasion of Albania, which would result in a complete loss. Might it not be better to salvage at least something from Greece, particularly if the West was offering it? Gromyko responded that the conversations of April 26 were too vague but that he had reported the matter to Moscow. In early May, he informed Rusk and British U.N. delegate Hector McNeil that he had permission from his government to discuss the matter.[138]

To the Soviets, the prospect was too good to be true: the West, which

[135]*Vafeiadis*, p. 50–51.

[136]Vontitsos-Gousias, *Aities gia tis Ittes, ti Diaspasi* 1:507.

[137]DSR 868.00/5-549, memorandum of conversation, in Kondis, *Angloamerikaniki Politiki*, pp. 473–78; see also, *Vafeiadis*, p. 51.

[138]DSR 868.00/5-549, memorandum of conversation, in Kondis, *Angloamerikaniki Politiki*, pp. 473–78.

only weeks ago was considering invading Albania, was now asking the Soviet Union for help in resolving the problem in Greece! This was clearly Stalin's last opportunity to restore influence in Greece; the prospect must have been tempting. Accordingly, Gromyko took up the issue in more detail with Rusk and McNeil on May 4, the date of Zachariadis' telegram to his military officers.[139] But why order the return to civil war? Since there is agreement on this point, it might be best to let available KKE sources provide the answer. According to Gousias, who by this time was head of military operations for the DSE, Zachariadis explained in a May 28 meeting that the Greek government was in serious difficulty, so the provisional government's proposals for a peaceful resolution had had a substantial impact. The Soviet Union, through Gromyko at the United Nations, had made proposals for peace and the cessation of war in Greece; it would not do for the enemy to view these proposals as made out of weakness, so offensive operations had to continue.[140]

Now it becomes clear what the Soviets had done: Stalin, seeing the opportunity to preserve a corner of Communist influence in Greece through a negotiated solution to the civil war, ordered Zachariadis to continue operations in order to avoid the appearance that the DSE was so weak it was suing for peace. Soviet policy in Greece had come full circle in 1949: initially, the civil war was to be a means of using the Macedonian issue against Tito; then, with the danger of an invasion of Albania looming, the retreat had to be sounded; finally, with a perceived softening of American attitudes, the Soviets needed a show of strength to bring about successful negotiations and preserve some pro-Soviet influence in Greece after the war.

Unfortunately, the DSE was already too weak to accomplish its task, and it is doubtful that American policymakers really meant to convey the impression of softening Stalin perceived. The immediate cause of Soviet policy failure at this time, however, was Tito, who began progressively closing the Yugoslav-Greek borders in June. Zachariadis apparently attempted to preserve the KKE's delicate stand toward Yugoslavia, but in 1949, Stalin would not allow it. In late July he ordered Zachariadis to denounce the Yugoslavs publicly. Beginning on July 23, Tito sealed off the border to Greek Communists entirely, trapping men in Yugoslavia and effectively robbing those remaining in Greece of their sanctuary. Within a

[139]Ibid.
[140]Vontitsos-Gousias, *Aities gia tis Ittes, ti Diaspasi* 1:516; Partsalidis, *Dipli Apokatastasi tis Ethnikis Antistasis*, p. 199.

month the final battle at Grammos was being fought, and by the end of August, the DSE was moving into Albania. The official Greek Communist declaration of the decision to stop the armed struggle came only later in 1949, but in reality, the defeat at Grammos ended the war.

Thus, despite several complicated shifts, the main thrust of Soviet policy during the civil war years after the collapse of the dual strategy was the containment of an overly militant Tito, who threatened to break Stalin's grip on all of southeastern Europe. To retain that grip, Stalin had to prevent a strategic commitment by the West in the eastern Mediterranean yet avoid appearing inactive to the party organizations with strong arguments for action. When the situation in Greece deteriorated, bringing on a U.S. response, Stalin was then free to manipulate the Greek Civil War to slow events in the Balkans and make time to recoup. While the effort was largely successful for Stalin, it was disastrous for the Greek Communists; for it produced the same fatal hesitancy that led to their defeat in December 1944. In the closing stages of the civil war, Stalin was able to turn the Greek situation into a weapon against Tito, but he never lost sight of his potential gain from preserving a pro-Soviet enclave in Greece; and when the opportunity appeared to arise, he took it. The dual strategy Stalin and Zachariadis had pursued created serious problems for the Soviets but also an important compensating benefit: although advising delay had given local Balkan forces the opportunity they needed to break free of Great Power interests, once Stalin had regained his preeminent position in the region, his persistent efforts to achieve a negotiated solution to the war provided Soviet policy with flexibility it would otherwise have lacked. In contrast, the Greek Communist experience was a bitter one—an example of how a great power's behavior, either through direct action or abstention from intervention, can affect regional and internal politics. Stalin certainly did not attain all to which he aspired, but far more than did the Greek Communists.

5

ELITE CONFLICT AND
SOVIET POLICY IN GREECE

Central to the foregoing analysis was the division between Stalin and Tito and its effect on Soviet policy during the Greek Civil War. The success with which the concept of elite conflict—"Stalinist" versus "Titoist"— has elsewhere been used to produce a plausible explanation of Soviet behavior in the Balkans suggests that this concept merits broader consideration. Did divisions within the Soviet leadership, possibly reflected among Greek Communist elites, significantly affect the performance of the KKE and its military arm, the DSE? The answer can be found in an analysis of two hypotheses: (1) the Stalin-Zhdanov dispute had a direct impact on the course of Soviet policy in Greece, and (2) as a consequence of the divisions within the Soviet Politburo and the close connections between Tito and Zhdanov, there existed a parallel division of the Greek Communist leadership into "Titoist" and "Stalinist" wings, with an effect on KKE policy. Investigation of elite conflict in the Soviet Politburo is, of course, a daunting task; the inner workings of the Soviet leadership are almost always inacessible to Western scholars, so personal accounts and occasional bits of information form the data for analysis. Despite this difficulty, several recent studies have attempted to analyze the power configurations within the Soviet elite after the close of World War II. Most of them focus predictably on the rise and fall of Andrei Zhdanov.[1]

---

[1]The role of Zhdanov in Kremlin politics has always been important to the study of the Stalin era. An early treatment can be found in Franz Borkenau, *European Communism*

The events surrounding Zhdanov's demise may be significant for the study of the Greek Civil War; for it is often alleged that Zhdanov was the leader of the "forward" line of Soviet policy, which stressed the need to expand the revolutionary struggle to confront the imminent collapse of capitalism. In this world view, Greece was a natural testing ground; there the forces of capitalism were staging the first of many battles against the inevitable spread of the international Communist movement. Stalin, according to several interpretations, held an opposing view; he realized that the world economic order was not about to collapse. Capitalism (American in particular) still possessed enormous strength. Thus any Soviet attempt to foment or support revolutionary activities would only provoke the United States and jeopardize hard-won gains.

A full understanding of what occurred in the Balkans during the last half of the 1940s must depend on knowing what forces in the Soviet Union created its policy. This knowledge would help as well in understanding the relationship between international conduct and the internal politics of the Soviet system. The scant references in the available KKE archives can shed some light on that relationship, although a brief chapter here can only touch upon what really should be the subject of a much larger study. Any effect of conflict within the Soviet leadership on foreign policy should be observable. Divisions within the Soviet Politburo, while they might have existed, are of little interest here if they cannot be shown to have affected policy; Soviet domestic conflict is relevant to foreign policy only in so far as it has a discernable impact on the outside world. The Greek case is particularly useful in this respect because it represents, as nearly as possible, the classic clash between "revolutionary" and "conservative" tactics. Such dichotomies are generally to be avoided because they obscure the texture of political activity, but in the Zhdanov case, this crude division of opposites certainly did form the basis for Marxist-Leninist polemics.

The second hypothesis is actually what has come to be accepted as the standard version of what occurred and has in fact become so ingrained in

---

(New York: Harper, 1953). Robert Conquest also deals with Zhdanov in his *Power and Policy in the U.S.S.R.: The Struggle for Stalin's Succession, 1945–1960* (New York: Harper & Row, 1967), pp. 79–94. More recent studies, each from different perspectives and with different interpretations, are William O. McCagg, *Stalin Embattled, 1943–1948* (Detroit: Wayne State University Press, 1978); Werner G. Hahn, *Post-War Soviet Politics: The Fall of Zhdanov and the Defeat of Moderation, 1946–1953* (Ithaca, N.Y.: Cornell University Press, 1982); and Gavriel Ra'anan, *International Policy Formation in the USSR: Factional 'Debates' during the Zhdanovshchina* (Hamden, Conn.: Shoe String, Archon, 1983).

studies of the KKE's policy that it is almost always unquestioned.[2] The
KKE leadership has been neatly described according the hypothesized
divisions: Zachariadis, the "Stalinist," is said to have supported a strategy
that entailed the creation of a regular army and excessive reliance on cities
as bases for revolutionary activity. Markos Vafeiadis is assumed to be the
"Titoist" who favored guerrilla-style tactics and exclusive use of the
mountains to sustain the rebellion. In this way, the hypothetical dispute
provides a rather neat division between guerrilla and conventional tactics,
making it possible to heap all the blame for Communist failure in the civil
war on Zachariadis.

Recently, however, the publication of new memoirs and materials have
led some scholars to begin reexamining this issue,[3] and the archival
excerpts that constitute the core of the present study show that the "standard" version simply does not conform to the facts. There was no crippling dispute over strategy until *after* the critical battles of 1947 had
already been fought. In the decisive years of 1946 and 1947, the KKE was
not torn by tactical or ideological conflict. Much of the standard version is
based upon the testimony of exiled KKE leaders who were in a position to
speak. Only now, in an atmosphere that allows "Stalinists" to present
their points of view, is it becoming apparent that this aspect of KKE
history is characterized by bitter recriminations, with interpretations advanced less to reveal the truth than to substantiate present political
positions.

Given this situation, the use of personal memoirs becomes very difficult. Nonetheless, the few extant excerpts from the archives, combined
with careful use of memoirs and the perspective of forty years' removal

---

[2]Because of its long-standing popularity, there are innumerable works that rely upon any
one of the various incarnations of the "Stalinist" versus "Titoist" thesis; mentioned here
are only a few of the most prominent. The most well-known non-Communist works, which
typically stress the division over strategy, are Christopher M. Woodhouse, *The Struggle for
Greece, 1941–1949* (London: Hart-Davis, MacGibbon, 1976), pp. 202 ff; and D. George
Kousoulas, *Revolution and Defeat: The Story of the Greek Communist Party, 1918–1949*
(London: Oxford University Press, 1965), pp. 249 ff. A recent version with a eurocom-
munist twist is Dominque Eudes, *The Kapetanios: Partisans and Civil War in Greece,
1943–1949* (New York: Monthly Review Press, 1972), esp. pp. 303–42. A revisionist
analysis of American involvement in the Greek Civil War that relies on the Markos-
Zachariadis conflict is Lawrence S. Wittner, *American Intervention in Greece, 1943–1949*
(New York: Columbia University Press, 1982), pp. 266–69. A work relying on more recent
materials which is especially helpful in beginning a much-needed reassessment of this
period is Ole L. Smith, "A Turning Point in the Greek Civil War 1945–1949," *Scandinavian Studies in Modern Greek*, no. 3 (1979), 35–46.
[3]The best job to date is in Smith, "Turning Point."

from the actual events, may provide insights surprisingly at odds with the conventional appraisals. In general, the evidence both casts doubt on the viability of the thesis that the Stalin-Zhdanov dispute was significant enough to disrupt Soviet foreign policy and indicates that the received truth about the "Titoist" heresy within the KKE must be reevaluated. This is not to say that disputes and divisions did not exist—the contrary is actually the case—but they did not substantially affect Stalin's relations with the KKE, and the Zachariadis-Markos feud was less a dispute over strategy and ideology than the inevitable mutual recriminations that accompany a Communist failure.

The Zhdanov Case

In order to evaluate the first hypothesis, it is first necessary to establish the extent of the relationships between Zhdanov, his East European allies, and the rest of the Soviet elite. The primary focus is, of course, on Josip Tito. The preceding analysis clearly reveals that Tito had succeeded in creating an independent base for pursuing an aggressive policy aimed at extending his influence throughout the Balkans. Stalin's heir apparent and the Yugoslav leader therefore appeared to have a common interest in a "militant" foreign policy.

From the end of the war through 1946, Zhdanov was ascendant. It was he, not Stalin, who presided over the 1946 annual celebration of the October Revolution in November, an occasion he took to give a speech that reflected his militant orientation in international affairs. The current situation of the world, Zhdanov asserted, was a result of its division into two camps, capitalist and socialist; the capitalist camp, while hostile to the very existence of the "democratic" socialist states, happened to be in a period of critical decline. This appraisal of the capitalist world was a key proposition in Zhdanov's international perspective. The 1946–47 period was also the time of the "Zhdanovshchina," a purge of Soviet society that sought to extirpate "pernicious" bourgeois traits and replace them with adulation of Slavic culture and Great Russian nationalism.[4] It was also Zhdanov's best chance to penetrate the Soviet bureaucracy with his protégés in order to solidify his domestic position.

In Bulgaria, there was a "Zhdanov connection" through Georgi Dimitrov, who had a previous personal tie to Zhdanov through their service

[4]Ra'anan, p. 54.

on the Ghost Comintern during the war, and through Dimitrii Manuil'skii, also apparently one of Zhdanov's followers.[5] This connection was probably most important to Dimitrov in late 1947, when Tito and the Bulgarian leader were drawing closer. The triumvirate of Zhdanov, Tito, and Dimitrov was a key faction in the founding meeting of the Cominform in September 1947.

At the Cominform meeting, according to Vladimir Dedijer, Zhdanov played a leading role in getting the Yugoslav delegates to criticize the French and Italian Communist delegations for their lack of revolutionary militancy and their stubborn pursuit of a parliamentary policy.[6] In addition, the Yugoslavs were accorded a place of high honor during the meetings; the choice of Belgrade as the permanent site for the Cominform was certainly indicative. Zhdanov was involving himself in policies and actions that went against Soviet policy. During the founding meeting at Szklarska Poreba, Kardelj (besides joining Djilas in an attack on the French and Italian Communists) specifically stated that partisan warfare was not a means of pressuring the bourgeoisie but of overcoming it,[7] an argument completely contrary to Stalin's advice to Zachariadis in 1946. Evaluated by the amount of attention they each received at the meeting, Zhdanov's chief rival, Georgii Malenkov, was reduced to a subordinate status.

Another event—this time, in May 1947—underscored the close connection between Zhdanov and his Yugoslav allies. The occasion was the attack (which took the form of a debate) on the work of economist Evgenii Varga. In 1946, Varga had published a study of the changes in world capitalism since World War II.[8] He made two points relevant to the present case. First, there was no crisis in the capitalist system because the development of state regulation during the war had allowed for a measure of control to be introduced over capitalist economies. Moreover, the crisis of overproduction confidently forecast by Zhdanovites would not soon develop because the war had left conditions favorable to the maintenance of high production and consumption levels. The United States was left

[5]Ibid., pp. 21, 53. Zhdanov also traveled several times to Yugoslavia and Bulgaria, allegedly solidifying his contacts with the Balkan leaders.
[6]Vladimir Dedijer, *Tito* (New York: Simon & Schuster, 1953), p. 295.
[7]Eugenio Reale, *Nascita del Cominform* (Milan: Arnoldo Mondadori, 1958), p. 38. Reale was one of the delegates from the Italian Communist party to attend the founding Cominform meeting, and his work, based on his notes of the meeting, remains the best source on what actually transpired.
[8]Evgenii S. Varga, *Izmeneniia v ekonomike kapitalizma v itoge vtoroi mirovoi voiny* (Moscow: Politicheskoi Literatury, 1946).

with a strong and relatively undamaged economy and could continue uninterrupted production at high levels; Europe, devastated by the war, would absorb U.S. overproduction. Until the economies of Western Europe had restored themselves, Varga implied, capitalism, far from destroying itself, would achieve a temporary stabilization. The present strength of capitalism dictated a cautious Soviet foreign policy. Second, Varga believed that countries in which the Communists had taken over were "democracies of a new type," state capitalist rather than socialist. To add insult to injury, he lumped Yugoslavia with such countries as Czechoslovakia (where the Communists were not yet in power) and Romania.

The Zhdanovites were bound to attack Varga and did so during the debates in May 1947. What is most interesting, however, is that the viewpoints of the Yugoslavs were very forcefully presented at this meeting despite the fact that foreigners were not invited to the debate. At least one analyst has concluded that there was an "informant" for Tito at the meetings.[9] But informants were hardly necessary; for the man who led the attack on Varga was Nikolai Voznesenskii, a close associate of Zhdanov and an acquaintance of Djilas. Djilas knew Voznesenskii's older brother (A. A. Voznesenskii) fairly well,[10] and it was apparently the elder Voznesenskii who was responsible for allowing the Yugoslav contact into the meetings.[11] Thus, the interests of the Yugoslavs were well-represented, making another instance of the close collaboration between the Zhdanov group and the Yugoslavs.

Nikolai Voznesenskii, who had also written an analysis of the wartime economy, attacked Varga on every fundamental point. In particular, he stressed that the crisis of capitalism was very near: "The high levels of productivity and of technology which were reached in the USA during the war make the contradiction peculiar to capitalism more acute, and created the basis for a new devastating economic crisis and chronic unemployment."[12] Of direct importance for the Yugoslavs and the situation in Greece was Voznesenskii's rebuttal of Varga on the likelihood of U.S. support for failing capitalist economies. Zhdanov's protégé argued that it would be impossible for the United States to prop up failing regimes

[9]Ra'anan, pp. 65–66.
[10]Milovan Djilas, *Conversations with Stalin*, trans. Michael Petrovich (New York: Harcourt, Brace & World, 1962), p. 150.
[11]Ra'anan, p. 66.
[12]Nikolai A. Voznesenskii, *Voennaia ekonomika SSSR v period otechestvennoi voiny* (Moscow: Politicheskoi Literatury, 1948), p. 32.

because the major capitalist states would be convulsed by the impending economic collapse.[13] The correlation of this statement with Yugoslav attitudes is striking: in September 1947, Deputy Foreign Minister Bebler argued along exactly the same lines and for that reason maintained confidence that Greece would collapse by virture of American inability to sustain foreign commitments.[14]

The Zhdanov faction therefore had extensive contact with the Yugoslav and Bulgarian Communist parties. The crucial point, however, is the significance of these contacts: Did Zhdanov's Balkan allies provide him with a base of support sufficient to challenge Stalin's control of foreign policy? Available evidence indicates the answer must be negative. First, as almost every analyst of Soviet politics has observed,[15] Zhdanov was not competing with Stalin but with Malenkov. What Stalin was actually doing was something at which he had become a pastmaster: deliberately creating overlapping spheres of administrative responsibility among the other Politburo members, keeping them at each other's throats and ensuring that they would not conspire against him.[16] To assume that Zhdanov's maneuvers were a serious threat to Stalin is to miss the point of elite conflict under Stalin.

In this competition between Stalin's two lieutenants, it is Zhdanov who is usually said to have had the upper hand at the founding Cominform meeting. A brief reconsideration of the activities of the two Soviet leaders indicates, however, that although Zhdanov was more prominent at the meeting, he was *not* in a dominant or uncontested position. There is the testimony of Eugenio Reale that the Yugoslav attack on the French and Italian Communists was arranged beforehand by Zhdanov *and Malenkov*.[17] Rather than supporting the Zhdanovite "forward line" thesis, the suggestion that both Soviet leaders orchestrated the event lends more credence to Kardelj's argument that the Cominform meeting was designed to ambush the Yugoslavs, who, by virture of their violent criticism of their comrades, were to find themselves isolated after the break with Stalin nine months later.[18] Existing analyses, moreover, have tended to regard the

[13]As cited in Ra'anan, p. 69.

[14]FO 371-57157 R13254, September 19, 1947.

[15]The exception is McCagg (in *Stalin Embattled*), who seems to argue that Stalin had genuinely to fear Zhdanov inside the Soviet Union.

[16]Ra'anan, p. 25.

[17]Reale, p. 41.

[18]Edvard Kardelj, *Memorie degli Anni di Ferro* (Rome, 1980), pp. 111–12; in Paolo Spriano, *Stalin and the European Communists,* trans. Jon Rothschild (London: Verso, 1985), p. 301.

Cominform meeting primarily as an outgrowth of Stalin's foreign policy dealings with the West. In this interpretation, Zhdanov's role stands out, since it was he who delivered the report on the international situation. But this view may reflect a misunderstanding of the manner in which Stalin adapted to the changed international realities. An equally plausible argument is that Stalin viewed the emerging Cold War as a threat to Soviet control of Eastern Europe, which made it essential to consolidate Soviet power in the region with a thorough Stalinization and an extirpation of independent, heretical parties. Hence, while the Yugoslavs exulted in their success by browbeating the French and Italians, Valko Chervenkov was lecturing East European Communists on how to monopolize power. And while Zhdanov openly supported his south Slav comrades and expounded on the "two-camp" thesis in foreign policy, Malenkov was quietly asserting that a fundamental problem in the near future would be the "coordination" of the activities of the various parties.[19] If Stalin was "ambushing" the Yugoslavs, then Malenkov appeared to be taking advantage of an opportunity to give his Soviet colleague the rope with which to hang himself. The situation less than a year later certainly appears to vindicate this interpretation: the Yugoslavs were isolated; bloc uniformity and monolithic Stalinism were in high gear; Western European Communist parties had fallen in line behind the Soviet leader; and Zhdanov was out of the picture entirely.

A more general point to bear in mind is that because of constant conflict among the members of the Politburo, ideological positions or alternative policies were espoused not for their inherent value but for their capacity to provide an immediate, short-term tactical advantage and thereby ensure the survival of the espouser. It is doubtful Zhdanov adhered to his policies because he truly believed in their merit. It is more probable that he adopted a militant pose to secure a tactical advantage over his chief

---

[19]Reale, p. 146. Fernando Claudin takes a position similar to that presented here in explaining the absence of certain Communist parties from the meeting at Szklarska Poreba: "Stalin's aim, contrary to the opinion held at the time by the politicians of the 'free world,' was not to unleash a world-wide revolutionary struggle against American imperialism. His strategic objective was still the same; only his tactics had changed. Stalin intended, by taking a 'hard' line, to force Washington to recognize the division into 'zones of influence' within the framework of a world-wide compromise guaranteeing bipartite control of the world by the two superpowers"; see Claudin, *The Communist Movement: From Comintern to Cominform*, pt. 2, *The Zenith of Stalinism* (New York: Monthly Review Press, 1975), p. 466. Stalin's prudent expansionism of 1945–46 was now transformed into a drive to ensure block control, and the best guarantee was monolithic control over Eastern Europe, not expansion into the West.

adversary. Such tactics are tolerable unless they encroach upon the security of the Soviet state, and Zhdanov's "forward" line did just that. Zhdanov, unlike Tito, could have had no *substantive* interest in a risky policy; hence, in his tactical moves, he was more or less accidental to the whole episode. Still, the connection, insofar as it incited and perhaps depended on the Titoists, is very important. His actions encouraged the Yugoslavs in their adventurist policy in Greece (and elsewhere), which threatened Soviet positions in the world, which then forced Stalin to break with Tito and (possibly) to eliminate Zhdanov—events of incalculable significance.

Second, the apparently close connections between the foreign Communists and Zhdanov could not possibly enhance his position relative to Stalin; for it was Zhdanov who was dependent upon the Yugoslavs and not the reverse. Tito had come to power through the efforts of the Partisans alone and required no assistance in running his own affairs, which most irritated and alarmed Stalin. It stands to reason, therefore, that Tito would have pursued his policies even if a Zhdanov faction had not existed. (Although he might have been less cocksure without the flattering entrée to Moscow.) Any harmony of interests between Tito and a sector of the Soviet bureaucracy reflects a fortuitous resonance rather than any real dependence. But Zhdanov was in search of support for his position. Since in 1947 the issues he fixed upon were concerned primarily with foreign policy, he naturally looked to allies outside of the Soviet Union to vindicate his position. Although Tito could live without Zhdanov, Zhdanov by virture of the issues he adopted, put himself in a position where his personal success conflicted with the interests of the Soviet state. In such a situation, Zhdanov was bound to lose.

Third, there is no available evidence that Zhdanov exerted independent influence in Greece. Evidently, Zachariadis had conversations about KKE strategy with Zhdanov, Molotov, and Stalin in April 1946. But if Lefteris Eleftheriou's account is correct, then it was at the second, private meeting in Crimea that Stalin apprised Zachariadis of the appropriate course of action (see chap. 3). There is good reason to accept this version of events because March 1946 was when the Soviets began dismantling their wartime politico-military institutions and initiated the massive task of reconstruction. This would have been the most likely time for conflict among the Soviet leadership, and Stalin would have wanted to keep a close watch on his subordinates, monitoring their activities and handling key policies personally. The Soviet dictator would have kept the closest watch on Zhdanov because he had emerged from the war as Stalin's heir apparent.

When Zachariadis requested aid for the armed struggle in the winter of 1946–47, he was rejected although this was supposedly the period of Zhdanov's greatest influence. Finally, while Zachariadis was in Moscow in May 1947, Zhdanov was said to have been an active participant in the discussions. It is conceivable that he had separate discussions with Zachariadis in a more "militant" vein, but if Zhdanov was really an ally of Tito, why would he have intimate conversations with the KKE's staunchest proponent of Stalinism? In any case, further evidence from Zachariadis' September 1, 1947, letter to Zhdanov indicates that the KKE general secretary provided him no special information. The Greek Communist leader even described the favorable preparations for transforming, the Greek rebels into a regular army. Again the question arises: Why, if Zhdanov was Tito's ally, would the supposedly Stalinist Zachariadis inform him of plans to adopt a strategy radically opposed to the guerrilla strategy advocated by the Yugoslavs? The records are incomplete, but the examples suffice to demonstrate the plausibility of the assertion that it could not have been possible for Zhdanov to influence the Greek Communists on his own.

Fourth, there is no evidence that Zhdanov had any supporters among the Soviet officials administering policy in Greece, nor any protégés in the KKE. Stalin's control over these officials and the fidelity of the KKE apparently precluded any real influence by Zhdanov in the civil war. Those actually responsible for Soviet policy in Greece were relatively few. The evidence presented indicates many Soviets had contact with the KKE between 1944 and 1949 (the Russian Military Mission; the "repatriation" mission; Soviet ex-POWs; CPSU officials in Belgrade, Sofia, and Tirana; the U.N. Commission of Inquiry; the numerous agents that filtered through the Greek frontier), but most of these were probably not in a position to direct Greek Communist policy.[20] Judging from existing

[20]The exact number is obviously impossible to obtain but certainly exceeds forty, an undeniably significant number for a small country supposedly assigned to the Western sphere-of-influence. The most interesting place to examine the interacting forces would be in the various Balkan capitals, particularly Belgrade. Some information regarding personnel concerned with the administration of Soviet policy when the Second Subcommittee of the KKE Politburo resided in Belgrade comes from available KKE archives. In Moscow, relations between the KKE, Tito and the Soviets were to some extent handled by Sergeiev, who ordered Zachariadis to leave Greece and enter Yugoslavia: *Avgi*, no. 6, December 8, 1979. Conceivably, this is Mikhail Sergeiev who was originally intended as the Soviet Ambassador to Greece and later replaced by Konstantin Rodionov (see chap. 2). According to the excerpts published in *Avgi*, there were still other Soviets in Belgrade. In June 1947 (*Avgi*, no. 12, December 15, 1979), Zachariadis wrote to "Baranov," and referred to "Chatouro[v] and the girl," and added that "we expect [await?] the remaining three

materials, the number of key Soviet officials may be safely limited to approximately a dozen. For some of these, the little evidence available reveals no tangible links to Zhdanov (although their fate after his demise remains unknown). Those in Greece and the Balkans for whom more information is available (Chernichev, Rodionov, Lavrishchev), certainly were not connected to Zhdanov since their actions reflect a faithful effort to implement the gradualist and (later) dualist policies. This leaves only five persons, Stalin, Molotov, Zhdanov, Baranov, and Petrov (first names of the last two unavailable) with the major responsibility for Greek-Soviet affairs. The fate of the first three is clear; only Baranov's position after the fall of Zhdanov is unknown. Petrov, the CPSU's official in charge of Balkan affairs, held his office before the crisis with Zhdanov and continued to do so long after Zhdanov had died. Vontitsos-Gousias asserts that Petrov was present at the KKE Fifth Plenum in January 1949 and then accompanied the KKE into exile in Tashkent and continued to oversee Greek-Soviet affairs.[21]

The overlapping territorial issues in the Balkans produced an atmosphere of distrust and anxiety which made it extremely difficult for Zhdanov's Yugoslav and Bulgarian protégés to have any influence in Greece. Although it depended on Tito's assistance, the KKE distrusted Yugoslav intentions in Macedonia; similarly, Hoxha was fearful of Greek (Communist or otherwise) aspirations to Northern Epirus. Bulgaria's wartime occupation of Greek territory and its minimal contribution to the DSE

---

comrades shortly." Later, in September 1947, Zachariadis shed some light on who these "three comrades" might be when, in a letter to Zhdanov, he stated that "comrades Giousoupof [Iusupov] and Lavro[v] have arrived. I am waiting for Chatouro[v]. Regarding Zhivko[v], we prefer if you did not send him to us": *Avgi,* December 30, 1979. (Zhivkov apparently did arrive in late September or early October, despite Zachariadis' distaste for him: *Avgi,* no. 32, January 12, 1980.)

[21]Some of Petrov's activities are discussed by several Greek Communists, but the account that clearly places him in an official capacity after the end of the civil war is in Giorgis Vontitsos-Gousias, *Oi Aities gia tis Ittes, ti Diaspasi tou KKE kai tis Ellinikis Aristeras* (Athens: Na Iperetoume to Lao, 1977), 2:1–30 passim. Baranov is more difficult to locate. A "Baranov" does appear in two different contexts in Soviet relations with Bulgaria. A letter to Bulgarian architect Trendafil K. Trendafilov dated August 18, 1945, mentions that "Baranov" visited Sofia several times with Soviet architect Aleksei V. Shchusev. In a June 1947 telegram congratulating Dimitrov on his sixty-fifth birthday, "Baranov" appears (along with Red Army Lieutenant-General A. S. Gundorov, [A. A.?] Voznesenskii, Korneichuk, Derzhavin, Kolas, Saevich, Tikhonov, Pilipchuk, and Komarov) as a member of the Pan-Slav Committee. It is impossible to determine whether the two Baranovs are the same person: *Sovetsko-Bolgarskie otnosheniia i sviazi: Dokumenty i materialy,* ed. L. B. Valev, vol. 2, *Sentiabr' 1944–Dekabr' 1958,* ed. R. P. Grishina (Moscow: Nauka, 1981), pp. 114, 213–14.

effort also failed to inspire confidence. Zhdanov may have had allies in the Balkans, but fundamental territorial and political differences among them produced mutual animosities that made it impossible to use them as a united and effective instrument of policy in Greece.

The scant evidence suggests that while Zhdanov had a clique of high-level Yugoslav, Bulgarian, and (possibly) Albanian Communists on his side, Stalin had a firm grip on the lower-level Soviet officials who actually administered policy on Greek Communism, and the undivided support of the KKE. Hence, basic political differences in the Balkans combined with Stalin's control and ability to manipulate lower level bureaucrats to vitiate any independent Zhdanovite initiative.

Converging lines of evidence impressively indicate that the Zhdanov affair did not significantly affect Soviet policy in Greece. While the Greek situation did force Stalin to take action to avoid losing what he had achieved during the war, his real concern in averting dangerous "adventurism" abroad was Tito and not Zhdanov.

Titoists versus Stalinists: An Ideological Fiction

If the Zhdanov angle is unhelpful in the Greek case, what of the hypothesis that there existed in the KKE divisions between "Stalinists," represented by Zachariadis, and "Titoists," represented by Markos, which seriously impaired the application of KKE policy? Several scholars have argued for this view. The following quotation from Woodhouse's work typifies the position: "It has reasonably been assumed that once the quarrel [the Soviet-Yugoslav dispute] became generally known Markos wished to align the KKE with Tito and Zachariades wished to align it with Stalin. *But their dispute had already been in existence for a long time,* not over Titoism but over tactics."[22]

Woodhouse bases this conclusion on the fact that Markos had wanted to fight using guerrilla-style tactics and Zachariadis chose instead to create a regular army. In addition, Woodhouse points to several examples of what he considers to be Markos's defiance of KKE directives. On September 5, 1947, for example, Markos sent a communication to the United Nations

[22]Woodhouse, *Struggle for Greece,* p. 231; emphasis added. Eudes, pp. 264–68, serves as an example of the view that Zachariadis sought to follow the "canonical" model of a revolution by relying on the urban proletariat, thereby crippling the insurgency in the mountains. This argument is a weak one at best, especially as Eudes provides no substantiation.

calling for a cease-fire and a coalition government. Woodhouse infers this was not sanctioned by the KKE because less than one week later the Third Plenum decisively turned the KKE toward civil war. Furthermore, Markos is portrayed as progressively hamstrung by the KKE leadership; Woodhouse asserts the last time Markos had undisputed control was just before the Third Plenum.[23] Thereafter Zachariadis is said to have begun encroaching on Markos, and soon the disputes between the two were to intensify.

Another argument has been that Markos resisted the transition to a regular army but was ultimately overruled. In this interpretation, the KKE's central problem was that the formation of a regular army was premature and ultimately entailed defeat for the DSE. In the fall of 1948, Markos is supposed to have presented this prospect to the KKE leadership, laying bare the weaknesses of the movement: poor recruitment, lack of mobilization in urban areas, and the success of "monarchofascism" in achieving a "temporary stabilization."[24] In sum, the entire failure of the KKE to carry out the civil war is said to have revolved around the continued dispute between Zachariadis, with his "Stalinist," regular-army approach, and the increasingly embattled "Titoist" and guerrilla-oriented DSE commander.

It is reasonable to conclude, in light of more recent sources, that the assumption of a simplistic Tito–Stalin division in the KKE, which subsequently caused its defeat because the Stalinist side won out, is at best exaggerated. In the wake of defeat, KKE leaders began to engage in sharp recriminations against each other that still continue to this day. As more former guerrillas return to Greece from the Soviet Union and Eastern Europe, more information fuels the dispute. What does seem to be a fact is that the KKE and DSE leaderships failed to perform some key functions properly, if at all. This failure combined with the Soviet action (or inaction) make it difficult to see how success could have been possible. In retrospect, the attempts to affix blame facilely employ the labels "Titoist" or "Stalinist," but whatever divisions existed in the KKE during the war were generally internally generated and had little or nothing to do with the dispute between Tito and Stalin. It is precisely the dispute between Zachariadis and Markos that so well illustrates the point.

There is fairly strong evidence that if there were any disputes between Markos and Zachariadis, they occurred only *after* the DSE defeat at

---

[23]Woodhouse, *Struggle for Greece,* pp. 216–17.
[24]Kousoulas, pp. 251–52.

Konitsa in December 1947–January 1948. The evidence is both from archives and memoirs. In the archival material there is absolutely no mention of disagreement between Markos and members of the KKE Politburo in Belgrade. In fact, the only division evident is that between the First Subcommittee of the KKE Politburo (in Athens) and the Second Subcommittee (in Belgrade), and it was due mostly to difficulty in communication but also to differences in interpretation of the dual strategy. Even after the decision of the Third Plenum, the Belgrade KKE Politburo had difficulty getting across to its counterparts in Athens that the KKE *was* firmly resolved to undertake civil war.[25]

More important, there is no evidence that Markos intentionally disobeyed orders or strongly dissented in any way. When the Third Plenum discussed military matters, Markos was the rapporteur; under his guidance the report on the military situation stressed that the DSE was pushing ahead boldly "in the transformation of our army into a regular army, beginning with the creation of brigades."[26] The idea of forming a regular army was by then at least six months old; had Markos wanted to disagree, would he not have already done so? In the military plan drawn up for the fall of 1947 at the Third Plenum, the basic objective of seizing and holding the territory of nothern Greece reflects an orientation toward forming a regular army and pursuing a conventional strategy, and Markos signed it.[27] It seems incredible that the commander of the entire Communist army would not, if he really wanted to, disagree with such plans.

The personal memoirs of Vasilis Bartziotas also indicate that the dissension between Markos and Zachariadis began only on December 2, 1947, when Zachariadis accused Markos of providing vastly exaggerated figures for the number of men in arms.[28] Markos himself states that the disagree-

[25]*Avgi*, no. 21, December 28, 1979; no. 27, January 5, 1980.

[26]*Avgi*, no. 24, January 1, 1980. Blanas is the exception here, arguing that Zachariadis' original orders for raising a partisan army in 1946 were changed after Markos's return from Belgrade; see Georgis Blanas, *Emfilios Polemos, 1946–1949: Opos ta Ezisa* (Athens: n.p. 1976), pp. 94–95. Blanas tries to blame Markos for this change in Zachariadis' orders, but he presents no supporting evidence. Markos's explanation that it was Ioannidis in Belgrade who changed the directive could be entirely correct.

[27]*Avgi*, no. 28, January 6, 1980.

[28]Vasilis Bartziotas, *O Agonas tou Dimokratikou Stratou Elladas*, 2d ed. (Athens: Sygchroni Epochi, 1982), p. 41. This date is significant, for it fixes the first open manifestation of the conflict between Zachariadis and Markos on the same day the KKE admitted serious problems in the development of its strategy: the Second Subcommittee of the KKE Politburo concluded that in general "there is a serious delay in the fulfillment of the decision of the Third Plenum and, more specifically, the plan of the politico-military leadership of the DSE": *To Kommounistiko Komma tis Elladas: Episima Keimena, 1945–1949*, vol. 6 (Athens: Sygchroni Epochi, 1987), p. 249.

ment first "came into the open" on December 2, when Zachariadis suddenly insisted that the DSE was a regular army. This assertion was made, according to Markos, in a manner that surprised him.[29] While both sources agree on the date, it is obvious that Markos was in no position to be surprised that the DSE should have been transformed into a regular army, having himself affirmed at the Third Plenum that progress was being made in that direction! There are other examples, but they all raise the same question: if the dispute between Markos and Zachariadis did not really arise during the first eighteen months of the civil war, then what caused it? The answer is that the "dispute" was invented after the fact and, given Stalin's desire to isolate Tito, may actually have been encouraged by the Soviet Union. If so, then it is a grave error to call anyone in the KKE a "Titoist."

Several more points regarding Markos help clarify the actual situation. Woodhouse is mistaken when he assumes that by broadcasting a peace offer on the eve of the Third Plenum, Markos was going against the party leadership. The policy of dualism, while clearly favoring the military option at that time, never explicitly abandoned the possibility of negotiations. This is evident from the stream of broadcasts, proposals, and secret approaches that the KKE and the Soviet Union made throughout the course of the civil war. In fact, the specific proposal Woodhouse mentions may have been intended to accompany the resolution to adopt more forceful means, thereby trying to convey to the Greek government the seriousness with which the KKE viewed the situation. In any event, to assume Markos was somehow breaking party discipline is dubious.

A second point is even more decisive. Immediately after the battle of Grammos in 1948, Markos became ill. He maintains that it was exhaustion,[30] while his erstwhile comrades maintain that the DSE commander had something on the order of a nervous breakdown.[31] Whatever the case, both Markos and other former KKE leaders agree on one key point: upon the onset of this disorder/exhaustion in late August 1948, Markos was sent to Moscow for therapy via Albania.[32] It only requires a moment's

---

[29]*Markos Vafeiadis: Martyries,* ed. Dimitris Gousidis (Thessaloniki: Epikairotita, 1983), (hereafter *Vafeiadis*), p. 18. This was the content of an interview Gousidis conducted with Vafeiadis in the late 1970s in Tetovo, Yugoslavia.

[30]Ibid., p. 22.

[31]Vontitsos-Gousias, *Aites gia tis Ittes, ti Diaspasi* 1:397–408.

[32]Ibid., pp. 400–1; *Vafeiadis,* p. 22. Vafeiadis' account of this period appears to change significantly over time. In an interview with the *New York Times* on October 19, 1986, the former DSE commander tells a quite different story from the one he told Gousidis in Tetovo. The 1986 account alleges that, in contrast to the "one month's rest" he supposedly

reflection to realize that if Markos was a supporter of Tito, this would have been his final journey; for he was traveling to the Soviet Union a full two months after the break with Tito. Not only did Markos survive the therapy in Moscow, but he returned to the DSE General Staff on November 15, 1948, and thereupon began to get involved in disputes of a much more serious nature. At that time it was revealed that he had sent a "platform" (letter) to the CPSU criticizing the errors of the KKE leadership. Among the points he made were that the DSE must return to subconventional tactics and that the effort to pursue KKE objectives using a regular army was bound to fail because monarchofascism had achieved a temporary stabilization.[33]

What is striking about this "platform" is that it employs an argument very similar to that made by Varga the previous year: Communists must not undertake aggressive activities because capitalism has stabilized and is therefore able to continue its support of the weaker capitalist regimes. The parallel suggests how incredible is the charge that Markos was Titoist. Indeed, the charge could hardly apply to any of the KKE hierarchy; for ultimately the entire leadership including Markos was forced to live in exile in the Soviet Union, and not a single major leader was purged in a period when Stalin's suspicious vindictiveness was at its height.

It can be added that Vafeiadis insists he never had any contacts with Tito.[34] Furthermore, if there was a "Titoist" wing in the KKE, it seems incredible that the Yugoslav leader would not have been informed of the KKE's decision to support the Soviets after Yugoslavia's expulsion from the Cominform. Certainly Markos had ample opportunity (about four weeks) to do so. The fact that Tito took no radical move in regard to the KKE indicates either he was unaware of the KKE decision or that no sharp division between pro- and anti-Tito forces existed. If "Titoists" were in the KKE Politburo, the former certainly could not have been the case. There is also no evidence that during 1943–44 Markos was in contact with Tempo or any other Yugoslav partisan commanders.[35] Furthermore, documents recently published in Skopje show Markos as cosignatory with

---

received in the Soviet Union after the battle at Grammos, he was "treated like a prisoner" and brought back "handcuffed to Greek territory." No other account to date supports his latest version.

[33]Vontitsos-Gousias, *Aities gia tis Ittes, ti Diaspasi* 1:452; Kousoulas, p. 252.

[34]*Vafeiadis*, p. 20.

[35]Elisabeth Barker, "Yugoslav Policy towards Greece 1947–1949," in *Studies in the History of the Greek Civil War, 1945–1949*, Lars Baerentzen, John O. Iatrides, and Ole L. Smith, eds. (Copenhagen: Museum Tusculanum Press, 1987), p. 265.

Bakirtzis of an October 16, 1944, order for the liquidation of the Slavo-Macedonian battalions that had gone over to the Yugoslavs.[36] The argument that there existed between different branches of the KKE some sort of rigid division over tactics is equally difficult to believe. Certainly, there were disputes over tactics, and they became worse as the DSE suffered further defeats. This is not abnormal in a disappointed leadership. To label these internal disputes Titoist, implying that they reflect the influence of external actors, in the absence of direct evidence, is unjustified. The Stalin-Tito dispute had no effect on the final determination of strategy, only on the ability of the KKE to implement strategy. The hypothesis that the rupture between Tito and Stalin produced a parallel rupture within the KKE therefore remains unsupported.

One final question remains: If the Stalin-Tito split had no impact on the internal structure of the KKE, then why has scholarly analysis focused on this issue? The answer is that it is extremely difficult to discriminate between the objective analysis of the past and its use as a weapon to gain political advantage in the present. The recriminations and counter-recriminations within the KKE have been so intense that it is hard to arrive at the truth. That, however, is a perennial problem in the analysis of conflict in Communist organizations: one can never be sure if statements purporting to present the historical truth are valid or deceptive.

In sum, the hypotheses about conflict within the Communist elites are not supported by examination of the evidence. While a dispute did center on Zhdanov, it had no significant bearing on the civil war in Greece. Similarly, the split between Yugoslavia and the Soviet Union did not precipitate a split within the ranks of the KKE. Rather, the rift became an excuse for assigning blame, a phenomenon that has obscured the fact that the real source of division was within the party: pressure arising from defeat under the most adverse conditions. Therefore, the only division of consequence for Greek affairs remains that between Stalin and the Yugoslavs.

[36]*Egejska Makedonija vo Nov 1944–1945*, vol. 1 (Skopje: Arhiv na Makedonija, 1971), pp. 496–97, in Barker, "Yugoslav Policy towards Greece," p. 265.

6

THE IMPACT OF SOVIET POLICY ON POSTWAR BALKAN POLITICS

The historical narrative is complete. One significant revelation is the concept of "prudent expansionism." Where previously it was only possible to refer vaguely to Stalin's "caution" or "flexibility" in the immediate postwar years, the case of the Greek Civil War lets us see the specific strategies the Soviets pursued, the tactics they employed, and the dynamics of intra-Communist relations. An equally important revelation is the degree to which the Soviet leader's limited control over events in the Balkans constrained his options, compelling him to respond to changing conditions. In fact, the politics of the region were so volatile they ultimately overwhelmed Stalin's basic effort to expand the political influence of communism in the West while keeping military forces in reserve. His need to respond to external developments while simultaneously pursuing his concrete goals explains much of the complexity in Soviet policy. The study also shows the impact of Soviet interests on the KKE in Greek communism's most dramatic decade. The record is an unhappy one; Soviet policy critically impaired the KKE's ability to pursue its own immediate interests. It was not Moscow's direct control that made the difference; rather, it was the Soviets' control over the *tempo* of events in the Balkans. Ironically, it was Stalin, the one person in whom Greek communism never lost faith, who played the decisive role in undermining the KKE's chances of success.

But questions remain. Is it not possible to explain the KKE's action (or inaction) on grounds other than Soviet influence? Stalin's control over the

Balkans was, after all, minimal compared with that which he exercised in other East European countries. In fact, the Soviet Union spent the better part of the 1944–49 period trying to regain its lost momentum in the region, which leads to a second, broader, question: Does the study not actually prove Moscow's *inability* to affect events in the Balkans significantly?

There is little doubt that Soviet policy adversely affected the policy of the Greek Communist party. As the narrative has shown, the impact of Soviet advice and actions was repeatedly to place the KKE in the position of taking action after the time for acting profitably had passed. In 1944, for example, the KKE rising took place several months after the best time for success. Similarly, in the third round in 1946–47, the KKE pursued its dual policy of political activity and military preparation until after the right time for force had passed.

On several critical occasions, the Greek Communists were restrained from resorting to arms by Soviet advice or explicit Soviet refusals to provide timely military assistance. In 1944, the dispatch of the Russian Military Mission to Greece, combined with Soviet pressure on the EAM delegation to accept the Lebanon agreement, powerfully indicated Soviet disapproval of any KKE military action. Soviet opinion prevailed because the KKE leadership felt obliged to await Soviet approval. In 1946, the desire for Moscow's blessing was outweighed by the even greater need for weapons. The KKE strategy of relying on the Yugoslavs in the interim was soon undermined by Yugoslav aspirations to Greek territory and by limited Yugoslav materiel support, forcing the KKE to turn to the Soviet Union. Zachariadis' unusual skill in eliciting from Stalin a promise of aid went for naught when that aid was so delayed as to fatally impair Greek Communist chances of success. The Soviet break with Tito also affected the KKE, as first reflected in their efforts to walk a narrow path between Stalin and the Yugoslavs. Once Zachariadis publicly supported the Soviet stand, the DSE's fate was sealed; the army became little more than a Soviet tool for applying pressure on Tito.

This is not to argue that Soviet actions were the *only* determinants of KKE policy; there was as well the need to respond to the deterioration of domestic conditions. This was compounded by the KKE failure to execute policy properly. In particular, the division of the Politburo in 1947 between Athens and Belgrade caused communication problems. The necessity of accommodating other leftist parties may also have distorted Zachariadis' analysis of the situation. Taken together, these factors still do not explain the whole of KKE policy. Once the option of civil war had been

chosen, it was clear, even to the Greek Communists, that Soviet diplomatic and material support was a prerequisite for success. It is here that
Stalin's behavior exerted a determining influence: through a combination
of outright rejection and dilatory tactics, he contributed significantly to the
defeat of the KKE and, by extension, to the overall course of events in
Greece.

Several important points must be stressed as a preliminary to an evaluation of the degree to which the Soviet Union was able to affect developments in the Balkans. In the analysis of Soviet foreign policy there is
always a temptation to move immediately to a balance sheet in which the
final outcome of Soviet efforts is labeled success or failure. The consequence of this approach is to reduce Soviet conduct to its final outcome
and miss entirely the complex environment in which policy developed.
The result, more often than not, is a deduced Soviet "line" although a
more balanced analysis would have revealed a series of shifts and turns.
Indeed, the Greek case indicates that any evaluation of Soviet performance depends upon the period chosen for examination. In 1945, Stalin
was reasonably successful in his objectives in Greece; for 1946–47, however, the evaluation changes dramatically. A serious assessment of Soviet
policy is therefore possible only if one takes into account the impact of a
complex international environment on major actors. Evaluations based on
this criterion may be less parsimonious than those focused solely on end
results, but they produce more realistic interpretations.

But there is another reason, embedded in the logic of the historical
narrative, for eschewing simplistic analyses. My goal has been to produce
a coherent appraisal of the Soviet contribution to the unfolding of a
critically important historical period. An analysis that provides nuanced
explanations that transcend political and intellectual boundaries is preferable to one that remains confined within preexisting inquiry. An examination, for example, of Greek communism confined to the domestic context
is valuable but does not begin to address the more basic question of the
relation between, on the one hand, the interests and activities of major
powers in the international system and, on the other hand, the political
environment of smaller states. No one can deny that major powers, either
by acting or abstaining from activity, exert profound influence on the
evolution of events in sensitive parts of the international system. Since
World War II, Soviet behavior—successful, failed, or indecisive—has
tangibly affected world politics. In Greece this impact is underscored by
the seemingly inexhaustible efforts of Greek Communists to come to
terms with a legacy of Soviet promises that remained unfulfilled. Hence,

the investigation should properly concentrate not merely on the existence or impact of a Soviet policy in Greece but on its effectiveness in advancing Soviet interests. By providing a plausible and defensible explanation of *Soviet* behavior, such an interpretation emerges as stronger and more narrowly focused.

On a more specific level, to argue that Moscow was able to affect the tempo of events in Greece crucially is not to say that this influence was uniformly successful from 1944 to 1949. Rather, the degree of Soviet influence varied with the relative success of Soviet policy and the extent to which events in the Balkan Peninsula were subject to Soviet control. The evidence reveals a dramatic decrease in Stalin's capacity to control developments as the civil war progressed, but even so, he still managed to affect the *pace* of events enough to produce a significant impact on KKE policy and on Greece generally. The analysis reveals not only the spotty Soviet success record but the manner in which the Soviets were forced to act to preserve their minimal gains (principally in Albania) in a region of the world where their control was limited.

It is safe to conclude that Soviet behavior had a general impact on the situation in Greece; it is less clear that the Soviets succeeded in attaining their objectives. On balance, the Greek Civil War was a failure for Soviet policy because once Stalin regained control over Balkan communism, the assets he had had in Greece had been all but destroyed. This conclusion should be tempered by the realization that the Soviets could have fared worse. The elimination of their assets in Greece did nothing to advance Soviet interests but was better than allowing Tito an independent hand in the Balkans, which could have led to greater losses.

Throughout the civil war, no single, sustained, impulse guided policy; the Soviets had to adjust to what they could not control. In 1944–45, strategic factors were dominant, so the Soviet dictator had to concentrate on winning the war, using Greece as a means of consolidating his control of Eastern Europe. Local Communist interests were subordinated to the fight against Hitler, and in return for his hands-off attitude toward Greece, Stalin acquired control of Romania under Great Power auspices. In 1945–46, a new set of strategic conditions obtained, and the Soviets were free to concentrate on exploiting differences between the United States and Britain over the Western presence in the Mediterranean. Stalin then moved to extend his influence into Western Europe. In Greece, his policy was one of political gradualism so as to establish a pro-Soviet presence without antagonizing the West. This policy, modestly successful at first, gradually gave way to one of simultaneous military preparations and political activity. The reason for this change was as much Stalin's desire to move toward a more aggressive long-term policy as it was the KKE inclination to military action.

Toward the end of 1946, regional and local circumstances began to overwhelm strategic considerations and constitute a threat to Soviet objectives. Stalin had evidently underestimated his ability to keep the KKE following its dualist policy. As Greek Communists turned toward military action, their cause found support in an increasingly independent and aggressive Yugoslav policy. Stalin, failing to restrain the insurgency, was forced to weigh the future value of the KKE organizations against the present threat they posed to Soviet objectives. Then in 1947–48, strategic factors were eclipsed completely, and the Soviets directed their attention toward preventing a loss of political influence to Tito in the Balkans and reestablishing the primacy of Great Power interests. To accomplish these objectives, the Soviets undercut Tito by agreeing to support the civil war (but delaying delivery to undermine KKE prospects) and simultaneously working to guarantee the political loyalties of Albanian and Bulgarian Communists. Soviet policy thus shifted from the pursuit of political influence in Western Europe to the preservation of hard-won gains in Eastern Europe threatened by Yugoslav actions.

After the Soviet-Yugoslav split and Stalin's success in retaining political control over all other Eastern bloc states, the Soviets could turn their attention to pressuring Tito. When this policy appeared to threaten the integrity of Albania, however, it was changed, as once more the *preservation* of gains took precedence over opportunities for expansion. In the final stages of the Greek Civil War, with Yugoslavia contained and the West apparently willing to negotiate, Stalin could return to strategic considerations. He ordered the DSE to continue fighting to provide a bargaining chip for a peaceful resolution of the "Greek question."

This series of policy shifts reveals a marked Soviet preference for dealing with issues at the strategic level—a preference particularly apparent in Stalin's efforts to get the KKE back to the bargaining table in the closing stages of the civil war. There are two possible reasons for the preference. First, Stalin's immediate postwar goal was removal of Western influence in the eastern Mediterranean. Sudden or decisive military action by local and regional actors would precipitate a strong Western response. Moreover, only the major Western powers, not the regional actors, could affect the strategic balance. Second, the Soviet dictator may have avoided operating at the regional and local level lest he lose control of the international Communist movement. The Soviet Union was the only Communist state that could operate at the strategic level, and by doing so, it effectively guaranteed that Communist objectives would be identical with Soviet objectives. The negative impact of Yugoslav behavior on Soviet policy demonstrated the validity of this reasoning.

The revelation that Stalin preferred to operate at the strategic level is of vital importance in demonstrating that Soviet activity made a difference in the outcome of events: had Stalin preferred to operate through actors at the regional and local level in pursuit of his objectives, his foreign policy would have been fundamentally different. Strategic considerations would have been secondary, opening the way for a more aggressive, militarily based policy in the Balkans. The conservatism inherent in a policy of prudent expansionism precluded a Soviet embrace of the civil war option.

This conclusion, that Stalin preferred to let strategic factors determine policy, would, if true, add significantly to our knowledge of the broader dynamics animating Soviet foreign policy. This point can only be established securely, however, if the problem of overexplanation is resolved: since strategic and regional factors, taken separately, are sufficient to account for Soviet policy, how is it possible to determine which category was more important? The difficulty is compounded because both operated simultaneously on Soviet interests during the Greek Civil War. A test of relative importance requires an instance in which either strategic or regional factors were nearly nonexistent, for example, the period from early 1949 to the conclusion of the civil war, when the impact of Tito on the Greek Communists had by then been minimized. If Stalin's cautious policy was determined by regional factors, that surely was the time for him to have taken a more aggressive approach; if strategic factors were dominant, prudence should then have prevailed. We know the Soviets ordered the civil war to continue—but only as a means of promoting a negotiated settlement among the Great Powers. The directive was strongly conditioned by Soviet perceptions of the United States. Regional factors *were* important in shaping the overall course of events in Greece, but it was *strategic* concerns that were central.

There is another, more indirect, method of evaluating the relative importance of strategic and regional factors in Soviet policy. Yugoslav conduct was directed at overturning the existing division of power in the Balkans, in clear conflict with U.S. interests in the region; in other words, Yugoslav policy sought a forceful modification of the strategic balance of power. A more cautious policy position would have been to accept the strategic status quo and try to work within the constraints of the system. Hence, a comparison of the benefits that could accrue to the Soviets from each policy should indicate which was preferable to the Soviets and, by implication, whether strategic or regional considerations were stronger.

In 1944–46 the Soviets had great political assets in Greece: a strong and relatively popular Communist party, a weak government, and tremendous prestige as a member of the Great Powers. The near-term benefit of working within a Western-dominated Greece was tempting: a strong pro-Soviet presence in Greek society, which could effectively neutralize any anti-Soviet initiatives. Under those circumstances a policy of cautious political gradualism was likely to yield significant results. In contrast, the option of civil war held out no such potential benefit: all political bases within Greek society would have to be severed; heavy material costs would have to be imposed to carry out the war; and there was always the strong possibility of losing more than the civil war, should the West intervene in Albania. Even if the Greek Communists should succeed, Stalin had no guarantee he would be able to retain any of the Balkan states under his control. A known evil is preferable to an unknown one. On the assumption, therefore, that a strong U.S. presence in Western Europe could be minimized by stabilizing the postwar status quo in the short-term, the Soviets stood to benefit more by working within the constraints imposed by strategic considerations.

A strategy of political activity made good sense in the Greek situation, and the advice to hold military forces in reserve assured the Soviet dictator of a means of capitalizing on any future instability. The results of the civil war bear this conclusion out; for not only did Stalin fail to achieve any victories, but he also lost the very substantial assets he had before the third round. In this sense, the civil war and its final outcome resulted in a clear loss for the Soviet leader: an area that was promising for the gradual expansion of his influence was now purged of any pro-Soviet presence.

Specific Soviet strategies also had direct impact on the Greek Civil War, by affecting KKE policy. Soviet consent to the expansion of military activities would have had a dramatic impact on KKE actions; it would have led to a rapid escalation of the civil war, perhaps in time to produce a KKE victory. Rapid mobilization, even as early as the October 1945 Seventh Congress, would have placed Greek Communist military forces in a position far superior to that in which they ultimately found themselves. Instead, the Soviets advised caution. What made good strategic sense for Stalin, however, proved fatal for the KKE. Zachariadis was compelled to adopt a sterile policy of "gradual" preparations for armed struggle in the vain hope that the British would view them not as a prelude to a seizure of power but as a defensive mobilization to be used in achieving a negotiated compromise. It was Stalin who encouraged the dual strategy, Stalin who refused aid. Had he chosen another policy, one that perhaps encouraged immediate military action, the consequences might not have been restricted to the Balkans. Soviet orders to pursue a purely parliamentary strategy would likewise have produced a different outcome (the experience of the French and Italian Communist parties is eloquent testimony on this point), although one also marked by bloodshed and violence.

This view of Soviet strategy permits a conclusion about the role the Soviet leader assigned to independent Communist military forces in the postwar world. The dual strategy implied that Stalin anticipated a period of quiet in the near-term, but then what? Political gradualism and its later replacement by the dual strategy suggest that Stalin envisioned a two-stage evolution of his policy. Greek Communists were to take advantage of the political instability in Greece in the immediate postwar period to entrench themselves firmly in the political system, producing a weak but just stable state. With this policy, the Soviets trod a fine line. If instability deteriorated into complete collapse (or what the West perceived as such), then a Western response was sure to follow. If the policy succeeded, however, a vigorous political campaign could then be waged to eliminate the Western presence, after which the Greek Communists could move aggressively with the military forces Stalin had counseled them to hold in reserve. This interpretation of Stalin's policy as intended to evolve through two stages is strengthened by the keen attention the Soviets paid to the disposition of British forces and by the change in Soviet demeanor after the Labour victory in Britain. The focus on strategic considerations further suggests that barring a strong American commitment to the region, Stalin was counting on an interim period of dealing with a deteriorating Western position in the eastern Mediterranean, succeeded by a period when Soviet forces would hold the strategic advantage. This interpretation is, of course, speculative, but it is grounded in evidence that Stalin did wish to preserve Communist military forces for some future, unspecified occasion.

There were, however, two crucial developments that overturned Stalin's long-term calculations: the failure of the Greek political system to achieve a degree of stability conducive to the reduction or elimination of Western forces, and the eagerness of the Yugoslavs (and many KKE military officers) for a militant policy. Hence, less than eighteen months after the war, Stalin found that events had changed so radically that earlier estimates were of little use; the volatile Balkan context, which had held great potential, had begun to threaten key Soviet gains.

Soviet policy in Greece is also useful in revealing the wide range of instruments used by Stalin. Perhaps the most valuable revelation in this regard has been the extent to which the Soviets employed direct contacts inside Greece in their efforts to gain information and guide policy at a time when Stalin professed to have little or no interest there. The many Soviets involved in intelligence activities or the oversight of policy were paralleled by Soviets acting on the diplomatic level to pressure an already fragile government in the direction of Soviet interests. Diplomatic activity at the level of Great Power relations further reveals that, despite Soviet professions of unwillingness to violate a state's sovereignty, Stalin evinced not the slightest hesitation in offering solutions that violated this principle when he felt it served his interests.

Inside Greece, the central focus of Soviet strategy was the Greek Communist party, which was enlisted to support Stalin's objectives at great cost to itself. Even more intriguing is the ability of the Soviet Union to insinuate itself and its demands into equally important non-Communist sectors of the Greek political system. Secret approaches were made to Royalist and Republican politicians such as Sofoulis, Tsaldaris, and Plastiras; more sympathetic persons, like Sofianopoulos, were manipulated through offers of political support. These contacts played to the vanity of established Greek politicians and fit neatly into the clandestine and secretive maneuvering characteristic of Greek domestic politics.

A less prominent yet not insignificant Soviet tactic was the manipulation of Balkan nationality conflicts. Stalin at first shunned such tactics because they clearly undermined the stability of the region in a manner unfavorable to Soviet strategic aims. During the period of peak Yugoslav independent activity, he also avoided this option because it played into the hands of Tito. In 1949, however, once Soviet predominance in Balkan Communist affairs was restored, Stalin adroitly manipulated the issue of Macedonian nationality to the disadvantage of the Yugoslav regime. The tactic's usefulness proved short-lived, as the unsettled situation began to threaten the integrity of Albania, and the prospect of a negotiated settlement in the civil war made the appearance of stability imperative.

The skill with which Stalin used these subtle tactics helps us appreciate why he chose the path of prudence in his policy toward the West. For the Soviet dictator, division of the world between the Soviet Union and the United States was inevitable. There could be no question of attempting to extend political influence and control into Western Europe in the immediate postwar era by military means. Not only would the West resist such an attempt; Stalin might lose areas he could not credibly defend. Thus, if

Stalin was to pursue an expansionist policy, he would have to do so through political means, leaving the military option open for the unspecified future. The Soviet leader was well aware that the route to power was different in the West than in the East. Instead of open hostility, the situation demanded a cautious approach that would make use of the complexities of political power in Western societies. This suggests that Stalin was initially willing to tolerate a degree of flexibility in East European Communist regimes because a slight blurring of lines between East and West would allow maximum access to Western societies. Once this flexibility proved to be a threat to Stalinist rule, the Soviet dictator had to cut off potential avenues in the West to preserve and consolidate control in the East.

Another telling aspect of the Soviets' behavior is the way they were able to replace one set of tactics with another. When direct contacts proved unproductive, the Soviets would turn to the United Nations to present their interests, as in their various attempts to pressure the British to leave Greece and especially in their efforts to promote a diplomatic solution to the civil war that would preserve some Communist influence in Greece. In their attempts to involve the U.N. general secretary in negotiations on Greece and in the talks among Gromyko, Rusk, and McNeil, the Soviets used the United Nations as a forum in which to pursue Great Power relations either through attacks on Western positions or through initiatives they otherwise would not have been in a position to make. In addition, the United Nations gave the Soviets contact with KKE leaders and sympathetic Greek politicians in order to make proposals and give instructions that would have been impossible in formal talks.

Finally, the strategy and tactics of Stalin's prudent expansionism permit brief reflection on some of the general principles that have often been presumed to guide policy. First, in relations with the West, the Soviets showed a preference for pursuing their objectives within the existing state system, a conclusion supported by Stalin's orientation toward strategic rather than regional or local considerations. In this respect, the Soviet Union was more a "conservative" than a "revolutionary" state. The revolutionary momentum in the aftermath of World War II had clearly swung in the direction of the various European Communist parties, while the Soviet dictator went to great lengths to stifle their independent initiatives. Second, the gains the Soviets made during the war served as a drag on their expansionist ambitions, a conclusion amply demonstrated by Stalin's volte face in the final stages of the civil war, when it appeared that the security of Albania was in doubt (to say nothing of his change in attitude about Yugoslav plans for the incorporation of Albania). Third, the developments in the Balkans during the civil war demonstrate both Stalin's desire to subordinate other Communist parties to the interests of the Soviet state and his inability to do so. Tito's heresy shattered the monolithic structure of international Communism; thereafter the Soviets had to focus on containing the damage from successful Yugoslav defiance and on learning how to manage relations with Communist parties no longer subject to outright control.

Fourth, the often-repeated argument that the Soviet Union moves to fill areas of perceived weakness is not entirely supported by Stalin's strategy and tactics in Greece. He eschewed direct involvement at a time when the Greek Communists could have acquired a militarily superior position. Apparently Stalin preferred to leave Greece to the West than risk the emergence of another Tito. Stalin was obviously aware, too, that forceful measures, even if taken by genuinely independent local Communist organizations, would be "proof" in the West of Soviet aggressive intent. This does *not* imply, of course, that Stalin was unwilling to move on weak areas under other circumstances. The Soviet leader's consent to the dual strategy left open the possibility that, should the Greek Communists eventually succeed in creating conditions favorable to the use of force (i.e., no Western response possible) Stalin could reconsider.

Last, Soviet policy was not consistently well integrated with the pace at which regional politics evolved. In the immediate aftermath of the war, Stalin overestimated his capacity to control the pace of developments to suit his prudently expansionistic policy. The Soviets' extreme concern for the strategic balance of power led them to respond to Western weakness so slowly that local and regional forces seized the initiative. Local initiative not only threatened to precipitate a strong Western response but challenged Soviet primacy in the revolutionary camp. By 1949, however, Stalin had successfully manipulated the evolution of developments in the Balkans to regain the momentum in the Communist world.

No analysis of Soviet policy in postwar Greece can ignore the implications for U.S.-Soviet relations in the formative period of the Cold War. The Truman Doctrine was born of U.S. policymakers' desire to rescue faltering societies from a perceived ideologically driven Soviet expansionism. Fearing Stalin would take advantage of the power vacuum in Europe at war's end to establish more Communist regimes, the United States adopted its policy of "containment," which sought to prevent Soviet access to Western societies. Stalin might maneuver freely in Eastern Europe but not in the West, especially its unstable areas, until his acquisitiveness had abated. Because of its chaotic condition, Greece became one of the first testing grounds for the new American policy. When in 1949, after several years of massive U.S. military assistance, the civil war ended in defeat for the Greek Communists, containment was deemed a success. In recent years a voluminous literature on the consequences and implications of containment has emerged.[1] This study adds a few points to these efforts to reclaim this crucial period from the rhetoric of the Cold War.

That Stalin was expansionist is well supported by the evidence, but it would be a fundamental mistake to conclude, as did U.S. policymakers, that this expansionism was rooted in Communist ideology. In reality, it was Yugoslavia that had an ideologically driven expansionist policy; the hubris resulting from Partisan victory fueled the Yugoslav Communists' conviction that they were riding a historical wave that would inevitably carry them to the Aegean Sea. Stalin's more subtle and prudent expansionism addressed strategic realities and the real possibility of a firm Western response. The distinction is vital; the result was two contrasting strategic outlooks with correspondingly different policies.

If Stalin's prudent expansionism was not militant or ideological, as the West believed, what does that reveal about the efficacy of U.S. policy in Greece? The United States stopped *Balkan* Communism in Greece; it never had the opportunity to stop the Soviet Union. When, in 1945, Stalin's policy was most successful, the United States had not yet firmly committed itself to containment. By late 1946, Stalin already realized his efforts were collapsing under the pressure of independent Yugoslav and Greek Communist activities. When American resolve became firm in 1947, the Soviet dictator's control over events was minimal.

This brings up the final question: what would have been an appropriate response to Soviet expansionism? It was Tito who inadvertently provided the answer, when his actions threatened existing Soviet assets, compelling Stalin to abandon his prudent expansionism to preserve what he already had. The best way for the United States to have countered Stalin's expansionism would thus have been to compel the Soviets to concentrate on preserving their wartime gains rather than try directly to prevent their

[1]Of special importance, besides the writings of George F. Kennan, are the works of John Lewis Gaddis; see, for example, Gaddis, *Strategies of Containment* (Oxford: Oxford University Press, 1982); and Terry L. Deibel and John Lewis Gaddis, eds., *Containing the Soviet Union* (Washington: Pergammon-Brassey's, 1987). The globalization of containment, the various forms the policy acquired, and a reassessment of Kennan's writings are taken up more fully in these works.

penetration of the West. The United States, had it capitalized on Stalin's sensitivity about Albania, might have accomplished more in a short time than it did with four decades of containment. But this alternative was never a real one, for by the time the United States perceived Stalin's expansionism as a global danger, the Soviet dictator had abandoned expansionism to try to contain the damage from the Yugoslav heresy by consolidating his grip on Eastern Europe.

APPENDIX

HISTORICAL NARRATIVE
AND PATH ANALYSIS

To use Greek evidence to support the propositions of this study, the obvious choice of method would have been a pure historical narrative approach that exploited the specificity of the evidence to construct an interpretation that reflected the mutability of Soviet policy. The essence of a narrativist approach is movement from an unstructured to a structured level of discernible truth. Individual historical occurrences and situations furnish "the evidence and the illustrations for a comprehensive interpretation of (an aspect of) a historical period."[1] The structure of an interpretation is a product, therefore, not of the actual historical past, but of the intellectual efforts of the analyst. Multiple and conflicting interpretations are thus possible, which is just one of the ways the historical narrative method differs from a social scientific one: the results of historical analysis are not cumulative; there is little possibility of testing the validity of an interpretation; and the hypothesized relationship among variables, which

---

[1] F. R. Ankersmit, *Narrative Logic: A Semantic Analysis of the Historian's Language* (The Hague: Martinus Nijhoff, 1983), p. 25. I rely heavily here on Ankersmit's analysis of historical narrative. While his purpose is to establish the internal logic by which historians narratively interpret the results of their research, Ankersmit also provides the basis for a methodological alternative that lies between social scientific approaches and speculative theories of history; both of these get the analyst into difficulties because the precise relationships among variables are specified *before* the analysis. In Ankersmit's view, historical narrative is a process of intellectual construction animated by actual historical events; the direction an investigation takes is guided only by the evidence and the interests of the scholar. Analysis thus proceeds inductively from empirical reality to historical interpretation.

forms the basis of the explanation, is not susceptible to generalization because it emerges from a specific historical context.

For several reasons I decided to use a method between this extreme and the social scientific one. After all, the historian's focus on specific situations does not preclude consideration of general explanatory categories. Almost any creditable historical analysis includes generous reference to such concepts as the balance of power, the structure of the international system, the power potential of states, and so on. The general explanatory concepts of historical investigation are quite similar to the variables of social science, except that the relationships among variables emerge only after historical analysis, whereas they are stipulated a priori in social scientific inquiry. Historical and social scientific approaches thus share the limited common ground of a set of general explanatory variables. The direction an investigation takes beyond this point depends on the interest of the analyst: an analyst concerned with the detailed examination of the past may proceed from the general to the specific historical reality, while one seeking general significance from specific cases can project results onto other cases through the medium of the common variables.

My flexible model for the analysis of Soviet policy therefore makes no assumptions about precise functional relationships until the evidence of the historical record has been examined closely. The analysis begins with the description of a set of general variables that can be assumed to exert a significant effect on the course of Soviet policy. My focus on the limited control the Soviets had over policy in the postwar Balkans dictated that the variables be exogenous to the Soviet domestic policy-making structure; otherwise, the central notion of a Soviet response to an imperfectly controlled environment would be meaningless.

Next, the exogenous factors have to have meaning in the specific context. This is established by selecting from the historical record a set of propositions on which to base an interpretation of the course of Soviet policy in Greece from 1944 to 1949. So conceived, the interpretation allows for the assumption that at certain junctures, the exogenous factors combined with Soviet interests and capabilities to produce a set of alternative "paths" the Soviet Union could pursue. I can then infer from historical evidence which "path" the Soviets actually chose. The advantage of this kind of interpretive path analysis is that it is sensitive to the specific environment and to the mutability of Soviet objectives.

Once the interpretation is constructed, I can use it to analyze two important aspects of Soviet policy. The actual historical record embedded in a narrative context lets me conclude which tactical alternatives and policy instruments the Soviets actually employed, and with what success. Similarly, I can determine the validity of the "principles" commonly assumed to guide Soviet foreign policy. This kind of analysis permits me to introduce and use data from areas that are objects of Soviet policy to evaluate larger patterns of Soviet international behavior.

Using such a method, one avoids, at least in part, the common error of viewing Soviet policy as monolithic, because the particular knowledge acquired in the study of a single case allows one to see with greater clarity the limits of Soviet power, knowledge, and control—all critically important in any analysis of foreign policy. That is why this kind of model is superior to earlier deductive approaches that analyzed from "principles" of Soviet conduct. The most interesting aspects of Soviet involvement in the Greek Civil War are the crucial and dramatic reversals of policy, but it is precisely these reversals that are impossible to explain from the deductive perspective, which assumes that a set of preexisting principles guided Soviet policy over the 1944–49 period. Path analysis avoids this dilemma entirely.

This method has wide applicability, but for two reasons it should not be extended to compare several cases in an effort to produce a rigid model of Soviet policy. First, the strength of such an approach emerges, ironically, from its *inability* to determine precisely the relationships among key variables. This is how the model allows for the incorporation of the vitally important elements of time, change, development, and learning. It is unrealistic to expect a situation to recur exactly; such an assumption rejects historical learning and development. Second, a more rigid model reduces the realism and power of historical interpretation. Any model distilled from historical analysis reflects to some degree the uniqueness of a historical period, and its application to another period will distort reality or fail to provide significant results. A flexible model reflecting Soviet preferences at specific times and places would be preferable. Parsimonious explanations are the ideal, but it is well to accept the fact that the complexity of explanations cannot be reduced without diminishing the realism of analysis. As Dostoevskii warned us in *Notes from Underground*, "Man is so partial to systems and abstract deduction that in order to justify his logic he is prepared to distort the truth intentionally."

BIBLIOGRAPHY

Newspapers and Periodicals

SOVIET UNION

Izvestiia
Krasnaia Zvezda
Krasnii Flot
New Times
Pravda
The War and the Working Class

GREECE

Anti
Avgi
Eleftheri Ellada
Eleftherotypia
Epikaira
Kathimerini
Kommounistiki Epitheorisi
Laiki Foni
I Machi
Ta Nea
Neos Kosmos
Rizospastis
Rizos tis Defteras
Tachydromos
To Vima

OTHER COUNTRIES

For a Lasting Peace, For a People's Democracy (Yugoslavia and the Soviet Union)
Humanité (France)
Nation (Britain)
News Chronicle (Britain)
New Statesman (Britain)
New York Herald Tribune (United States)
New York Times (United States)
Politika (Yugoslavia)
The Times (Britain)

Archival Materials

UNITED STATES

National Archives, Washington, D.C.
    Record Group 59: General Diplomatic Correspondence
    Record Group 226: Office of Strategic Services Reports

BRITAIN

Public Records Office, Kew Gardens, London
    Foreign Office File 371: General Diplomatic Correspondence

GREEK COMMUNISTS

Archives of the Democratic Army of Greece
    Excerpts from the archives of the DSE were published in the newspaper *Eleftherotypia* in a twenty-five part series from December 12, 1978 to January 11, 1979; a second series (108 installments) appeared from January 20 to September 7, 1986.
Archives of the Communist Party of Greece
    Excerpts from the archives of the Greek Communist party, in the possession of the Greek Communist Party of the Interior, published in the newspaper *Avgi* in a forty-part series from December 2, 1979 to January 23, 1980.

UNITED NATIONS

Organization Archives, documents on the Balkans question:
    DAG-1/1.3.1.1 (2–5)
    DAG-1/1.3.2.0 (1, 4, 5)
    DAG-1/2.1.3 (6–8)
    DAG-1/2.1.4 (1, 2)
    RAG-1/91, 103–109, 111
    RAG-2/35 (1, 3, 4)
    RAG-2/102 (8, 10, 14)
    RAG-2/141, 142
    RAG-2/264 (9–16)

Published Documentary Materials

UNITED STATES

Department of State. *Foreign Relations of the United States, 1943,* vols. 1, 3, Washington, D.C.: USGPO, 1963; vol. 2, 1964. *1944,* vols. 3, 5, 1965; vol. 4, 1966; vol. 2, 1967. *1945,* vols. 1, 5, 1967; vol. 4, 1968; vol. 8, 1969. *1946,* vols. 5–7, 1969; vols. 2–4, 1970; vol. 1, 1972. *1947,* vol. 5, 1971; vols. 3, 4, 1972; vol. 1, 1973. *1948,* vols. 3, 4, 1974; vol. 5, pt. 1, 1975; vol. 5, pt. 2, 1976. *1949,* vol. 3, 1974; vol. 4, 1975; vol. 5, 1977.

_____. *Foreign Relations of the United States: The Conferences at Cairo and Teheran, 1943.* Washington, D.C.: USGPO, 1961.

_____. *Foreign Relations of the United States: The Conferences at Malta and Yalta, 1945.* Washington, D.C.: USGPO, 1955.

_____. *Foreign Relations of the United States: The Conference of Berlin (The Potsdam Conference), 1945.* Vols. 1, 2. Washington, D.C.: USGPO, 1960.

SOVIET UNION

Berlinskaia (Potsdamskaia) konferentsia rukovoditelei trekh soiuznykh derzhav SSSR, SShA i Velikobritanii: Sbornik dokumentov. Sovetskii Soiuz na mezhdunarodnykh konferentsiiakh perioda velikoi otechestvennoi voiny, 1941–1945 gg. Vol. 6. Ed. A. A. Gromyko. Moscow: Politicheskoi Literatury, 1980.

Correspondence between the Chairman of the Council of Ministers of the USSR and the Presidents of the USA and the Prime Ministers of Great Britain during the Great Patriotic War of 1941–1945. 2 vols. Ed. A. A. Gromyko. Reprint. Moscow: Progress, n.d.

Konferentsiia Ob"edinennykh Natsii v San-Frantsisko: Sbornik dokumentov. Sovetskii Soiuz na mezhdunarodnykh konferentsiiakh perioda velikoi otechestvennoi voiny, 1941–1945 gg. Vol. 5. Ed. A. A. Gromyko. Moscow: Politicheskoi Literatury, 1980.

Sovetsko-Bolgarskie otnosheniia i sviazi: Dokumenty i materialy. Ed. L. B. Valev. Vol. 1, *Noiabr' 1917–Sentiabr' 1944.* Ed. L. B. Valev. Vol. 2, *Sentiabr' 1944–Dekabr' 1958.* Ed. R. P. Grishina. Moscow: Nauka, 1976, 1981.

The Soviet-Yugoslav Dispute. London: Royal Institute of International Affairs, 1948.

GREEK COMMUNISTS

Episima Keimena. To Kommounistiko Komma Elladas sto Polemo kai stin Antistasi. N.p.: KKE Esoterikou, 1974.

To Evdomo Synedrio tou KKE: Part III. Dokumenta tou Ellinikou Proodeftikou Kinimatos no. 17. Athens: Mnimi, n.d.

Keimena tis Ethnikis Antistasis. 2 vols. Athens: Sygchroni Epochi, 1981.

To Kommounistiko Komma tis Elladas: Episima Keimena. Vol. 1, *1918–1924.* 2d ed. Athens: Sygchroni Epochi, 1974. Vol. 2, *1925–1928.* 2d ed. Athens: Sygchroni Epochi, n.d. Vol. 3, *1929–1933;* vol. 4, *1934–1940;* vol. 5, *1940–1945.* Athens: Sygchroni Epochi, 1981. Vol. 6, *1945–1949.* Athens: Sygchroni Epochi, 1987.

I Panelladiki Organotiki Syskepsi. Dokumenta tou Ellinikou Proodeftikou Kinimatos no. 5. Athens: Mnimi, n.d.

PEEA: Episima Keimena. Praxeis kai Apofaseis. Dokumenta tou Ellinikou Pro-odeftikou Kinimatos no. 15. Athens: Mnimi, n.d.
Saranta Chronia tou KKE, 1918–1958: Epilogi Dokumenton. N.p.: Politikes kai Logotechnikes Ekdoseis, 1958.
VIII S"ezd Kommunisticheskoi Partii Gretsii. Moscow: Politicheskoi Literatury, 1962.

BRITAIN

Fakellos Ellas: Ta Mystika Archeia tou Foreign Office. Athens: Nea Synora, 1972.

UNITED NATIONS

Documents of the United Nations Conference on International Organization: San Francisco, 1945. 16 vols. New York: United Nations Information Organizations, 1945.

Books and Articles

Allison, Graham T. *Essence of Decision.* Boston: Little, Brown, 1971.
Anonymous. "Otan Irthe o Zachariadis sto Boulkes . . . ," *Anti,* January 2, 1981.
Archer, Laird. *Balkan Journal.* New York: Norton, 1944.
———. *Balkan Tragedy.* Manhattan, Kan.: MA-AH, 1983.
Argyropoulos, Savvas. *Prosfygia, Andartiko, Exoria: 1924–1949.* Athens: Grammi, 1980.
Arsh, G. L., ed. *Osnovnye problemy balkanistiki v SSSR.* Moscow: Nauka, 1979.
Auty, Phyllis, and Richard Clogg, eds. *British Policy towards Wartime Resistance in Yugoslavia and Greece.* London: Macmillan, 1975.
Averoff-Tossizza, Evangelos. *By Fire and Axe: The Communist Party and the Civil War in Greece, 1944–1949.* New Rochelle, N.Y.: Caratzas Brothers, 1978.
Baerentzen, Lars. "Anglo-German Negotiations during the German Retreat from Greece in 1944." *Scandinavian Studies in Modern Greek,* no. 4 (1980).
———, ed. *British Reports on Greece, 1943–44.* Documents on Modern Greek History 1. Copenhagen: Museum Tusculanum Press, 1982.
Baerentzen, Lars, John O. Iatrides, and Ole L. Smith, eds. *Studies in the History of the Greek Civil War, 1945–1949.* Copenhagen: Museum Tusculanum Press, 1987.
Banac, Ivo. *With Stalin against Tito.* Ithaca, N.Y.: Cornell University Press, 1988.
Barker, Elisabeth. *The British between the Superpowers, 1945–50.* London: Macmillan, 1983.
———. *Macedonia: Its Place in Balkan Power Politics.* 1950. Reprint. Westport, Conn.: Greenwood, 1980.
Barmine, Alexander. *One Who Survived: The Life Story of a Russian under the Soviets.* New York: Putnam's, 1945.
Barros, James. *Trygve Lie and the Cold War: The U.N. Secretary-General Pursues Peace, 1946–53.* DeKalb: Northern Illinois University Press, forthcoming.
Bartziotas, Vasilis G. *O Agonas tou Dimokratikou Stratou Elladas.* 2d ed. Athens: Sygchroni Epochi, 1982.

_____. *Ethniki Antistasi kai Dekemvris 1944: Istoriko Dokimio.* 4th ed. Athens: Syg-chroni Epochi, 1983.
_____. "I Politiki mas ton Stelechon sto KKE ta Teleftaia Deka Chronia." *Deka Chronia Palis.* 1950. Reprint. Athens: Poreia, 1978.
Battaglia, Roberto. *The Story of the Italian Resistance.* London: Odhams, 1957.
Bethell, Nicholas. *Betrayed.* New York: Times Books, 1984.
Black, Cyril E., and Thomas P. Thornton, eds. *Communism and Revolution: The Strategic Uses of Political Violence.* Princeton, N.J.: Princeton University Press, 1964.
Blanas, Giorgis. *Emfilios Polemos, 1946–1949: Opos ta Ezisa.* Athens: n.p., 1976.
Borkenau, Franz. *End and Beginning.* Ed. Richard Lowenthal. New York: Columbia University Press, 1981.
_____. *European Communism.* New York: Harper, 1953.
Brzezinski, Zbigniew. *The Soviet Bloc: Unity and Conflict.* Cambridge: Harvard University Press, 1967.
Burks, R. V. *The Dynamics of Communism in Eastern Europe.* Princeton, N.J.: Princeton University Press, 1961.
_____. "Hellenic Time of Troubles." *Problems of Communism* 33 (November–December 1984).
_____. "Statistical Profile of the Greek Communist." *Journal of Modern History* 27 (1955).
Capell, Richard. *Simiomata: A Greek Notebook, 1944–45.* London: Macdonald, 1945.
Chandler, Geoffrey. *The Divided Land: An Anglo-Greek Tragedy.* London: Macmillan, 1959.
Chatzis, Thanasis. *I Nikifora Epanastasi pou Chathike.* 4 vols. 2d ed. Athens: Dorikos, 1982.
Churchill, Winston S. *The Second World War.* Vol. 6. London: Cassell, 1954.
Claudin, Fernando. *The Communist Movement: From Comintern to Cominform.* 2 pts. New York: Monthly Review Press, 1975.
Clogg, Richard. *A Short History of Modern Greece.* Cambridge: Cambridge University Press, 1979.
Conquest, Robert. *Power and Policy in the U.S.S.R.: The Struggle for Stalin's Succession, 1945–1960.* New York: Harper & Row, 1967.
Dallin, David J. *Soviet Foreign Policy after Stalin.* Philadelphia: Lippincott, 1960.
Dedijer, Vladimir. *Tito.* New York: Simon & Schuster, 1953.
Deibel, Terry L., and John Lewis Gaddis, eds. *Containing the Soviet Union.* Washington: Pergammon-Brassey's, 1987.
Deltio tou Dimokratikou Stratou Elladas DSE. Dokumenta tou Ellinikou Proodeftikou Kinimatos no. 20. Athens: Mnimi, n.d. [1979?].
Dennett, Raymond, and Joseph E. Johnson, eds. *Negotiating with the Russians.* Boston: World Peace Foundation, 1951.
Dimitriou, Panos, ed. *I Diaspasi tou KKE.* 2 vols. Athens: Themelio, 1978.
Dimitrov, Georgi. *I. Ki Omos Kineitai . . . ; II. To Eniaio Metopo; III. Synendevksi sto Rizospasti.* Dokumenta tou Pangkosmiou Proodeftikou Kinimatos no. 1. Athens: Mnimi, 1976.
Djilas, Milovan. *Conversations with Stalin.* Trans. Michael Petrovich. New York: Harcourt, Brace & World, 1962.

———. *Vlast*. London: Naša Reć, 1983.

Dritsios, Thomas. *I Exegersi tis Taskendis: Ekei pou Ragise i Kardia mas*. Athens: Glaros, 1984.

Eleftheriou, Lefteris P. *Synomilies me ton Niko Zachariadi*. Athens: Kentavros, 1986.

Esche, Matthias. *Die Kommunistische Partei Griechenlands, 1941–1949*. (Munich and Vienna: R. Oldenbourg, 1982.

To Ethniko Mas Provlima kai to Kommunistiko Komma tis Elladas. Dokumenta tou Ellinikou Proodeftikou Kinimatos no. 13. Athens: Mnimi, n.d.

Eudes, Dominque. *The Kapetanios: Partisans and Civil War in Greece, 1943–1949*. New York: Monthly Review Press, 1972.

"To Evdomo Synedrio tou KKE." *Anti*, June 17, 1978.

Fleischer, Hagen. *Greece in the 1940s: A Bibliographic Companion*. Hanover, N.H.: University Press of New England, 1981.

Gaddis, John Lewis. *Strategies of Containment*. Oxford: Oxford University Press, 1982.

Gousidis, Dimitris, ed. *Markos Vafeiadis: Martyries*. Thessaloniki: Epikairotita, 1983.

Griffith, William E. *Albania and the Sino-Soviet Rift*. Cambridge: M.I.T. Press, 1963.

Grigoriadis, Foivos N. *Istoria tou Emfiliou Polemou, 1945–1949: To Deftero Andartiko*. 4 vols. Athens: Kamarinopoulos, n.d.

Grigoriadis, Solon. *O Emfilios Polemos: I Ellada tou 1945–1949*. 2 vols. Athens: Typos, 1979.

———. *Istoria tis Sygchronis Elladas, 1949–74*. 7 vols. Athens: Kapopoulos, 1978.

Gromyko, A. A., and Boris Ponomarev, eds. *Soviet Foreign Policy, 1917–1980*. 2 vols. Moscow: Progress, 1980.

Hahn, Werner G. *Postwar Soviet Politics: The Fall of Zhdanov and the Defeat of Moderation, 1946–53*. Ithaca, N.Y.: Cornell University Press, 1982.

Halperin, Morton H., and Arnold Kantor, eds. *Readings in American Foreign Policy: The Bureaucratic Perspective*. Boston: Little, Brown, 1973.

Hammond, Thomas T., ed. *The Anatomy of Communist Takeovers*. New Haven, Conn.: Yale University Press, 1975.

———. *Witnesses to the Origins of the Cold War*. Seattle: University of Washington Press, 1982.

Harris, Jonathan. "The Origins of the Conflict between Malenkov and Zhdanov: 1939–1941." *Slavic Review* 35 (June 1976).

Hondros, John Louis. *Occupation and Resistance: The Greek Agony 1941–44*. New York: Pella, 1983.

Horelick, Arnold L., A. Ross Johnson, and John D. Steinbruner. *The Study of Soviet Foreign Policy: A Review of Decision-Theory–Related Approaches*. R-1334. Santa Monica, Calif.: Rand Corp., 1973.

Hoxha, Enver. *The Titoites*. Tirana: "8" Nentori, 1982.

———. *With Stalin: Memoirs*. Tirana: "8" Nentori, 1979.

Iatrides, John O. *Revolt in Athens: The Greek Communist "Second Round," 1944–1945*. Princeton, N.J.: Princeton University Press, 1972.

———, ed. *Greece in the 1940s: A Nation in Crisis*. Hanover, N.H.: University Press of New England, 1981.

Ideologiki Pali Anamesa sto KKE kai stis Parafyades tou Ellinikou Trotskismou, 1946–1947. Athens: Ekdoseis tou Laou, 1947.

Ioannidis, Iannis. *Anamniseis: Provlimata tis Politikis tou KKE stin Ethniki Antistasi, 1940–1945.* Athens: Themelio, 1979.

Jecchinis, Christos. *Trade Unionism in Greece: A Study in Political Paternalism.* Chicago: Roosevelt University, Labor Education Division, 1965.

Johnson, A. Ross. *The Transformation of Communist Ideology: The Yugoslav Case, 1945–1953.* Cambridge: M.I.T. Press, 1972.

Katsoulis, Giorgis D. *Istoria tou Kommounistikou Kommatos Elladas.* 7 vols. Athens: Nea Synora, 1976–78.

Kir'iakidis, G. D. *Grazhdanskaia voina v Gretsii, 1946–1949.* Moscow: Nauka, 1972.

Kirjazovski, Risto. *Narodnoosloboditelniot Front i drugite organizatsii na makedontsite od egejska makedonija, 1945–1949.* Skopje, Macedonia: Kultura, 1985.

Kitrinos, Robert W. "International Department of the CPSU." *Problems of Communism* 23 (September–October 1984).

Kofos, Evangelos. *Nationalism and Communism in Macedonia.* Thessaloniki: Institute for Balkan Studies, 1964.

Kohler, Beate. *Political Forces in Spain, Greece and Portugal.* London: Butterworth, 1982.

Kondis, Vasil [Basil]. *I Angloamerikaniki Politiki kai to Elliniko Provlima, 1945–1949.* Thessaloniki: Paratiritis, 1984.

———. "Aspects of Greek American Relations on the Eve of the Truman Doctrine." *Balkan Studies* 19 (1978).

Kousoulas, D. George. *Revolution and Defeat: The Story of the Greek Communist Party, 1918–1949.* London: Oxford University Press, 1965.

Kozlov, M. M., ed. *Velikaia otechestvennaia voina, 1941–1945: Entsiklopediia.* Moscow: Sovetskaia Entsiklopediia, 1985.

Krasner, Stephen D. "Are Bureaucracies Important? (Or Allison Wonderland)." *Foreign Policy,* no. 7 (1972).

Kuniholm, Bruce R. *The Origins of the Cold War in the Near East: Great Power Conflict and Diplomacy in Iran, Turkey, and Greece.* Princeton, N.J.: Princeton University Press, 1980.

Loulis, John C. *The Greek Communist Party, 1940–1944.* London: Croom Helm, 1982.

McCagg, William O. *Stalin Embattled, 1943–1948.* Detroit: Wayne State University Press, 1978.

Mackintosh, John M. *Strategy and Tactics of Soviet Foreign Policy.* New York: Oxford University Press, 1963.

McNeill, William H. *America, Britain & Russia: Their Co-operation and Conflict, 1941–1946.* London: Oxford University Press, 1953.

———. *The Greek Dilemma: War and Aftermath.* Philadelphia: Lippincott, 1947.

———. *The Metamorphosis of Greece since World War II.* Chicago: University of Chicago Press, 1978.

MacVeagh, Lincoln. *Ambassador MacVeagh Reports: Greece, 1933–1947.* Ed. John O. Iatrides. Princeton, N.J.: Princeton University Press, 1980.

Maltezos, Gerasimos. *DSE: Dimokratikos Stratos Elladas.* Athens: n.p., 1984.

Manousakas, Iannis. *O Emfilios: Sti Skia tis Akronafplias*. Athens: Dorikos, 1977.

Mastny, Vojtech. *Russia's Road to the Cold War: Diplomacy, Warfare, and the Politics of Communism, 1941–1945*. New York: Columbia University Press, 1979.

Mathieu, Gilbert. "The French and Belgian Communist Parties in Relation to Soviet Objectives towards Western Europe in 1940 and 1944." Ph.D. diss., University of Wisconsin, 1971.

Matthews, Kenneth. *Memories of a Mountain War: Greece, 1944–1949*. London: Longmans, Green, 1972.

Mavrogordatos, George T. *Stillborn Republic: Social Coalitions and Party Strategies in Greece, 1922–1936*. Berkeley and Los Angeles: University of California Press, 1983.

Mertzos, N. I. *Svarnout: To Prodomeno Andartiko*. 6th ed. Thessaloniki: n.p., 1984.

Meyer, Alfred G. *Leninism*. Cambridge: Harvard University Press, 1957.

Moore, Barrington. *Soviet Politics: The Dilemma of Power*. Cambridge: Harvard University Press, 1950.

Mosely, Philip E. *The Kremlin and World Politics*. New York: Knopf, Vintage, 1960.

Myers, E. C. W. *Greek Entanglement*. London: Hart-Davis, 1955.

Myridakis, Michalis I. *Agonas tis Fylis: I Ethniki Antistasi EDES-EOEA, 1941–1944*. 2 vols. Athens: Sideris, 1976.

Naltsas, Christoforos A. *To Makedoniko Zitima kai i Sovietiki Politiki*. Thessaloniki: Institute for Balkan Studies, 1954.

Nefeloudis, Pavlos. *Stis Piges tis Kakodaimonias: Ta Vathitera Aitia tis Diaspasis tou KKE, 1918–1968*. 5th ed. Athens: Gutenberg, 1974.

Nikitin, S. A., ed. *Slaviano-Balkanskie issledovaniia: Istoriografia i istochnikovedenie. Sbornik statei i materialov*. Moscow: Nauka, 1972.

Novikov, Nikolai V. *Puti i pereput'ia diplomata: Zapiski o 1943–1944 gg*. Moscow: Nauka, 1976.

O'Ballance, Edgar. *The Greek Civil War, 1944–1949*. London: Faber & Faber, 1966.

Oikonomidis, Foivos. *Oi Prostates: I Alithini Istoria*. Athens: Kaktos, 1984.

Papadakis, V. P. *Diplomatiki Istoria tou Ellinikou Polemou, 1940–1945*. Athens: n.p., 1957.

Papaioannou, Achilleas. *I Diathiki tou Niko Zachariadi*. Athens: Glaros, 1986.

Papapanagiotou, Alekos. *I Alitheia gia to "Pisoplato Chtipima": Martyria*. Athens: Kazantza, 1974.

———. "O Rolos ton Xenon stin Antistasi kai ton Emfilio." *Anti*, May 8, 22, June 19, 1981.

Papastratis, Prokopis. *British Policy towards Greece during the Second World War, 1941–1944*. London: Cambridge University Press, 1984.

Partsalidis, Dimitris [Mitsos]. *Dipli Apokatastasi tis Ethnikis Antistasis*. Athens: Themelio, 1978.

———. "O Mitsos Partsalidis Mila gia tin Periodo 1943–49." *Anti*, May 14, 1977.

Pederson, James Henry. "Focal Point of Conflict: The United States and Greece, 1943–47." M. A. thesis, University of Michigan, 1974.

Pijade, Moša. *About the Legend That the Yugoslav Uprising Owed Its Existence to Soviet Assistance*. London: n.p., 1950.

Pospelov, P. N., ed. *Istoria velikoi otechestvennoi voiny Sovetskogo Soiuza, 1941–1945*. 6 vols. Moscow: Voennoe Izdatel'stvo, Ministerstva Oborony Soiuza SSR, 1960.

Protopopov, A. S., ed. *Sovetskii Soiuz v Organizatsii Ob"edinennykh Natsii*. Vol. 1. Moscow: Nauka, 1965.

Psimmenos, Takis. *Andartes St'Agrafa*. Athens: Sygchroni Epochi, 1983.

Psomas, Andreas. *The Nation, the State, and the International System: The Case of Modern Greece*. Athens: n.p., 1977.

Ra'anan, Gavriel D. *International Policy Formation in the USSR: Factional "Debates" during the Zhdanovshchina*. Hamden, Conn.: Shoe String, Archon, 1983.

Reale, Eugenio. *Avec Jacques Duclos au Banc des accuses*. Trans. Pierre Bonuzzi. Paris: Plon, 1958.

———. *Nascita del Cominform*. Milan: Arnoldo Mondadori, 1958.

Richter, Heinz. *British Intervention in Greece: From Varkiza to Civil War, February 1945 to August 1946*. London: Merlin, 1985.

Rieber, Alfred J. *Stalin and the French Communist Party, 1941–1947*. New York: Columbia University Press, 1962.

Roberts, Henry L. *Rumania*. New Haven, Conn.: Yale University Press, 1951.

Roberts, Walter R. *Tito, Mihailović and the Allies*. New Brunswick, N.J.: Rutgers University Press, 1973.

Ross, Graham, ed. *The Foreign Office and the Kremlin: British Documents on Anglo-Soviet Relations, 1941–1945*. Cambridge: Cambridge University Press, 1984.

Rousos, Petros. *I Megali Pentaetia*. 2 vols. 2d ed. Athens: Sygchroni Epochi, 1978.

Sarafis, Marion, ed. *Greece: From Resistance to Civil War*. Nottingham: Spokesman, 1980.

Sarafis, Stefanos. *ELAS: Greek Resistance Army*. London: Merlin, 1980.

Secchia, Pietro. *Archivo Pietro Secchia, 1945–1973*. Milan: Feltrinelli, 1979.

Semiriaga, M. I. *Bor'ba narodov tsentral'noi i iugo-vostochnoi evropy protiv nemetsko-fashistskogo gneta*. Moscow: Nauka, 1985.

Shulman, Marshal D. *Stalin's Foreign Policy Reappraised*. New York: Atheneum, 1965.

Smith, Ole L. "The Boycott of the Elections 1946: A Decisive Mistake?" *Scandinavian Studies in Modern Greek*, no. 6 (1982).

———. "The Memoirs and Reports of British Liason Officers in Greece, 1942–1944: Problems of Source Value." *Journal of the Hellenic Diaspora* 11 (Fall 1984).

———. "On the Beginning of the Greek Civil War." *Scandinavian Studies in Modern Greek*, no. 1 (1977).

———. "The Problems of the Second Plenum of the Central Committee of the KKE, 1946." *Journal of the Hellenic Diaspora* 12 (Summer 1985).

———. Review of *Die Kommunistische Partei Griechenlands 1941–1949*, by Matthias Esche. *Journal of the Hellenic Diaspora* 11 (Spring 1984).

———. "A Turning Point in the Greek Civil War 1945–1949." *Scandinavian Studies in Modern Greek*, no. 3 (1979).

———. "On Zachariades' Theory of the Two Poles." *Scandinavian Studies in Modern Greek*, no. 5 (1981).

Sofianopoulos, Iannis. "Greece Needs an All-Party Government to End Terrorism." *New Chronicle*, July 28, 1945.

Spriano, Paolo. *Stalin and the European Communists*. Trans. Jon Rothschild. London: New Left, Verso, 1985.

Stavrianos, Leften S. *Greece: American Dilemma and Opportunity*. Chicago: Regnery, 1952.

Steinbruner, John. *The Cybernetic Theory of Decision*. Princeton, N.J.: Princeton University Press, 1974.

Strugar, Valdo. *Iugoslaviia v ogne voiny, 1941–1945*. Moscow: Nauka, 1985.

Svoronos, Nikos G. *Episkopisi tis Neoellinikis Istorias*. Athens: Themelio, 1976.

Sweet-Escott, Bickham. *Greece: A Political and Economic Survey, 1939–1953*. London: Royal Institute of International Affairs, 1954.

Telesheva, L., ed. *Pravda o Gretsii: Golubaia Kniga*. Moscow: Inostrannoi Literatury, 1949.

Tillon, Charles. *On Chantait Rouge*. Paris: Laffont, 1977.

Triska, Jan F., and David Finley. *Soviet Foreign Policy*. New York: Macmillan, 1968.

Trukhanovskii, Vladimir G. *Sovetsko-Angliiskie otnosheniia, 1945–1978*. Moscow: Mezhdunarodnye Otnosheniia, 1979.

_____. *Vneshniaia politika Anglii v period vtoroi mirovoi voiny*. Moscow: Nauka, 1965.

_____, ed. *Istoriia mezhdunarodnykh otnoshenii i vneshnei politiki SSSR, 1917–1967*. 3 vols. Moscow: Mezhdunarodnye Otnosheniia, 1967.

Truman, Harry S. *Memoirs*. 2 vols. Garden City, N.Y.: Doubleday, 1955.

Ulam, Adam B. *Expansion and Coexistence: The History of Soviet Foreign Policy, 1917–67*. New York: Praeger, 1971.

_____. *Titoism and the Cominform*. Cambridge: Harvard University Press, 1952.

Vafeiadis, Markos. *Apomnimonevmata*. Vol. 1. Athens: Difros, 1984. Vols. 2, 3. Athens: Nea Synora, Livani, 1985.

_____. Interviews in *Epikaira*, December 9, 16, 1976.

_____. "O Markos Vafeiadis Apanta sto Mitso Partsalidi gia ti 'Synantisi me ton Stalin' ti Varkiza kai tin 'katangelia' Zachariadi." *Anti*, September 4, 1976.

Valeva, L. B., and G. M. Slavina, eds. *Sovetskii Soiuz i bor'ba narodov tsentral'noi i iugo-vostochnoi evropy za svobody i nezavisimost', 1941–1945 gg*. Moscow: Nauka, 1978.

Varga, Evgenii S. *Izmeneniia v ekonomike kapitalisma v itoge vtoroi mirovoi voiny*. Moscow: Politicheskoi Literatury, 1946.

Vlantas, Dimitris. *Emfilios Polemos, 1945–1949*. Vol. 3, pt. 1. Athens: n.p., 1979. Vol. 3, pt. 2. Athens: Grammi, 1981.

_____. *I Prodomeni Epanastasi, 1941–1944*. Athens: Evangelios, 1977.

_____. *Tragodia tou KKE, 1950–1967*. Athens: Grammi, 1976.

Voithima gia tin Istoria tou KKE. 2d ed. Reprint. Athens: Ekdoseis tou Laou, 1975.

Vontitsos-Gousias, Giorgis. *Oi Aities gia tis Ittes, ti Diaspasi tou KKE kai tis Ellinikis Aristeras*. 2 vols. Athens: Na Iperetoume to Lao, 1977.

_____. "O Zachariadis Mou Eipe . . . ," *Anti*, February 25, 1978.

Votsikas, Dimos K. *I Ipeiros Xanazonetai T'Armata*. Athens: n.p. 1983.

Vournas, Tasos. *I Diaspasi tou KKE*. Athens: Tolidis, 1983.

_____. *Istoria tis Sygchronis Elladas: O Emfilios*. Athens: Tolidis, 1981.

Voznesenskii, Nikolai A. *Voennaia ekonomika SSSR v period otechestvennoi voiny*. Moscow: Politicheskoi Literatury, 1948.

Vukmanović-Tempo, Svetozar. *How and Why the People's Liberation Struggle of Greece Met with Defeat*. 1950. Reprint. London: Merlin, 1985.

Wittner, Lawrence S. *American Intervention in Greece, 1943–1949*. New York: Columbia University Press, 1982.

Woodhouse, Christopher M. *Apple of Discord: A Survey of Recent Greek Politics in Their International Setting*. London: Hutchinson, 1948.

------. *The Struggle for Greece, 1941–1949*. London: Hart-Davis, MacGibbon, 1976.

Xydis, Stephen George. *Greece and the Great Powers, 1944–1947*. Thessaloniki: Institute for Balkan Studies, 1963.

Zachariadis, Nikos. *Deka Chronia Palis: Symberasmata, Didagmata, Kathikonta. Pros tin Triti Syndiaskepsi tou KKE*. 1950. Reprint. Athens: Poreia, 1978.

------. *Ta Provlimata Kathodigisis sto KKE*. 1952. Reprint. Athens: Poreia, 1978.

------. *Provlimata tis Krisis tou KKE*. N.p.: Laikis Exousias, n.d.

------. *Theseis gia tin Istoria tou KKE*. Athens: Gnoseis, n.d.

Zafeiropoulos, D. G. *O Antisymmoriakos Agon, 1945–1949*. Athens: n.p., 1956.

Zapantis, Andrew L. *Greek-Soviet Relations, 1917–1941*. New York: Columbia University Press, 1982.

Zhdanov, Andrei Alexandrovitch. *The International Situation*. Moscow: Foreign Languages Publishing, 1947.

Zotiades, George B. *The Macedonian Controversy*. Thessaloniki: Institute for Balkan Studies, 1954.

INDEX

Adriatic Sea, 83
Aegean Macedonia, 128–29, 130n. *See also* Macedonia; *entries for individual nations*
Aegean Sea, 51, 128, 214
Aftoamina. See Self-defense groups
Albania, 49, 144n, 155, 156n, 157n, 166–67, 178, 185, 200, 206–7; aid to Greek Communists, 106, 162–63, 173; and Greek demands for Northern Epirus, 62, 67; possible support for Zhdanov, 197; prospect Western invasion of, 5, 179, 181–84, 182n, 209; Soviet concern for integrity of, 4, 52n, 83, 134–35, 143, 168, 170–71, 171n, 211–13, 215; Workers' Party of, 129, 180. *See also* Commission of Investigation Concerning Greek Frontier Incidents; Foreign Communist assistance to Greek Communist insurgency; Yugoslavia
Allied Control Commission–Sofia (ACC), 63–64
Allied Military Mission to Greece, 129n
Allied Mission for Observing the Greek Elections, 138–39, 174; Soviet refusal to participate in, 77–78. *See also* Greek elections

Allied Powers. *See* Great Powers; *entries for individual nations*
Andartes (guerrillas), 108, 123, 140, 179, 198. *See also* Armed forces; Communist Party of Greece; Democratic Army of Greece; Greek Popular Liberation Army
Angelopoulos, Angelos, 22
Ankersmit, F. R., 217n
Antifascist Army Organization (ASO), 17
Antifascist Assembly of the National Liberation of Macedonia (ASNOM), 130–31
Antifascist Council for the National Liberation of Yugoslavia (AVNOJ), 10, 17, 44, 131
Ardahan, 61
Argentina, 77, 80
Armed forces (Greek Communist): penetration of government armed forces by, 88, 111, 114, 123–25; strength estimates of, 113, 114–15, 123–25, 138, 144, 161. *See also* Bartziotas, Vasilis; Blanas, Giorgis; Coup d'etat; Democratic Army of Greece; Foreign Communist assistance to Greek Communist insurgency; Greek Popular Liberation Army; Self-defense groups;

The index was prepared with the assistance of Jennifer Adams and Ann Parker.

Armed forces (Greek Communist) (*cont.*)
   Vontitsos-Gousias, Giorgis; Votsikas,
   Dimos
Armenians, 117
Askoutsis, Nikolaos, 22
Athens, 14n, 33, 37, 53–54, 62, 64, 66–
   68, 116, 130, 132, 143, 149, 155, 164,
   175, 199
Attlee, Clement, 73

Badoglio, Pietro, 46
Bakirtzis, Evripidis, 30, 39, 58, 155, 202
Balkan Commission of Inquiry. *See*
   Commission of Investigation
   Concerning Greek Frontier Incidents
Balkan Federation, 168
Balkans, 203; factors affecting Soviet
   policy in, 2–5, 62, 166, 181, 182n,
   203–4, 206; percentages agreement
   regarding, 27–28, 31, 34; postwar
   objectives in, 9–11, 48, 70, 93; Soviet
   prospects in, 20, 205, 210, 213;
   Yugoslav aims in, 139, 189, 208, 214.
   See also entries for individual nations
Baltic States, 9–10
Baranov, 152, 162–63, 164n, 195n, 196
Barker, Elisabeth, 8n, 19, 169
Barros, James, 156n
Bartziotas, Vasilis, 14n, 68n, 92n, 93,
   103n, 104–8, 113, 114n, 120, 121n,
   175–77, 199
Bebler, Aleš, 159, 167
Belenkov, 82
Belgrade, 116, 138n, 145, 147, 148n,
   149, 151, 154, 157n, 160, 162, 164,
   169, 182n, 195, 199; Soviets in, 116n,
   195n, 196n. *See also* Communist Party
   of Greece; Foreign Communist
   assistance to Greek Communist
   insurgency
Bevin, Ernest, 72–73
Bigart, Homer, 175
Biriuzov, Sergei, 62
Blanas, Giorgis, 68, 101n, 103n, 106–8,
   111–14, 120n, 121, 124, 138
Bled Conference, 134, 166. *See also*
   Bulgaria; Dimitrov, Georgi; Tito, Josip
   Broz; Yugoslavia
Blum, Leon, 41
Border incidents, on Greek-Bulgarian
   Frontier, 62–64
Borkenau, Franz, 46

Boulkes, 150, 158
British Military Mission (Sofia), 61n, 119
Brynes, James F., 84
Brzezinski, Zbigniew, 5n
Bucharest, 40
Bulgaria, 34, 78, 144n, 157n, 166n, 167,
   171; and contact with KKE, 37–38, 52,
   145, 158, 162–63; and contact with
   Zhdanov, 190n, 196–97; and
   Macedonian question, 180–81; Soviet
   objectives in, 49, 170, 178, 207; Soviet
   presence in, 61–64; and Yugoslavia,
   134–35, 146, 166. *See also* Border
   incidents; Commission of Investigation
   Concerning Greek Frontier Incidents;
   Foreign Communist assistance to Greek
   Communist insurgency; Greece; Soviet-
   Yugoslav dispute

Cadogan, Alexander, 117n
Cairo, 28, 116
Cairo Government. *See* Greece:
   government-in-exile
Cannon, Cavendish, 167
Caserta Agreement, 33
Chatourov, 195n, 196n
Chatzis, Thanasis, 24
Chatzivasileiou, Chrysa, 164–65
Chernichev, Nikolai P., 29–30, 58, 117,
   118n, 196
Chetniks, 43
Churchill, Winston S., 26–27, 31, 34, 79,
   122, 132
Clark Kerr, Archibald, Sir, 91
Cold War, 193, 214, 312. *See also* Great
   Powers; *entries for individual nations*
Cominform, 46n, 171–74, 190, 192–
   93, 201. *See also* Soviet-Yugoslav dis-
   pute
Comintern, 11
Commission of Investigation Concerning
   Greek Frontier Incidents, 143, 144n,
   148n, 154–56, 158–60; Albanian,
   Yugoslav, and Bulgarian liaison officers
   of, 155, 156n; meeting with Markos,
   155–56, 157n; Polish delegation on,
   155; Soviet delegation on, 94n, 155;
   Subsidiary Group of, 157. *See also*
   Lavrishchev, A. A.; United Nations
   Organization; Vafeiadis, Markos;
   entries for individual countries

Communist Organization of the Army and Security Forces (KOSSA), 88, 114. *See also* Armed forces; Coup d'etat

Communist Organization of Athens (KOA), 14n, 53–54, 75

Communist Party of Belgium (PCB), 44–45

Communist Party of France (PCF), 44–45, 114n, 171n, 190, 193, 210

Communist Party of Greece (KKE), 11–12, 70, 101, 176, 196, 214; attitude toward Greek government, 13, 16, 68, 71–73, 85, 87–89, 160, 174; and British presence, 66, 68, 85; and civil war plans, 135, 147, 161, 183–84; conflict with European Communists, 169–70; conflict with Soviet policy, 97, 99, 101, 127–28, 143–44; dissatisfaction with Soviet assistance, 142, 162; divisions within leadership, 6, 102, 103, 105, 107–8, 112–13, 119–20, 122–24, 175, 188–89, 197–202; fidelity to Soviet Union, 12–13, 21, 41, 170, 195, 203; impact of Yugoslav policy on, 37, 138n, 139, 144, 146, 148, 166n, 208; as instrument of Soviet policy, 5, 49–50, 207; labor policy of, 76–77, 96–97; and Macedonia, 173, 179–80, 182; orientation of policy, 32–33, 35–36; post-Varkiza policy, 52–56, 74–75, 102–5; response to Lebanon agreement, 23–25, 31; and second round, 4, 13, 130, 132, 196; Soviet contacts and advice to, 28–30, 38–39, 58, 66, 92, 110n, 119, 126, 140n, 141, 148n, 155, 157, 164–65, 178, 180, 182, 184, 189, 203–5. *See also* Armed forces; Coup d'etat; Dual strategy; Foreign Communist assistance to Greek Communist insurgency; Greek elections; National Liberation Front; Neutralization of Greece; Party Congresses; Plenary sessions; Politburo of the Communist Party of Greece; Political gradualism; Political parties; Reconciliation; Zachariadis, Nikos

Communist Party of Italy (PCI), 45–46, 114, 171n, 190, 193, 210

Communist Party of Macedonia, 102

Communist Party of the Soviet Union, 95, 109n, 110n, 140n, 141, 152n, 201;

International Department of, 90, 91n, 180; Politburo of, 186, 193

Containment, U. S. policy of, 213–15

Coup d'etat: fears of rightist attempt at, 82, 122; KKE preparations for, 120n, 122–25. *See also* Armed forces; Greek elections

Crete, 117

Cult of personality (*prosopolatria*), 106, 120. *See also* Zachariadis, Nikos

Cyprus, 91

Czechoslovakia, 19; Communist Party of, 163; Communist Party Congress, 95n, 109; Communist Party support for Civil War, 109, 163. *See also* Foreign Communist assistance to Greek Communist insurgency

Dachau, 66

Damaskinos, Archbishop: regent of Greece, 72, 98

Dedijer, Vladimir, 190

de Gaulle, Charles, 44–46

Democratic Army of Greece (DSE), 6, 148n, 149, 153n, 155–56, 173, 176–85, 195; changes in strategy of, 95n, 148, 154, 158, 160–61, 165, 174, 197–202, General Staff of, 145, 162, 172, 182; and Macedonians, 179–80; materiel and recruitment problems of, 149, 151–53, 161–64, 166n, 171–72; personnel of, 106–7, 137, 138n, 158n, 168; Soviet and Albanian assistance to, 176–78, 181; Stalin orders termination of operations of, 182–84; and Stalin-Tito split, 166, 168, 171–73; and Yugoslavia, 158, 196; Zachariadis orders formation of, 137. *See also* Armed forces; Foreign Communist assistance to Greek Communist insurgency; Vafeiadis, Markos; Zachariadis, Nikos

Denisov. *See* Ioannidis, Iannis

Dilaveris, Nikos, 58

Dimakis, Ilias (Gotsi), 130–32. *See also* Slavo-Macedonian National Liberation Front

Dimitrov, Georgi, 139, 141n, 145, 162, 166n, 171; advice to KKE, 52, 89, 95, 140–41; links to Zhdanov, 189–90; rapprochement with Tito, 135–36, 166,

Dimitrov, Georgi (*cont.*)
190; and Soviet policy, 168, 178. *See also* Bulgaria
Dionysis. *See* Ioannidis, Iannis
Djilas, Milovan, 100, 169, 170n, 171n, 172n, 182n, 190–91
Dodecanese, 83, 99
Doxiadis, Konstantinos, 75
Dual strategy (Greek Communist), 92, 96, 101, 104–6, 111, 120–21, 128, 133, 200; defined, 50–51; and drift toward civil war, 144, 147; impact of Soviet interests on, 110, 115, 120, 142, 206–7, 209–10; precursor to, 103; reemergence of, 136, 170, 173, 176; Soviet attitude toward, 95n, 99, 109–10, 139–41, 159, 185, 209–10, 213. *See also* Democratic Army of Greece; Neutralization of Greece; Plenary sessions; Political gradualism; Reconciliation; Self-defense groups; Zachariadis, Nikos

Eastern Europe, 70, 100, 122, 193n, 198, 202, 206–7, 215; Communist parties of 193
Eden, Anthony, 9, 15, 26–27
Egypt, 36
Eighth Division, Government Army, 123. *See also* Greece: armed forces of
Eighth Pan-Hellenic Labor Congress, 96
Eleftheriou, Lefteris P., 95n, 109n, 110n, 139n, 194
Eleventh Plenum of the Central Committee of the Communist Party of Greece. *See* Plenary sessions
Elite conflict, 6, 186–202. *See also* Communist Party of Greece; Stalin, Josef V.; Vafeiadis, Markos; Zhdanov, Andrei A.
Epirus, 36, 124, 145
Epirus Regional Office. *See* Regional Committee of Epirus
Erythriadis, Giorgis, 165
Ethridge, Mark, 49, 156
Ethridge Commission, 49
Evans, P. H., 130n

Feather, Victor, 77
Fifth Plenum of the Central Committee of the Communist Party of Greece. *See* Plenary sessions

Finland, 9–10
First Plenum of the Central Committee of the Communist Party of Greece. *See* Plenary sessions
First Subcommittee of the Greek Communist Politburo. *See* Politburo of the Communist Party of Greece
Florina, 130n, 131–32
Foreign Communist assistance to Greek Communist insurgency, 114n, 138, 140, 149–50, 152–53, 163, 176–78. *See also* Zachariadis, Nikos; *entries for individual nations*
"Forward line," of Soviet policy, 187, 192, 194. *See also* Tito, Josip Broz; Zhdanov, Andrei A.
Fourth Plenum of the Central Committee of the Communist Party of Greece. *See* Plenary sessions
France, 10, 44, 69, 77, 151, 167; Ambassador in Yugoslavia, 167; Embassy in Athens, 167; Minister at Tirana, 176
"Free" Greek state. *See* Provisional Democratic Government

Gaddis, John Lewis, 214n
Gheorghiu-Dej, Gheorghe, 40
General Confederation of Greek Workers (GSEE), 76, 96; Confederation of Workers and Clerks, 35
George, king of the Hellenes, 13, 16, 136, 141n
Germany: Nazi, 4, 7, 11, 41, 125, 206; postwar, 100
Ghost Comintern, 190
Gotsi. *See* Dimakis, Ilias
Gorbachev, Mikhail S., 31n
Gottesman, Gustav, 156
Government Army, Eighth Division of, 123. *See also* Greece: armed forces of
Grammos, 170n, 172, 175n, 177, 181, 183, 185, 200, 201n
Graur, Andrei, 155, 156n. *See also* Commission of Investigation Regarding Greek Frontier Incidents
Great Britain, 50, 100, 146, 148n, 169, 182n; armed forces of, 63, 84–86, 90, 107, 143; and deterioration of presence in Mediterranean, 49, 52, 65, 70, 84; diplomatic posts and personnel of, 118n, 141n, 157, 167–68, 176; Foreign

Great Britain (*cont.*)
 Office of, 16, 38, 57–58, 60n, 130n,
  141n, 158, 181; General Headquarters
  in Cairo, 129; and Greek government,
  4, 35, 55, 71, 87, 97; intelligence
  service of, 115, 130; and invasion of
  Albania, 182n; and KKE, 36, 56, 70,
  81–86, 108, 130; and mutiny in the
  Middle East, 21; policy under Labour
  government, 73, 80–81; Special
  Operations Executive, 14; and USSR,
  9–10, 14, 19n, 26–28, 38, 49, 63–64,
  70, 116, 118, 142, 183. *See also*
  Border incidents; Soviet "repatriation"
  mission
Great Powers, 9, 13, 48, 58–59, 69n, 82,
  91, 140, 174, 185, 206
Greece, 177, 187, 194, 198, 209, 218;
  armed forces of, 35–36, 40, 88, 148n,
  152, 155, 171, 179; Emergency
  Measures Act, 135–36; fears of coup,
  82; government of, 69n, 153, 164–65,
  170, 173n, 184; government-in-exile
  (Cairo government), 13, 15–18, 22,
  24–25; government of national unity
  (Papandreou government), 22, 30, 32,
  34–35, 76; National Bank of, 75;
  neutrality of, 69n; recognizes Tito's
  regime, 97–98; relations with Western
  Powers, 181, 193. *See also* Coup
  d'etat; Greek elections; *entries for
  individual nations*
Greek Civil War, 1, 183, 203, 206–8,
  219
Greek Communist strategy. *See* Dual
  strategy; *Limnes*; Neutralization of
  Greece; Political gradualism;
  Reconciliation
Greek elections, 124–25, 138; Greek
  Communist attitudes toward, 68, 72,
  86–87, 89–90, 99, 101, 126, 135,
  150–51; Soviet view of, 77, 84, 94.
  See also, Allied Mission for Observing
  the Greek Elections; Zachariadis, Nikos
Greek Macedonia, 130. *See also*
  Macedonia
Greek Popular Liberation Army (ELAS),
  11–15, 24–25, 35–36, 52, 138; conflict
  with other resistance groups, 14, 24–
  25, 56; contact with Soviets, 28–30,
  31n, 32, 129n; former officers' views
  on insurgency, 103, 106–7, 112–13;
  and hidden weapons, 113, 152;

reconstruction of, 115; Soviet opinion
  of, 11, 32–33, 39, 41–42; tensions
  with Yugoslavs over Macedonia, 129–
  30, 132. *See also* National Liberation
  Front
Gromyko, Andrei A., 142–43, 154, 183–
  84, 212
Gurskii, 117n
Gusev, Fedor, 26

Hadziiossif, Christos, 74n
Hagia Paraskeve, 132
Halara, 131
Historical narrative, 205, 217
Hitler, Adolf. *See* Germany
Hoxha, Enver, 52n, 67, 166, 171, 178,
  181, 182n, 196. *See also* Stalin, Josef
  V.
Hungary, 34, 164

Iatrides, John O., 18n, 21, 33, 37
Iliou, Filippos, 109n, 140n, 146–47
Imbros, 67
Inter-Allied Commission: KKE demands
  for intervention of, 53, 55–56, 61, 69–
  70, 72, 77–78, Soviet view on, 61, 70;
  U.S. proposal for, 77–78, 143. *See
  also* Allied Mission for Observing the
  Greek Elections; Commission of
  Investigation Concerning Greek Frontier
  Incidents
Ioannidis, Iannis (Denisov, Dionysis), 22,
  30, 106, 113n, 131–32, 138n, 140–42,
  145, 147–149, 152–53, 161, 163,
  177n, 199n
Istanbul, 20
Italy, 45–46

Kalinin, Mikhail, 98
Kanellopoulous, Panagiotis, 86;
  government of, 87
Karamanov, Vladimir D., 117, 118n
Kardelj, Edvard, 168, 171n, 190, 192
Karpenisi, 179
Kars, 61
Kasparov, G. B., 155n, 157n
Kastoria, 129
Kavala, 64
Kennan, George F., 214n
Kirkos, Michalis, 159
Koldonov, A. I., 31n
Kondis, Vasil, 128n, 166n, 182n

Konitsa, 164–65, 199
Korçe, 176
Korfu, 102n
Koukos. See Zachariadis, Nikos
Koula, 64
Kousoulas, D. George, 37
Kozani, 131
Krystalopighi, 131
Kukin, Konstantin, 117n, 118

Labour party (British): election victory of, 71, 79–80, 210; policy of, 73. See also Union of Soviet Socialist Republics
Lambrakis, Dimitris, 75
Lavrent'iev, Anatolii I., 90n, 91n, 94n
Lavrishchev, A. A., 155–57, 159–60, 165–66, 196
League of National Resistance Fighters, 114
Lebanon Charter, 22–23, 25, 27–28, 30–31, 59, 204
Leeper, Reginald, 33n, 54n, 57, 65, 80, 87, 118, 130n
Lenin, Vladimir Ilych, 127
Leonidas. See Stringos, Leonidas
Lie, Trygvye, 176, 183, 212
Limnes, 161. See also Democratic Army of Greece
Longo, Luigi, 46n
Loulis, John, 18n, 24, 37n

Macedonia, 31, 34n, 36, 58, 114–15, 117n, 119, 128–33, 145, 156n, 161, 173; question of independence of, 50, 130–33, 146, 179; Yugoslav republic of, 179. See also Plenary sessions; entries for individual nations
Macedonian autonomy, 5, 37, 89, 117n; Stalin's use of, 179–84. See also Plenary sessions
McCagg, William O., 192n
Macmillan, Harold, 34, 55
McNeil, Hector, 87, 183–84, 212
McNeill, William H., 29
MacVeagh, Lincoln, 18–20, 54–55, 59, 62, 65, 71, 73–74, 77, 81, 84, 86–87
Maiskii, Ivan, 9
Malenkov, Georgii, 190, 192–93
Malinovskii, Rodion, 62n
Maltezos, Gerasimos, 95n, 138n
Mantakas, Emmanuil, 36, 131
Manuil'skii, Dimitrii, 81, 142, 154, 190

Markos. See Vafeiadis, Markos
Markos government. See Provisional Democratic Government
Marshall Plan, 171n
Marxism-Leninism, 127, 187
Mastny, Vojtech, 8
Mathieu, Gilbert, 45
Mediterranean, 69, 135, 185, 206–7, 210
Metaxist government, 11, 60
Meyer, Alfred G., 127
Michael, king of Romania, 40
Mihailović, Draža, 43
Molotov, Vyacheslav M., 9–10, 15, 19–20, 26–27, 41, 61, 78, 81, 94, 95n, 97, 109, 126, 139, 144, 168, 182n, 192, 196
Montreux Convention, 61
Moscow, 149, 153, 169, 178, 195, 200–201
Moscow Conference (October 1944), 34–35. See also Percentages agreement
Moscow Foreign Ministers Conference (October 1943), 9–10, 15
Mountain Brigade, 35. See also Greece: armed forces of
Mount Athos, 117n
Mussolini, Benito, 45
Mutiny in the Near East, Soviet involvement in, 4, 18–20, 26. See also Antifascist Army Organization; National Liberation Front (EAM); Romania

Naousa, 73, 111, 178
National and Social Liberation (EKKA), 14, 23
National Liberation Army of Yugoslavia, 44
National Liberation Front (EAM), 13–15, 32, 36, 39, 58–59, 69, 93, 99, 132, 140; Central Committee of, 34–35; control of by Greek Communists, 11–12, 52; creation of, 11; Executive Committee of, 71; post-Varkiza policy of, 54, 56, 71–72, 77–78, 85–89, 92; and proposals for cessation of hostilities, 148n, 155; response to Lebanon conference, 22–25; sends delegation abroad, 89–91; Soviet contacts with, 28–29, 90–91, 125, 157, 159–60; Soviet opinion of, 33n; Soviet support for, 42, 60–61, 77, 81–82; tensions between political parties in, 31,

National Liberation Front (*cont.*) 94–95, 136. *See also* Greek elections; Greek Popular Liberation Army; Political parties; Stalin, Josef V.

National Liberation Front (NOF). *See* Slavo-Macedonian National Liberation Front

National Liberation Military Democratic Organization, 17

National Republican Greek League (EDES), 14–15, 24, 56n

Nefeloudis, Pavlos, 28n

Nefeloudis, Vasilis, 75

Neutralization of Greece, Zachariadis' proposal for, 69, 140–42, 174. *See also* "Two poles," theory of

Northern Epirus, 62, 67, 82n, 83, 91, 102, 106

Novikov, Nikolai, 19, 28, 116

October Revolution: 1946 Anniversary of, 189

Office of Strategic Services (OSS), 12, 39, 62, 119

Panhellenic Military Committee, 104, 106, 120–21. *See also* Dual strategy; Party Congresses; Plenary sessions

Panhellenic Union of Fighters, 114

Pan-Slav Committee, 196n

Path analysis, 217–19

Patras, 86

Pauker, Ana, 40

Papandreou, George, 22–23, 25, 27, 30n, 31, 36; government of, 28n, 34–35, 76

Papapanagiotou, Alekos, 17, 50n, 68, 90n, 106

Paris, 67, 80n

Partsalidis, Dimitris (Mitsos), 52, 54, 87, 89–90, 91n, 93, 94n, 107, 110n, 114n, 121n, 169, 182n

Party Congresses: Seventh Congress of the Communist Party of Greece, 88, 92n, 103–4, 106–7, 109n, 116, 119–20, 209. *See also* Self-defense groups

Peake, Sir Charles, 176

Peloponnese, 36, 53, 159, 177

Percentages agreement (October 1944), 4, 10, 34, 80, 193n, 195n

Peter, king of Yugoslavia, 44

Petrov, [P.], 180, 196

Philby, Kim, 182n

Plaka Agreement, 15

Plastiras, Nikolaos, 55–56, 159–60, 211; government of, 53, 57–58, 60–61

Plenary sessions (Central Committee of the Communist Party of Greece): Eleventh Plenum (1945), 56–57, 92n; Twelfth Plenum (1945), 92n, 103; First Plenum (1945), 92n; Second Plenum (1946), 92, 95n, 96n, 104–7, 109, 111–12, 115n, 120–21, 123–26; Third Plenum (1947), 147n, 154, 157, 160–61, 173, 176, 199–200; Fourth Plenum (1948), 172–73; Fifth Plenum (1949), 180, 196; Seventh Plenum (1957), 95n, 115n, 138n

Poland, 9–10, 164; delegates on Balkan Commission of Inquiry, 155

Politburo of the Communist Party of Greece, 153, 160, 201, 204; First Subcommittee of (Athens), 149, 163–64, 199; Second Subcommittee of (Belgrade), 154, 160–61, 164, 195n, 199

Political Committee of National Liberation (PEEA), 15, 17, 24, 28, 30–32; and Lebanon Agreement, 22–23, 25, 28, 31; National Council of, 24. *See also,* Greek Popular Liberation Army; National Liberation Front

Political gradualism, Greek Communist strategy of, 48–49, 61, 65, 69n, 73, 77, 80–83, 87, 89, 92, 100, 103n, 206. *See also* Dual strategy; Stalin, Josef V.; Zachariadis, Nikos

Political parties, division between Greek Communist and other leftist, 23, 94, 104

Popov, Grigorii, 29–30, 32, 33n, 58, 117

Popular Democratic Federation of the Balkan Peoples, 180

Porfyrogenis, Miltiadis, 22, 28n, 30n, 76, 151

Potsdam Conference, 70, 78, 81–82, 126, 143n

Prague, 109, 144n, 168

Prespa, 153

Providence (U.S. Cruiser), 84

Provisional Democratic Government (Markos government), 151, 161, 164–66, 168, 180, 184. *See also* Communist Party of Greece; Democratic Army of Greece

Prudent expansionism, Stalin's policy of, 5–6, 100, 193n, 203, 208, 211–12, 214–15. *See also* Dual strategy; Political gradualism
Psarros, Dimitris, 23

Rafail, Rafail, 79, 97
Reale, Eugenio, 146n, 171n, 192
Reconciliation (*symfiliosis*), KKE policy of, 110, 136–37, 148. *See also* Dual strategy; Stalin, Josef V.; Zachariadis, Nikos
Regional Committee of Epirus (KKE), 102, 120n, 123
Rennos. *See* Tzimas, Andreas
"Repatriation" mission. *See* Soviet "repatriation" mission
Richter, Heinz, 92n
"Rightist terror," 55, 133, 135; KKE demand for end to, 61
Rodionov, Konstantin K., 57–58, 83, 97–98, 116, 118n, 143, 159, 195n
Romania, 49, 62n, 78, 191, 206; Communist Party assistance to KKE, 164; in discussions with British, 18–20, 26n; Soviet objectives in, 3–4, 9–10, 26, 28, 32, 34, 40–41, 52, 99
Roosevelt, Franklin D., 9, 27
Roumeli, 145, 177
Rousos, Petros, 22, 28, 38, 140, 145, 175
Rubiq, 158
Rural Police (*chorofilakis*), 124
Rusk, Dean, 183–84, 212
Russian Military Mission, 13, 27–33, 37, 58, 195, 204. *See also* Greek Popular Liberation Army
Rust, Mathias, 31n
Ryan, Stanley, 156n

Sacred Squadron, 35. *See also* Greece: armed forces of
San Francisco Conference. *See* United Nations Organization
Sarafis, Stefanos, 13, 22, 32, 129n
Sarper, Selim, 61
Schuyler, Cortlandt, 40
Scobie, Ronald, 33, 118
Secchia, Pietro, 39n
Second Plenum of the Central Committee of the Communist Party of Greece. *See* Plenary sessions
Second Subcommittee of the Greek

Communist Politburo. *See* Politburo of the Communist Party of Greece
Security Battalions, 55
Self-defense groups (*aftoamina*), 68, 85, 88–90, 93, 103–4, 109, 112, 115, 119, 123–24. *See also* Bartziotas, Vasilis; Blanas, Giorgis; Plenary sessions; Zachariadis, Nikos
Sergeiev, Mikhail, 57, 195n
Seventh Plenum of the Central Committee of the Communist Party of Greece. *See* Plenary sessions
Shehu, Mehmet, 166, 171, 178, 180
Siantos, Giorgis, 14, 17, 23, 30n, 35–36, 38, 52, 60, 72, 86, 93n, 129n, 131
Siatistis, 131
Siderokastro, 64
Skopje, 201
Slavo-Macedonian National Liberation Front (SNOF), 129–30, 180; Second Plenum of Central Committee of, 180–81. *See also* Macedonia; *entries for separate nations*
Slavo-Macedonians, division of, 131
Smith, Ole L., 50n, 68n, 104n, 109n, 134n, 138n, 139n
Sofia, 63, 141, 145, 195
Sofianopoulos, Iannis, 57, 59–60, 80–81, 87, 98–99, 126, 211
Sofoulis, Themistoklis, 160, 176, 211; government of, 71n, 81n, 87, 89, 97, 100, 116, 118
Soviet Military Mission. *See* Russian Military Mission
Soviet press, 81–83, 91
Soviet "repatriation" mission, 58, 64n, 116–18, 195. *See also* Great Britain; Greece
Soviet-Yugoslav dispute: expulsion of Yugoslavia from Cominform, 171; friction prior to split, 43–44, 133–35, 151, 157, 165–66, 170, 207, 213; impact on KKE, 133–34, 171–73, 198–202; Soviet policy after break, 173, 178–79, 184, 194, 197, 200–201.
Spheres-of-influence agreement. *See* Percentages agreement
Spiru, Nako, 168
Spriano, Paolo, 171n
Stalin, Josef V., 4–5, 7–8, 108, 122, 126, 203, 214; and alleged approval of KKE policy, 109, 172; attitude to

Stalin, Josef V. (*cont.*)
  Greek government, 38–39, 57–58;
    attitude to independent Communist
    militaries, 41–42, 45n, 46–47, 99–100,
    171n, 203, 210, 212; and Balkans, 3,
    31, 48, 178, 206; and conflict with
    Zhdanov, 186–87, 189, 192–97; con-
    tact with Zachariadis, 95n, 109, 139,
    147, 149, 170n, 177–78, 182, 184,
    190; and dual strategy of KKE, 51, 94,
    99, 125; and Eastern Europe, 8, 10,
    122, 193, 207, 212, 215; and efforts to
    restrain KKE, 31, 110, 133, 135, 139,
    143–44, 150, 160, 209; and gradualist
    policy of KKE, 51, 65, 80, 100–102,
    121, 125; and Great Britain, 3–4, 11,
    13, 15, 25–26, 49, 56, 83, 99, 117,
    125, 129n, 140; and Great Powers, 6,
    10, 15, 26–29, 61, 82, 125–26, 150;
    impact on KKE policy, 93, 178, 184,
    205; and Macedonian question, 179,
    182, 211; meets with Partsalidis, 52n,
    182n; orders shutdown of DSE
    operations, 182; pressure on Turkey,
    51–52; promises aid to DSE, 178; and
    reaction to independent KKE initiatives,
    15, 17; sensitivity to Albania, 62, 170,
    182, 212, 215; and Yugoslavia, 3,
    43, 134–35, 158, 165–66, 171–172,
    186, 198, 202–4, 207–8. *See also*
    Inter-Allied commission; Prudent
    expansionism; Soviet-Yugoslav dispute
Stalinists, 188, 195, 197
Stalinization, 193
Stergios. *See* Tzimas, Andreas
Straits (Dardanelles), 61–62, 67n, 83, 99
Strasbourg, 151
Stratis, Dimitris, 22
Stringos, Leonidas, 131–32
Šubašic, Ivan, Dr., 44
Svolos, Alexander, 22, 28
Symfiliosis. See Reconciliation
Szklarska Poreba, 190, 193n

Tashkent, 196
Teheran Conference, 10, 44
Tenedos, 67
Theos, Kostas, 75n, 92
Thessaloniki, 13, 38, 63–64, 89, 117,
    155n, 156–57, 160–61, 173n
Thessaly-Sterea, 35–36
Third Plenum of the Central Committee of

the Communist Party of Greece. *See*
    Plenary sessions
Thorez, Maurice, 45
Thrace, 161; Eastern, 67, 91; Western,
    156n
Tillon, Charles, 45n
Tirana, 157n, 195
Tito, Josip Broz, 21, 34n, 146, 166n,
    178–79, 200, 204, 213; contact with
    KKE, 17n, 129n, 139; contacts with
    Zachariadis, 109, 144, 148–49, 154,
    161, 177n; and divisions within the
    KKE, 201–2; independent policy of, 4–
    5, 17, 127–28, 185, 189, 206; meeting
    with Šubašic, 44; and Stalin, 150–51,
    157, 169, 171n, 185; and support for
    civil war, 4, 37–38, 138, 146, 149,
    162, 184, 196; and the USSR, 7–8,
    43–44; and Zhdanov faction, 186, 189–
    90, 194–95, 197. *See also* Balkans;
    Dimitrov, Georgi; Macedonia; *entries
    for individual nations*
Titoists, 188, 200–202
Togliatti, Palmiro, 39n, 46
Tolbukhin, Fedor, 62n
Trikala, District of, 156n
Truman, Harry, 84; fact-finding
    commission of, 49
Truman Doctrine, 128, 150, 155n, 156,
    159, 213
Tsaldaris, Konstantinos, 174–75, 211
Tsotylio, 129
Tsouderos, Emmanuil, 18–19, 22, 160,
    174
Turkey, 10, 40, 49, 57–58, 61–62, 80,
    83
Twelfth Plenum of the Central Committee
    of the Communist Party of Greece. *See*
    Plenary sessions
"Two camp" thesis, 189, 193. *See also*
    Zhdanov, Andrei A.
"Two poles," theory of, 69–70, 102,
    103n, 106–7. *See also* Dual strategy;
    Zachariadis, Nikos
Tzimas, Andreas (Rennos, Stergios), 14n,
    37–38, 129, 155

"Ukranian complaint." *See* United Nations
    Organization
Ulam, Adam, 5n
Union of Soviet Socialist Republics
    (USSR), 80–81, 103n, 144n, 166n,

Union of Soviet Socialist Republics (*cont.*)
187, 198, 201, 218–19; advice to Greek Communists, 29–32, 39, 90, 91n, 95n, 142n, 155n; and Albania, 67, 83, 135, 182; assessment of British policy in Greece, 168, 206; contact with Greek Communists 28–29, 90–91; effect of British Labour victory on, 79–80; efforts to restrain insurgency, 140–41, 143, 146, 150, 151n, 154; embassy in Athens, 117, 118n, 174; and Europe, 8, 61, 206; and Greek elections, 78, 84, 90, 94; and Greek government, 57, 77, 81, 97, 116, 154, 159, 173–74; and impact on Greece, 41, 206–7; and inter-Allied commission, 65, 143; linkage of Romania and Greece, 19, 26–27; order to terminate civil war, 183; and postwar objectives, 8–9, 211–12; presence in Greece, 63–64, 116–17, 119, 125, 129n, 155–56, 195–96, 211; and relation to Greek Communist strategies, 65, 69, 99, 108–9, 126, 148, 150, 184, 204, 209; response to Greek Communist actions, 15, 17, 38–39, 195n, 196n; and support for Communist insurgency, 153, 168–69, 176–77, 207–8; and Truman Doctrine, 155n, 156–57, 213–14; and Turkey and the Balkans, 10–11, 48, 51–52, 61–62, 65, 67, 83, 205; and the United Nations, 83, 91, 142–44, 154–55, 176, 212; willingness to intervene in Greece, 78–79; and Yugoslavia, 135, 157, 207. *See also* Border incidents; Prudent expansionism; Russian Military Mission; Soviet "repatriation" mission; Soviet-Yugoslav dispute
United Nations Commission of Investigation. *See* Commission of Investigation Concerning Greek Frontier Incidents
United Nations Organization, 77, 80–81, 83, 91, 98–99, 142–44, 154, 156n, 183, 197, 212; Conference on International Organization (San Francisco Conference), 57, 62, 75, 80–81; General Assembly of, 154; Security Council of, 91, 142–43; "Ukranian complaint," 142–43. *See also* Commission of Investigation Concerning Greek Frontier Incidents; Inter-Allied Commission; *entries for individual nations*
United Nations Relief and Rehabilitation Administration (UNRRA), 96
United States, 156, 169, 174, 187, 191, 209, 211; agrees to participate in observation of Greek elections, 65; attitude toward the Balkans, 84; and crisis of capitalism, 190–92; embassy in Moscow, 169; intelligence, 113; offer of international mission of investigation, 65; relations with Greece, 27, 38, 86–87, 130, 152, 168, 171, 185; reluctance to become involved in Greece, 65, 84; and the Soviet Union, 84, 99, 117n, 150, 174, 183, 214–15; and Yugoslavia, 166–67

Vafeiadis, Markos (Markos), 38n, 93, 137, 138n, 147–48, 153, 155, 156n, 157, 158n, 163, 167, 169, 175–77, 180, 188, 197–201. *See also* Democratic Army of Greece; Elite conflict; Plenary sessions; Titoists; Zachariadis, Nikos
Varga, Evgenii, 190–91, 201
Varkiza Agreement, 39–40, 42, 47–48, 52–56, 58–60, 71, 78–79, 103n, 105, 107, 126, 140, 152
Varvaresos, Kyriakos, 73–76, 81, 98
Velichonskii, N., 58, 61
Venizelos, Sofoklis, 22
Veterans' Associations (Veterans' Groups), 36
Vinogradov, Sergei, 10n, 79–80, 97
Vitsi, 177, 183
Vlantas, Dimitris, 175
Volokhov, Konstantin, 156
Vontitsos-Gousias, Giorgis (Gousias), 28n, 68, 103n, 109n, 120n, 123–24, 142n, 145, 150, 152, 153n, 169, 172, 175, 177, 184, 196, 198
Votsikas, Dimos, 68n, 111, 124
Voulgaris, Petros, 60, 72, 85, 122; government of, 72n, 73, 77, 81, 86, 98
Voznesenskii, A. A., 191, 196n
Voznesenskii, Nikolai, 191, 196n
Vukmanović-Tempo, Svetozar (Tempo), 129–30, 132, 180, 201
Vyshinskii, Andrei, 9, 40, 91, 99, 116, 154–55

Western powers, 70, 143, 193, 206, 209, 213. *See also entries for individual nations*
Wittner, Lawrence S., 169n
Woodhouse, Christopher, M., 29, 68n, 102n, 143, 179, 198, 200
Workers' Antifascist League (ERGAS), 76, 96
Workers' National Liberation Front (EEAM), 76
World Federation of Trade Unions, 96
World War II, 212. *See also entries for individual nations*

Xoxe, Koçi, 134, 171, 178
Xydis, Stephen G., 49, 79

Yalta Agreement, 41, 44, 54, 56, 78; Declaration on Liberated Europe of, 40
Yugoslavia, 8n, 29, 48, 65, 134n, 142–44, 151, 190, 201–2; and Albania, 4, 182n, 213; assistance to KKE, 106, 114n, 115, 127, 138, 145–46, 149–50, 154, 158n, 162–63; and Cominform, 171, 173; and creation of AVNOJ, 10–11; Greek Communist Politburo in, 140, 155n; independent policy of, 50, 166–68; and Macedonia 34n, 128–33, 179–82, 211; recognition by Greek government, 98; royal government of, 43–44; tensions with KKE, 37, 138n, 139, 150, 170, 184; and the USSR, 3, 5, 39, 42–44, 134–35, 143–44, 146, 159, 165, 170, 207, 211; and United Nations, 144, 155–58; and Zhdanov faction, 191–93, 195–97. *See also* Balkans; Foreign Communist assistance to Greek Communist insurgency; Soviet-Yugoslav dispute; Zachariadis, Nikos; *entries for individual nations*

Zachariadis, Nikos, 61–62, 72, 92, 94, 101–16, 141n, 150, 152, 166n, 170, 180, 197n, 199n, 204; and abstention from elections, 86, 93, 95–96, 106n, 110; contact with European Communists, 109, 114n, 125, 137–38, 144, 147–48, 154, 158, 161–62, 169, 177n; contact with Soviet leadership, 80n, 95, 109, 118–19, 139, 147, 149, 152n, 153, 165–66, 168–69, 170n, 177–78, 182–83, 194–95, 196n; and decision for civil war, 147–48; development of KKE policy, 68, 86, 88–89, 103n, 104, 110, 115–16, 122, 136–37, 138n, 147; and dual strategy, 92, 99, 104–5, 121, 133, 140, 176; and limited mobilization, 137–38; and Macedonian question, 89–90; management of intraparty conflict, 102, 105–6, 112–13, 119–23, 126; and neutralization of Greece, 69–70, 141–42, 174; and political gradualism, 104; relation to Soviet objectives, 50–51, 66–67, 95, 102, 110n, 173, 184; and rivalry with Markos, 148, 158n, 175, 188–89, 197–200; and Soviet-Yugoslav dispute, 134; and territorial claims, 67. *See also* Foreign Communist assistance to Greek Communist insurgency; Reconciliation; Self-defense groups; "Two poles," theory of
Zafeiropoulos, D. G., 155n
Zervas, Napoleon, 14–15, 24–25
Zevgos, Iannis, 38
Zhdanov, Andrei A., 80n, 95n, 109, 139n, 153, 165, 186–87, 189, 191, 192n, 194, 196n; competition with Malenkov, 192–93; contact with Balkan Communist parties, 190; impact on Soviet policy toward Greece, 194–97. *See also* Elite conflict; "Forward line"; "Two camp" thesis
Zhdanovites, 190, 192
Zhdanovshchina, 189
Zhivkov, 162, 196n
Zukov, 63

Library of Congress Cataloging-in-Publication Data

Stavrakis, Peter J., 1955–
    Moscow and Greek communism, 1944–1949.

    Bibliography: p.
    Includes index.
    1. Soviet Union—Foreign relations—Greece.
2. Greece—Foreign relations—Soviet Union. 3. Greece—
History—Civil War, 1944–1949. 4. Soviet Union—
Foreign relations—1945–   . 5. Communism—Greece.
6. Greece—Politics and government—1935–1967.
I. Title.
DK67.5.G8S73   1989   327.470495   88-47767
ISBN 0-8014-2125-X (alk. paper)